my **revisi**

Edexcel A-level
BUSINESS

Andrew Hammond

HODDER EDUCATION
AN HACHETTE UK COMPANY

Hachette UK's policy is to use papers that are natural, renewable and recyclable products and made from wood grown in sustainable forests. The logging and manufacturing processes are expected to conform to the environmental regulations of the country of origin.

Orders: please contact Bookpoint Ltd, 130 Park Drive, Milton Park, Abingdon, Oxon OX14 4SE. Telephone: (44) 01235 827827. Fax: (44) 01235 400401. Email education @bookpoint.co.uk Lines are open from 9 a.m. to 5 p.m., Monday to Saturday, with a 24-hour message answering service. You can also order through our website: www. hoddereducation.co.uk

ISBN: 978 1 4718 8322 4

© Andrew Hammond 2017

First published in 2017 by
Hodder Education,
An Hachette UK Company
Carmelite House
50 Victoria Embankment
London EC4Y 0DZ
www.hoddereducation.co.uk

Impression number   10 9 8 7 6 5 4 3 2 1
Year   2021 2020 2019 2018 2017

Cover photo reproduced by permission of Kirill Cherezov/123RF.com

Typeset in Bembo Std Regular, 11/13 pts. by Aptara, Inc.

Printed in Spain

A catalogue record for this title is available from the British Library.

Get the most from this book

Everyone has to decide his or her own revision strategy, but it is essential to review your work, learn it and test your understanding. These Revision Notes will help you to do that in a planned way, topic by topic. Use this book as the cornerstone of your revision and don't hesitate to write in it — personalise your notes and check your progress by ticking off each section as you revise.

Tick to track your progress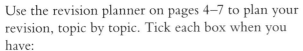

Use the revision planner on pages 4–7 to plan your revision, topic by topic. Tick each box when you have:

- revised and understood a topic
- tested yourself
- practised the exam questions and gone online to check your answers and complete the quick quizzes

You can also keep track of your revision by ticking off each topic heading in the book. You may find it helpful to add your own notes as you work through each topic.

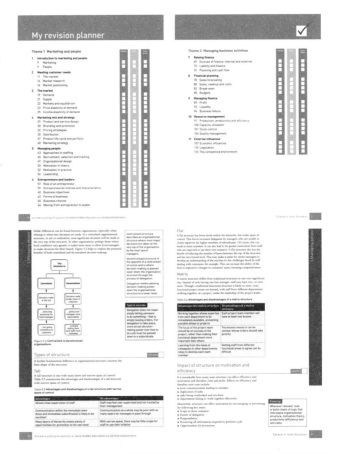

Features to help you succeed

Exam tips

Expert tips are given throughout the book to help you polish your exam technique in order to maximise your chances in the exam.

Typical mistakes

The author identifies the typical mistakes candidates make and explains how you can avoid them.

Now test yourself

These short, knowledge-based questions provide the first step in testing your learning. Answers are online at the Hodder website, as below.

Definitions and key words

Clear, concise definitions of essential key terms are provided where they first appear.

Key words from the specification are highlighted in colour throughout the book.

Revision activities

These activities will help you to understand each topic in an interactive way.

Exam practice

Practice exam questions are provided for each topic. Use them to consolidate your revision and practise your exam skills.

Summaries

The summaries provide a quick-check bullet list for each topic.

Online

Go online to check your answers to the Now test yourself questions and the exam questions and try out the extra quick quizzes at **www.hoddereducation.co.uk/myrevisionnotes**

My revision planner

Answers and quick quizzes at **www.hoddereducation.co.uk/myrevisionnotes**

Theme 2 Managing business activities

REVISED | TESTED | EXAM READY

Theme 3 Business decisions and strategy

REVISED   TESTED   EXAM READY

Theme 4 Global business

REVISED   TESTED   EXAM READY

Answers and quick quizzes at
www.hoddereducation.co.uk/myrevisionnotes

Countdown to my exams

6–8 weeks to go

- Start by looking at the specification — make sure you know exactly what material you need to revise and the style of the examination. Use the revision planner on pages 4 and 5 to familiarise yourself with the topics.
- Organise your notes, making sure you have covered everything on the specification. The revision planner will help you to group your notes into topics.
- Work out a realistic revision plan that will allow you time for relaxation. Set aside days and times for all the subjects that you need to study, and stick to your timetable.
- Set yourself sensible targets. Break your revision down into focused sessions of around 40 minutes, divided by breaks. These Revision Notes organise the basic facts into short, memorable sections to make revising easier.

REVISED ☐

2–6 weeks to go

- Read through the relevant sections of this book and refer to the exam tips, exam summaries, typical mistakes and key terms. Tick off the topics as you feel confident about them. Highlight those topics you find difficult and look at them again in detail.
- Test your understanding of each topic by working through the 'Now test yourself' questions in the book. Look up the answers at the back of the book.
- Make a note of any problem areas as you revise, and ask your teacher to go over these in class.
- Look at past papers. They are one of the best ways to revise and practise your exam skills. Write or prepare planned answers to the exam practice questions provided in this book. Check your answers online and try out the extra quick quizzes at **www.therevisionbutton.co.uk/ myrevisionnotes**
- Use the revision activities to try out different revision methods. For example, you can make notes using mind maps, spider diagrams or flash cards.
- Track your progress using the revision planner and give yourself a reward when you have achieved your target.

REVISED ☐

One week to go

- Try to fit in at least one more timed practice of an entire past paper and seek feedback from your teacher, comparing your work closely with the mark scheme.
- Check the revision planner to make sure you haven't missed out any topics. Brush up on any areas of difficulty by talking them over with a friend or getting help from your teacher.
- Attend any revision classes put on by your teacher. Remember, he or she is an expert at preparing people for examinations.

REVISED ☐

The day before the examination

- Flick through these Revision Notes for useful reminders, for example the exam tips, exam summaries, typical mistakes and key terms.
- Check the time and place of your examination.
- Make sure you have everything you need — extra pens and pencils, tissues, a watch, bottled water, sweets.
- Allow some time to relax and have an early night to ensure you are fresh and alert for the examinations.

REVISED ☐

My exams

A-level Business Paper 1

Date:...

Time:...

Location:...

A-level Business Paper 2

Date:...

Time:...

Location:...

A-level Business Paper 3

Date:...

Time:...

Location:...

1 Introduction to marketing and people

Marketing

Marketing is the term used to describe the range of activities that businesses undertake to try to create a demand among consumers for their products or services. Marketing managers must ensure that they understand what is happening in the markets they sell to and how and why consumers behave the way in which they do. In order to gain this understanding, marketing departments carry out market research aimed at developing a genuine understanding of consumer behaviour. This allows them to make better decisions on how to entice consumers to decide to buy the products and services. In a modern marketing department, much of this research is gathered in real time from social media and minutely detailed analyses of sales data.

A summary of the work done by marketing departments can be seen in Table 1.1.

Table 1.1 Work done by marketing departments

Understanding markets	Making marketing decisions
Market research	Designing products and services
Analysing factors affecting demand in a market	Deciding on a price
Deciding which markets to sell to	Deciding where to distribute
Spotting changes within markets	Communicating with customers
Understanding consumer behaviour within markets	

People

Businesses need many different resources to enable them to meet their objectives. Physical resources such as buildings and equipment, as well as financial resources, must be well managed. Research shows that in the long run human resources are the most important. This is why so much time and attention is given to ensuring that businesses get as much from their people as possible.

Human resources departments are likely to take charge of the following activities:
- recruitment of new staff
- selection of applicants for jobs/promotions
- training new and existing staff
- designing and administering payment systems
- planning future workforce needs.

In smaller firms, without a specialist HR department, the boss will need to handle all these tasks, and others relating to the people who work for the business. Some larger businesses will also expect departmental managers and supervisors to take responsibility for other people-related tasks including:
- working out shift rotas
- coaching staff

- providing on-the-job training
- motivating staff on a day-to-day basis
- delegating authority.

A business can secure an advantage over its rivals through expert use of marketing and people in many ways. A selection of these is shown in Figure 1.1.

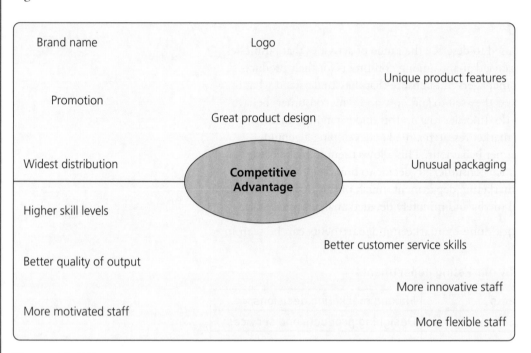

Figure 1.1 **Different ways in which businesses have advantages over their rivals**

Now test yourself

TESTED

1 Briefly explain what makes the following successful products or services stand out from their rivals:
   (a) Apple's iPhone
   (b) Heinz Tomato Ketchup
   (c) John Lewis department stores
   (d) Cadbury's chocolate

Answers online

Summary

- Marketing is the business function whose role is to create a demand for a firm's products or services.
- The people in a business are a critical resource that needs to be used effectively.
- Marketing and people can both provide a competitive advantage.

2 Meeting customer needs

The market

A market exists where buyers and sellers meet in order to exchange goods or services. Though some markets can be identified as having a physical location, markets are best thought of as any occasion where a buyer and seller can interact and can therefore be online, by post or in a shopping centre or trade fair.

Mass markets and niche markets

Some businesses will produce products and services aimed at satisfying the needs of a whole market, rather than any specific section of the market. Attempting to sell to the whole market is called mass marketing. Other businesses select a **segment** of the market and sell products specifically to suit the needs of consumers in that segment. This process is called **niche** marketing.

> A **market segment** is a subsection of a larger market in which consumers share similar needs and wants.
>
> A **niche market** is a small segment of a larger market.

Table 2.1 **Benefits of different marketing strategies**

Benefits of mass marketing	Benefits of niche marketing
Huge potential number of customers	Meeting consumer needs more precisely allows higher prices to be charged
Higher production levels allow economies of scale – lower production costs	Higher profit margins
Can use mass media advertising	Easier to enter for firms with limited financial resources

There are notable differences between mass and niche markets as shown in Table 2.2.

Table 2.2 **Differences between mass and niche markets**

	Mass market	Niche market
Characteristics	Generic products which are broadly similar in form and function	Specialist products and services are required. Changes in consumer preferences can be rapid and devastating to the market
Market size and share	Huge markets in which large firms can operate successfully even though their market share may be low, e.g. Ferrero's 5% share of the UK chocolate market	Smaller markets mean successful firms may achieve far higher shares of their niche than mass market firms
Brands	Huge brands can develop with the name/logo representing a key point of differentiation	Differentiation is more likely to be achieved through product features and functions

Exam tip

Choosing a mass or niche market approach is a strategic choice. In other words this choice will affect the whole business, from the approach to marketing through to decisions on scale of production and production methods and locations. Try to ensure that, when writing about a firm using mass or niche marketing, you acknowledge the impact of the choice of marketing strategy on other business decisions.

Dynamic markets

REVISED

No business can afford to stand still because markets are dynamic, they tend to change over time. There are four major issues to consider.

Online retailing

Continued growth in online retailing has varied between different markets, with clothing growing tremendously but growth in online sales of books slowing to a virtual halt. This unpredictability of growth adds to the unpredictability of dynamism in online retailing. What history has shown us is that retailers who fail to switch to online retailing can fail completely as online rivals steal sales. Above all, it is vital to ensure that your product or service is available to buy wherever consumers want to buy it. In some cases it is vital to have an online presence, or if consumers want to buy online and collect from their local store, a click-and-collect service is needed.

How markets change

Markets change as a result of major external influences, as summarised by the **PESTLE** acronym.

Examples of market changes include the following:
- Political: In 2016 the government's new 'Living Wage' was brought in, pushing the legal minimum (for over-25s) from £6.70 to £7.20 an hour; this was great for low-paid employees, but tough on employers in low-wage industries such as care homes.
- Economic: The economic recession of 2008–09 led to major changes in UK grocery retailing, as price-conscious shoppers opted for Aldi and Lidl.
- Social: An increased desire for convenience has driven the rise in online retailing.
- Technological: 'Apps' did not exist ten years ago, prior to the advent of the smartphone; by 2016 they were capable of turning century-old markets on their head, as with taxis and the arrival of Uber.
- Legal: Growth in the market for e-cigarettes is being affected by the introduction of new laws relating to who can buy, how they can be advertised and where they can be consumed.
- Environmental: The car industry is facing major changes in order to try to minimise the damaging impact of exhaust fumes on the environment.

PESTLE highlights the major sources of external changes faced by businesses: Political, Economic, Social, Technological, Legal and Environmental.

Innovation and market growth

A major cause of change within markets is innovation. With competing firms continually trying to develop new products and services that offer features that no rivals offer, consumer loyalties can change dramatically. Once one innovation has been successful, other companies may be forced to try to adapt their offerings in order to keep pace with rivals.

Furthermore, many companies will try to come up with their own innovations in order to try to benefit from leading change in the market.

Adapting to change

Market research and an understanding of general trends in the market are vital to successfully adapting to change. Identifying subtle changes in what consumers are looking for in their products allows businesses to adapt their products to better suit these needs. Whether it be removing sugar from food products or adding features to mobile phone handsets, changing earlier than rivals offers a major source of competitive advantage.

> **Typical mistake**
>
> Too often exam answers imply that adapting to change is a simple process for a business. These responses fail to show an appreciation of the impact on all four business functions: marketing, people, finance and operations. Required changes may include production methods, finding new suppliers, redeploying workers and adopting new advertising and distribution methods.

How competition affects the market

REVISED

Competition is the feature of business that most stimulates change and development. This is especially clear in the battle between Apple and Samsung in the smartphone market. Neither can sit back for a moment. That was clear when the market was disappointed by Apple's iPhone 5, leading to significant gains for Samsung. It took a huge development effort for Apple to regain its supremacy with the iPhone 6.

Increased levels of competition create various pressures for businesses:
- The need to drive down costs.
- The need to maintain competitive prices.
- The need to develop innovative products and services.
- The need to maintain high quality of products and services.

The difference between risk and uncertainty

REVISED

Operating a business in any market involves facing up to risk and coping with uncertainties. The key difference lies in the predictability of events occurring. A risk is quantifiable, so if statistics show that only 1 in 20 new consumer goods succeed, the risk involved in launching a new product can be identified and quantified. The factors causing the risk are the uncertainties – those factors that cause a lack of certainty in future events – such as reactions of rivals, reactions of consumers, reactions of retailers and such unexpected events as currency movements and economic downturns.

> **Typical mistake**
>
> Too many answers use the terms 'risk' and 'uncertainty' interchangeably – they are not the same thing.

TESTED

> **Now test yourself**
>
> 1 State two benefits of mass marketing.
> 2 State two benefits of niche marketing.
> 3 What are the six major external forces that lead to change in markets?
> 4 State three benefits experienced by consumers as a result of increased competition in a market.
> 5 What marketing activity tends to be the key to successfully adapting to change in markets?

Answers online

2 Meeting customer needs

Edexcel A-level Business 13

Market research

Product and market orientation

REVISED

Product orientation is an approach to making decisions that considers internal factors before worrying about changes in the market. This means that product-orientated businesses can focus on their own key strengths and this can lead to revolutionary new ideas that consumers would never have dreamed of. However, the danger is that the business fails to adapt its products in line with what consumers are looking for, which could lead to huge problems.

The opposite approach – market orientation – is more likely to lead to marketing success since it places consumers' views and behaviours at the heart of decision-making within the business.

Primary and secondary research

REVISED

Market research can use either secondary data or primary data, with **primary research** being new research carried out for the first time, and **secondary research** being research that uses data that had already been gathered for some other purpose.

The data gathered may be **quantitative** or **qualitative**. Quantitative data contains factual, often numerate data that is intended to be statistically representative of the whole market. Qualitative data contains opinion and is unlikely to have been gathered on a large enough scale to give statistically reliable data. It is designed to give insight into why customers behave the way they do.

> **Primary research** is new research conducted for a particular purpose.
>
> **Secondary research** uses pre-existing data that has been gathered for another purpose.

Table 2.3 Advantages and disadvantages of primary and secondary research

	Secondary research	Primary research
Advantages	• Often free • Provides a good market overview • Usually based on large-scale, reliably produced research	• Addresses the specific issues you are interested in • Data is up to date • Can help to understand customer psychology
Disadvantages	• Information may be out of date • Not tailored to suit your particular needs • Can be expensive to buy published research reports on markets	• Expensive, costing thousands of pounds to do properly • Risk of bias from questionnaire and interviewer • May need to compare with other information to understand the meaning of findings

Typical mistake

Primary research does not have to be carried out by individual businesses. They can hire a market research company to do the research for them. If it is new research, it is still primary.

Quantitative research is research conducted on a large-enough scale to provide statistically reliable data, usually aimed at discovering factual information about how customers behave.

Qualitative research is unlikely to be carried out on a large-enough scale to give statistically valid data, but is instead aimed at providing insights as to why customers behave the way they do.

Exam tip

Generally most firms will use a combination of secondary and primary research, with secondary often conducted first to help design the primary research needed without incurring the high cost of primary research first.

Table 2.4 Different primary and secondary research methods

Secondary research methods	Primary research methods
The internet	Surveys
Trade press	Retailer research
Government statistics	Observation
Past internal sales figures	Group or individual discussions

Limitations to market research

REVISED

If all market research provided accurate and reliable data, then all businesses would succeed. There are two major reasons why market research data may be unreliable:

● Sample size too small: This means that there is more chance that respondents who do not reflect the overall views of the market are over-represented in the sample.
● Sample bias: The way that respondents are selected may over-represent certain types of people whose views may skew the overall findings away from the views of the total population being researched.

Exam tip

Using the wrong research method may not be the major mistake made by a business whose research seems to let them down. Analysing and then interpreting market research data correctly is the most common problem within the marketing process. The best marketing decision-makers use surveys to provide insights – but they still take the key decisions based as much on experience and intuition as on research.

Use of ICT to support market research

REVISED

There are three main ways in which ICT can support market research:

● Company websites can gather data on visitors to the website which can provide some information about online shoppers' or browsers' interests.
● Social media can also offer information on consumer attitudes to a product or service, and even allow for an element of relationship building between the business and consumers.
● Database technology, which has advanced so far in recent years, allows vast quantities of data relating to consumers to be trawled in order to identify patterns that can help to explain how consumers actually behave, with much of this data being generated by loyalty cards.

Typical mistake

Despite their name, a major purpose of loyalty schemes is to gather information on customers' buying habits.

Market segmentation

REVISED

One main function of market research is to help to decide on useful ways to **segment markets**. Splitting markets up helps to target specific groups of consumers who share similar needs and wants, enabling a firm to meet these more closely. Market research can unearth insights that allow firms to identify segments that they can fulfil profitably.

Benefits of segmenting a market include:

● Products and services can be designed to suit specific customers.
● Meeting customers' needs precisely allows a higher price to be charged.
● Promotional activity is easier to target.

Market segmentation means discovering useful ways to split up a market into different groups of consumers who share similar characteristics and needs.

TESTED

6 What type of research is aimed at finding out about customer attitudes in the hope of gaining insights into consumer behaviour?
7 What type of research uses data that has already been gathered for another purpose?
8 What type of research gathers brand new data?
9 What type of research is aimed at delivering statistically reliable information?
10 Is a product-orientated or market-orientated business more likely to come up with brand new, revolutionary product ideas?
11 State two reasons why market research may give misleading results.
12 List three ways that ICT can help with market research.
13 State three benefits of segmenting a market.

Answers online

Market positioning

Decisions over fine tuning the product being sold must follow earlier, strategic decisions about what products to sell to which markets. This fine tuning is the process of **market positioning**.

> **Market positioning** means deciding exactly what image you are trying to create for your product relative to its rivals.

Market mapping

REVISED

The two key judgements required in successful market mapping are:
● choosing the right variables to place on each axis
● placing rival brands in the right place on the map, truly reflecting consumer perceptions of those brands (see Figure 2.1).

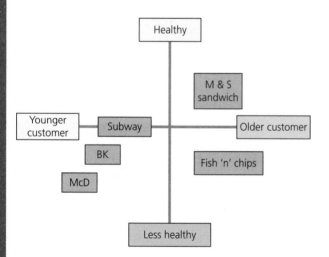

Figure 2.1 **Market map of the UK fast food industry**

With a market map produced, a business can identify the gaps in the market more easily. Following this is a check to ensure that the gap can be filled profitably. For example, drawing a map of the UK car market can identify a gap for a truly luxurious sports car selling for £10,000. Of course, the reason why this gap exists is that no firm is capable of making the product at a cost that will let them make a profit at a price of £10,000.

With a gap identified, the firm must then decide how to use the marketing tools at its disposal. Managers will want to create an image that matches the product to the gap that has been identified.

Competitive advantage

REVISED

Products without any competitive advantage over their rivals have been proven time and again to have no long-term future. The two major generic routes to finding a competitive advantage are to:

- be the lowest cost producer, e.g. Ryanair in the European airline market
- find a sustainable point of differentiation, e.g. KFC in the market for fast food.

Producing your product more efficiently and thus more cheaply than any rivals will ultimately allow a business to sell at a lower price than any other firm, yet still make a profit. Generally, in any given market there is space for one firm to fulfil this role of lowest-cost producer.

The key to competitive advantage is that it should be sustainable in the long term. A really strong brand name and image can achieve this, but only if the whole business focuses on providing the products and services that match or even enhance the brand.

Product differentiation

REVISED

Standing out from rivals can be achieved through actual, tangible differences between products or through manipulating consumer perceptions of your product – a kind of psychological differentiation. Possibilities are shown in Table 2.5.

Table 2.5 Tangible differences between products

Actual product differentiation	Perceived product differentiation
Design	Branding
Different functions	Advertising
Taste	Sponsorship
Performance	Celebrity endorsement

> **Product differentiation** means attempting to make your product seem different, in the minds of consumers, to any other rival in the market.

The purposes of **product differentiation** are:

- insulating the product from the actions of competitors
- allowing prices to be increased without a major fall in demand or sales.

As we will see later, in Chapter 3, differentiation is the key to reducing a product's price elasticity.

> **Typical mistake**
>
> Be careful not to over-use the term 'unique selling point'. Many product features can differentiate a product without being actually unique.

Adding value

REVISED

Product differentiation generally helps to add value to products and services. The ability to push prices higher without increasing the costs of producing a product will naturally add value. Once more, **added value** may come about through tangible, engineering methods, such as creating a great design or finding a way to produce in a far cheaper manner, or it may be added through perception, generally through promotional methods such as advertising and branding. L'Oréal's slogan 'Because I'm worth it' is the company's clever way of persuading customers that paying a higher price for L'Oréal products is 'worth it', i.e. it adds value.

> **Added value** is the difference between the cost of bought-in goods and services and the selling price of a product.

Now test yourself

14 What is market mapping designed to reveal?
15 What are the two main routes to competitive advantage?
16 Explain the effects that the arrival of Aldi and Lidl have had on Tesco in the UK grocery market.
17 Explain the main sources of competitive advantage for each of the following:
   (a) iPhone   (b) Yorkie   (c) Nando's
18 How can being the most efficient producer of a product create long-term success?
19 What are the two main benefits of successful product differentiation?
20 How can advertising add value to a product?

Answers online

Exam practice

The market for toys in the UK is highly seasonal. It is a market that has a strong record of innovation, especially in the development of electronic toys that use the latest audio-visual technology, and can often throw up surprise success stories. Over the past three years the market has grown as the UK's economy has recovered. As well as new toy products, some old products are also making a return. In the niche market of sports games, a Spanish company Netcam has relaunched Subbuteo table football in the UK. It decided to go ahead after studying the results of some quantitative research among boys. The game, which was first launched in the 1950s, had been withdrawn from the market in 2007. With the game beginning to appear in major toy retailers such as Argos and John Lewis, the relaunch seems to be proving a modest success. Nevertheless, many commentators have suggested that the company's failure to launch an e-commerce site through which Subbuteo products can be bought directly may be harming sales growth.

Questions

1 What is meant by quantitative research?   (2)
2 What is meant by niche market?   (2)
3 Explain how the use of a familiar brand name can help Netcam relaunch Subbuteo products.   (4)
4 Assess the major influences on the market size of the toy market examined in the item.   (10)

Answers and quick quiz 2 online

ONLINE

Summary

- Mass marketing and niche marketing are alternative approaches to marketing that both offer benefits and drawbacks.
- Markets are dynamic. They change, raising the following issues for businesses: how markets change, the rise of online markets, innovation in markets and adapting to change in markets.
- Competition is a key driving force behind features within markets such as prices, quality and innovation.
- Risk is quantifiable; uncertainty is unquantifiable and unpredictable.
- Market research can allow businesses to understand the customers to whom they plan to sell, enabling better marketing decisions to be made.
- Market research can gather fresh information (primary) or be based on information already gathered (secondary).
- Market research can be carried out on a large enough scale to give statistically reliable results (quantitative) or can be small scale, in-depth and designed to give insights (qualitative).
- Market research methods can undermine the reliability of research results if sample sizes are small or samples are poorly selected.
- ICT can help gather and analyse market research data.
- Market research can help to segment markets.
- Market mapping helps to make decisions over where to try to position a product in the market.
- Successful market mapping requires good decisions on what to plot on the map's axes and where to place existing products.
- Having some kind of competitive advantage is crucial for the success of any product.
- Competitive advantage can come from lowest costs or product differentiation.
- Differentiation may be tangible or perceived.
- Differentiation helps to lessen the effects of competitors' actions, allows firms greater price flexibility and helps to add value to products and services.

3 The market

Demand

Demand is such a fundamental concept in business that understanding the factors that affect demand is critical to running a successful business. The main factors affecting demand are listed below.

> **Demand** is the term used to describe the level of interest customers have in a product.

Price

Higher prices lead to lower **effective demand**, since fewer customers can afford to pay. Price also affects consumers' decisions on relative value of the product compared to alternatives – higher prices make alternatives seem better value. On the other hand, prices give off a signal about the product being sold – so lower prices may damage consumer perceptions of quality.

> **Effective demand** is interest backed by the ability to pay.

Changes in prices of substitutes and complements

A clear relationship exists between demand for a product and the price of its **substitutes**. If the price of a tin of *Roses* falls, demand for *Quality Street* will fall as consumers switch to buying the cheaper substitute. The same relationship holds if the price of the substitute rises; demand for *Quality Street* will increase as consumers switch away from *Roses*, the more expensive substitute.

> A **substitute** is a similar, rival product that consumers may choose instead.
>
> A **complement** is a product whose use accompanies another, so petrol is a complementary product to cars.

The relationship between demand for a product and the price of its **complements** works in the other direction. Should the price of a complementary product rise, demand for the original product is likely to fall. Often complementary products can represent the 'running costs' of another product, such as petrol for cars, or coffee capsules for coffee machines. If the price of the complementary product rises, demand for the original will fall, and vice versa.

> **Typical mistake**
>
> Too many candidates under pressure confuse the terms 'complement' and 'substitute' – pause before choosing the appropriate term.

Changes in consumer incomes

As income levels rise, demand for most products (normal goods) rises in line, as consumers have more income to spend. For luxury goods such as Porsche cars, demand will rise even faster than incomes. Of course, incomes do not always rise. As economies go through recession, incomes will fall, and for normal and luxury goods, demand falls as consumers try to save money. However, some products, known as inferior goods, see demand rise when incomes fall, as happened to Poundland in the recession-affected years 2008–13. Inferior goods, as their name suggests, tend to be cheaper alternatives to normal goods, which consumers can switch to in order to save money when their income is falling. As incomes rise again, consumers will switch back to normal and luxury goods, leading to a fall in demand for inferior goods.

Fashions, tastes and preferences

REVISED

Subject to change over time, factors such as attitudes to diet (for example, no sugar or low fat) change unpredictably but can have a major impact upon demand for products, either positive or negative.

Advertising and branding

REVISED

Successful advertising can lead to major short-term increases in demand. Consistent advertising linked to other marketing activity may help to build a brand, protecting it from direct competition and making sales volumes relatively stable.

Demographics

REVISED

Changes in the make-up of populations, which form the basis of any market's demand, can affect demand for individual products. Major demographic trends in the UK in recent years have seen a growing population of over-60s, a rising birth rate and increased numbers of European migrants. All these groups provide opportunities for increased demand for carefully targeted products.

External shocks

REVISED

Natural disasters, changes in the law, unexpected traffic problems or a major customer not renewing a contract are all examples of events that can have a hugely damaging impact on demand for small or large businesses. The major problem with many external shocks is their unpredictability. They are outside the business's control.

Seasonality

REVISED

Seasonal factors affect demand for many products, whether they are related to the weather and nature's seasons or due to special events during the course of a year, such as Christmas.

Now test yourself

TESTED

1 List seven factors that could affect demand for a product.
2 If the price of petrol falls, what is likely to happen to demand for cars?
3 If the price of Adidas trainers increases, what is likely to happen to demand for Nike trainers?
4 Give two examples of external shocks that could damage demand for a local independent coffee shop.

Answers online

Supply

Along with demand, the amount that businesses are willing and able to supply will have a major impact on the price of all products. The general rule governing the amount firms are willing to supply is that the more profit they can make by supplying a product, the more they are willing to supply.

Changes in costs of production

REVISED ☐

If the cost of making a product changes, the amount that a business is willing to supply will adjust accordingly:
● If production costs rise, the amount supplied will fall.
● If production costs fall, the amount supplied will rise.

Introduction of new technology

REVISED ☐

New technology used in production, such as industrial robots, tends to reduce the costs of production:
● The introduction of new technology should lead to an increase in supply
● Firms willing to supply more with lower production costs offering higher profits

Indirect taxes

REVISED ☐

Indirect taxes act just like another component of the cost of producing a product or service. Therefore:
● An increase in indirect tax rates will increase cost and therefore reduce supply.
● A decrease in indirect tax rates will cut total costs and therefore increase supply.

> **Indirect taxes** are taxes that the government imposes on goods and services, for example VAT.

Government subsidies

REVISED ☐

These are the opposite of taxes. When the government wants to encourage the supply of a product such as wind-powered energy, it may offer subsidies to businesses. This cuts the cost of production faced by the business, meaning that subsidies will increase supply.

External shocks

REVISED ☐

Unexpected events such as economic crises, poor harvests or natural disasters can reduce the total quantity of an item available. This would lead to an increase in the price of the item, meaning that production costs rise and firms reduce the amount they are willing to supply.

> **Revision activity**
>
> Produce a mind map, with 'Supply' in the centre, which summarises the major factors affecting supply and then *how* that factor affects supply. So you will have one branch for each factor and each branch will break off to explain how changes in that factor might increase or decrease supply.

Now test yourself

5 Explain the relationship between costs of production and supply.
6 How might the invention of a new, more efficient production robot affect the supply of cars?
7 Give an example of an external shock that may reduce the supply of wheat.
8 Explain two reasons why governments might offer subsidies to firms supplying wind turbines.
9 What would be the effect of a reduction in the rate of VAT on supply?

Answers online

Markets and equilibrium

The interaction of supply and demand

REVISED

In **commodity markets**, price is determined simply by the interaction of supply and demand. Simply stated:

● If demand is higher than supply, the price of the product will rise, until demand falls back to the level of supply.
● If supply is higher than demand, price will fall, stimulating more demand to ensure that all that is supplied is sold.

What is happening is that price adjusts until demand and supply are in **equilibrium**. This is the natural state for all markets in which price is determined simply by demand and supply.

> **Commodity markets** are markets for undifferentiated products, generally raw materials such as gold, crude oil or rice.
>
> **Equilibrium** describes a situation in a market where supply and demand are balanced, making the price stable.

Supply and demand diagrams

REVISED

Drawing a demand curve simply involves plotting a series of points showing how much of a product would be demanded at a range of different price levels. In a similar way, a supply curve can be plotted, showing how much of a product businesses are willing to supply at a range of price levels.

Table 3.1 shows the demand and supply of sacks of coffee beans at a range of prices.

Table 3.1 Demand and supply of sacks of coffee beans

Price ($ per sack)	Demand (million sacks)	Supply (million sacks)
210	175	125
230	165	140
250	155	155
270	145	170
290	135	185

This information can be used to plot both a demand curve and a supply curve on a diagram that will show the market for coffee beans (Figure 3.1).

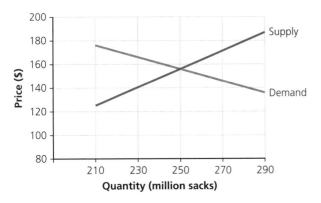

Figure 3.1 Equilibrium in the market for coffee beans

As Figure 3.1 clearly shows, the current equilibrium price is at $150 per sack, i.e. the place at which the level of demand and supply are the same.

If there is a significant change in the factors that determine the demand or supply of coffee, the lines will change. Possible reasons for these changes are examined on pages 17–19. These will cause leftward or rightward shifts in the demand and supply curves. Table 3.2 summarises the effect on price of shifts in the curves.

Table 3.2 Effect on price of shifts in the demand/supply curves

If this changes	Price will move
Demand curve moves to the right (rises)	up
Demand curve moves to the left (falls)	down
Supply curve moves to the left (falls)	up
Supply curve moves to the right (rises)	down

Now test yourself

TESTED

10 What name is given to products that cannot be differentiated?
11 Why does a demand curve slope downwards from left to right?
12 Why does a supply curve slope upwards from left to right?
13 What name is given to the point at which demand and supply curves cross?
14 State two factors that may cause a demand curve to shift.
15 State two factors that may cause a supply curve to shift.

Answers online

Price elasticity of demand

Price elasticity of demand measures the responsiveness of demand for a product to a change in its price.

Calculation

REVISED

Price elasticity of demand can be calculated by measuring the percentage change in demand that follows a change in price:

$$\text{Price elasticity of demand} = \frac{\%\ \text{change in demand}}{\%\ \text{change in price}}$$

Interpreting price elasticity

REVISED

Once elasticity has been calculated, the result can be interpreted, as shown in Table 3.3.

Table 3.3 Differences between price elasticity and inelasticity

If price elasticity is between 0 and −1	If price elasticity is a negative number greater than 1
Product is price inelastic	Product is price elastic
Changes in price have proportionately smaller effect on demand/sales	Changes in price have a proportionately larger effect on sales/demand

Price elasticity and revenue

REVISED

Depending on a product's price elasticity it is possible to make definitive statements about the effect of price changes on its revenue (Table 3.4).

Table 3.4 Price elasticity and revenue

If the product is:	Change in price:	Effect on revenue:	Explanation:
Price elastic	Increasing price	Fall in revenue	Because a small increase in price leads to a large fall in demand
Price elastic	Decreasing price	Increases revenue	Because a small cut in price leads to a large increase in demand
Price inelastic	Increasing price	Increases revenue	Because an increase in price leads to a small fall in demand
Price inelastic	Decreasing price	Fall in revenue	Because a price cut will only cause a small increase in demand

This predictability gives the opportunity to generate clear advice to offer in answer to questions asking for recommendations about a product's selling price.

Factors influencing price elasticity

REVISED

The major factors affecting price elasticity all boil down to whether the product seems different to its rivals. They are:
- degree of product differentiation
- availability of direct substitutes
- branding and brand loyalty.

Answers and quick quizzes at **www.hoddereducation.co.uk/myrevisionnotes**

If price is a central factor in the decision, price elasticity will be high ('elastic'). If it's got to be *Nike*, price elasticity will be low ('inelastic').

Significance of price elasticity

REVISED

Price elasticity is a useful concept for managers for two major reasons:
- Price elasticity can help in forecasting sales, by considering the likely impact of planned future price changes.
- Knowledge of price elasticity can help to decide on the best pricing strategy for increasing revenue, as shown in Table 3.4 above.

However, it is important to consider that price elasticity values tend to change over time since in a competitive market many firms' actions will affect the extent to which one product stands out from its rivals (just think how many chocolate bars there are).

> **Exam tip**
>
> Most businesses prefer to have price inelastic products because they are able to increase their price if necessary as a result of perhaps an increase in costs. This helps to explain why so much marketing activity can be traced back to attempts to make the product stand out from its rivals, reducing price elasticity.

Now test yourself

TESTED

16 Would a well-known popular branded product be likely to be price elastic or inelastic?
17 To increase revenue on a price elastic product, should price be increased or decreased?
18 What three factors determine price elasticity?
19 What are the two major uses of price elasticity for marketing managers?
20 What is the major limitation to the use of price elasticity?

Answers online

> **Real income** is the amount by which average incomes have adjusted for inflation – the amount by which prices have risen. For example: average household incomes up 3% in the past year; inflation at 1.2% – so real incomes are up by 3% – 1.2% = 1.8%.

Income elasticity of demand

Income elasticity of demand measures the responsiveness of demand for a product to a change in **real incomes**.

Calculating income elasticity

REVISED

Income elasticity of demand can be calculated by measuring the percentage change in demand that follows a change in real incomes:

$$\text{Income elasticity of demand} = \frac{\% \text{ change in demand}}{\% \text{ change in real incomes}}$$

> **Typical mistake**
>
> Unlike calculations of price elasticity, the result of an income elasticity calculation can be either positive or negative. It is important to make sure you pay attention to whether the changes in demand and income are positive or negative and carefully note the sign of your answer.

> **Typical mistake**
>
> Always use percentage change figures. Do not simply use the absolute changes in income (£s) or demand (units sold).

Interpreting income elasticity

REVISED

When categorising products and services according to their income elasticity there are three possible types:
- Inferior goods: These will have a negative income elasticity.

- Normal goods: These are products with a positive income elasticity between 0 and 1.
- Luxury goods: These goods and services have a positive income elasticity that is greater than 1.

Table 3.5 Effect of changes in income on different types of product

Type of product	Change in real incomes	Change in demand	Explanation
Inferior good	Increase	Decrease	Consumers stop buying cheaper substitutes and trade up now they have more money
	Decrease	Increase	Consumers switch to these products to save money as their incomes fall
Normal good	Increase	Increase at the same rate as real income or a little slower	Increasingly affluent consumers are now able to buy a little more of this type of product
	Decrease	Decrease at the same rate as real income or a little slower	As consumers tighten their belts, they will cut back a little on these products
Luxury good	Increase	Increase at a faster rate than real incomes	As consumers' incomes rise, these luxuries are the ones that most of their extra income will be spent on
	Decrease	Decrease at a faster rate than real incomes	These will be the first products to disappear from consumers' shopping baskets when they feel the need to tighten their belts

Factors affecting income elasticity

REVISED

Necessity or indulgence?

The indulgences – those things we can easily live without, but love to treat ourselves to when we can afford to – will be those that are most sensitive to changes in income. Necessities are those more basic items that we would always expect to buy, even when times are tight, therefore they are not as sensitive to changes in real incomes.

Significance of income elasticity

REVISED

Sales forecasting

Knowledge of the likely reaction of a product to a change in real incomes allows a business to forecast sales *if* it has reliable economic forecasts available. Of course, the reliability of economic forecasts is not always strong.

Financial planning

If income elasticity gives sales forecasts, then this information can be factored into budgets and financial plans. If a recession is forecast, a firm producing luxuries can plan ways to reduce costs in advance of a probable sharp fall in sales.

Product portfolio management

Having a product portfolio consisting entirely of luxuries *or* inferior goods increases the danger of changes in real income having a critical impact on sales. Firms intending to spread their risk will look to ensure that their product portfolios contain products with a range of income elasticities.

> **Typical mistake**
>
> Income elasticities change over time. As a result, a company can never be 100% confident that what happened to sales last time real incomes changed will be repeated. Add to this the fact that most economic forecasts tend to be a little inaccurate (at best) and writing about using elasticity to forecast sales should be accompanied by words such as 'may' or 'could' instead of 'will'.

Now test yourself

21 If average earnings rise by 4% and prices rise by 2.5%, what is the change in real income?
22 If a 3% fall in real income leads to a 6% rise in demand for potatoes, what is their income elasticity?
23 What are the two main factors affecting the income elasticity of a product?
24 State two reasons why sales forecasts based on income elasticity may prove inaccurate.
25 What name is given to a product with a negative income elasticity?
26 Will the demand for a product go up or down if:
  (a) The price of a substitute rises
  (b) The price of a substitute falls
  (c) The price of a complementary good rises
  (d) The price of a complementary good falls?

Answers online

Exam practice

The UK market for milk

Demand and supply of milk in the UK at different price levels

Price (pence per litre)	Demand (billion litres)	Supply (billion litres)
42	15.0	14.0
43	14.8	14.3
44	14.6	14.6
45	14.4	14.9
46	14.2	15.2

The estimated income elasticity of milk in the UK is +0.1.

Questions

1 On one diagram, draw a demand and supply curve for milk in the UK using the data in the table above. (4)
2 Using the data in the table for demand at a price of 44p per litre and 45p per litre, calculate the price elasticity of demand for milk. (3)
3 Calculate the impact on demand for milk in the UK if incomes fell by 5% in a year, if price was 42p per litre. (3)
4 Explain two possible factors affecting supply of milk in the UK. (10)

Answers and quick quiz 3 online

ONLINE

Summary

- In addition to price there are seven other major factors that could affect demand for a product. They are:
  - changes in the prices of substitutes and complementary goods
  - changes in consumer incomes
  - fashions, tastes and preferences
  - advertising and branding
  - demographics
  - external shocks
  - seasonality.
- Decisions on how much to supply are governed by how much profit a business can make.
- Changes that would increase the amount of profit a firm can make lead to an increased willingness to supply and vice versa.
- The major factors affecting supply in most markets are: changes in the costs of production, introduction of new technology, indirect taxes, government subsidies, external shocks.
- In markets with undifferentiated products, price is determined by the interaction of demand and supply.
- A demand curve shows the amount of the product that would be demanded at a range of price levels.
- A supply curve shows the amount of a product that firms would be willing to supply at different price levels.

- The point where the two curves cross is the equilibrium position, i.e. the point at which the price will be stable in the short term.
- Demand and supply curves shift due to a range of different causes.
- Shifts in demand or supply cause changes in the equilibrium price in a market.
- Price elasticity measures the responsiveness of demand to a change in price.
- All price elasticities are negative values.
- Price inelastic products have an elasticity between 0 and –1.
- Price elastic products are those with a price elasticity greater than –1.
- Price elasticity depends on the extent to which a product stands out from its rivals.
- Increasing the price of a price inelastic product will lead to an increase in revenue.
- Income elasticity of demand

$$= \frac{\% \text{ change in demand}}{\% \text{ change in real incomes}}$$

- According to their income elasticity, products are classified as luxury goods, normal goods or inferior goods.
- Income elasticity depends on whether the product is an indulgence or a necessity and on who buys the product.
- Income elasticity information can be used to forecast sales, aid financial planning and design a balanced product portfolio.

Answers and quick quizzes at **www.hoddereducation.co.uk/myrevisionnotes**

4 Marketing mix and strategy

The marketing mix is the collective term for the four major marketing decisions that a firm faces when trying to build a coherent plan, or strategy, for how its product will be marketed. Each of the Ps (product, place, promotion and price) should work in harmony to generate a coherent, credible image for the product.

Product and service design

Design is everywhere – any product that has been made has been designed, including products that are used to make other products. Services are also designed, perhaps in a less obvious way and using slightly different principles from, say, designing a sports car. The process by which services are purchased also has to be planned and therefore designed – perhaps designing an easy-to-use, attractive-looking app for ordering that pizza. So the principles of the design mix still apply.

The design mix

REVISED

Design is a compromise. Product and service designers must consider each of the points of the triangle in Figure 4.1.

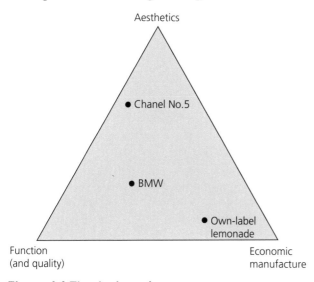

Figure 4.1 **The design mix**

- *Aesthetics* is the word used to describe the look, taste, texture or feel of an item.
- *Function* relates to whether the item actually does what it is expected to do and the extent to which it surpasses expectations of quality of performance.
- *Economic manufacture* considers the ease and economy with which the item can actually be made on the scale required.

However, for many firms, one aspect will take priority over the other two, so own-label drinks manufacturers will be far more concerned about designing a product that can be manufactured very cheaply than quality or aesthetics. However, not all businesses will head for the edges. As can be seen, BMW tries to strike a fine balance between all three aspects of the mix.

Benefits of good design

- Can add value
- Can provide a point of differentiation
- Can reduce manufacturing costs, boosting profit margins
- Improves brand image and therefore brand loyalty

Changes in the design mix to reflect social trends

Environmental concerns

As acceptance of the need to be aware of the environmental impact of business activity grows, product design has increasingly focused on two key environmental concerns:

- Design for waste minimisation or reuse: This describes a growing awareness of the need to design products from the outset with the end of their lives in mind. Designers are trying to minimise the parts of a product that cannot be reused and must be thrown away.
- Recycling: Even those parts of products that cannot be reused may be able to be recycled for another use.

Ethical sourcing

Media coverage over recent years has begun to examine the sources of components and finished goods used by businesses. Reports of child labour being used to make clothing, or unethical fishing methods used to catch tuna, have encouraged designers to ensure that the components or ingredients used in their products come from ethical sources.

Now test yourself

TESTED

1 What are the three points of the design mix?
2 What type of business may be most concerned with economy of manufacture?
3 State three possible benefits to a business of great design.
4 List three environmental concerns increasingly considered in product design.
5 How can design help to ensure ethical sourcing?

Answers online

Branding and promotion

Both branding and **promotion** are methods of communicating, explicitly or implicitly, information about a product or service to consumers.

> **Promotion** describes methods used by the business to communicate information and persuade consumers to purchase a product.

Types of promotion

These are best categorised into two groups: those that are aimed at boosting sales in the long term and those that are simply expected to generate a short-term effect.

Long-term methods

- Persuasive advertising
- **Public relations**

Short-term methods

- Buy one get one free (BOGOF)
- Seasonal price-cutting promotions

> **Public relations** describes attempts by a business to create publicity that is reported as news, such as staging a glitzy launch party for a new product.

> **Exam tip**
>
> Think carefully when answering a question about an appropriate form of promotion. Ask yourself about the goals of the business: a short-term boost in sales? Or are they willing to invest in long-term sales growth?

Types of branding

Individual brand

These are single product **brands**, such as *Marmite* or *Penguin* (biscuits). The firm that manufactures these brands may make little or no attempt to push their company name, focusing instead on the single brand to provide focus. Which company makes *Penguins*? And which makes *Marmite*?

> A **brand** is a recognisable name or logo that helps to differentiate a product or business.

Brand family

This is a brand name that is used across a range of related products, with Cadbury being a prime example. The benefit of this is the ability to use the umbrella brand name to encourage sales of each product within the family through association with others. A strong brand family also makes it much easier to get retail distribution when launching new products.

Corporate brand

Using the company name as a brand, in the way that Nestlé does, can convince consumers that all products across the entire range share similar benefits (or drawbacks!). Even for Nestlé, though, there may be individual products that seem stronger without the corporate brand logo, such as Nespresso (a Nestlé innovation that keeps quiet about the brand connection).

Ways to build a brand

- Advertising: This works best as a way of reinforcing the messages the company wants to send about its brand.
- **Unique selling point (USP)**: This may well provide the key stimulus that launches a brand, and although the unique feature may be copied in time, the brand may already be well established before this happens.
- Sponsorship: This is a way of brand building by association. Sponsoring an event, a sports team or even a TV programme can help to create

> A **unique selling point (USP)** is a particular feature of a product or service that no rival provides.

attachments in consumers' minds that build the brand's personality: for example, Red Bull sponsoring extreme sports.

● Digital media: From using social media to build relationships with customers to using Google Adwords to pop up every time a particular search is carried out, digital media offer a range of methods to help build a brand, some of which have not even been developed yet.

Changes in branding and promotion to reflect social trends

REVISED

Viral marketing

Traditionally, businesses loved creating 'word of mouth' promotion, where happy customers recommended a business to their friends and family – the good reputation of the business was spread like a virus. In a digital world, word of mouth became supercharged, with social media offering a faster and wider way to spread good (and bad) recommendations about a product.

Social media

Social media, just like traditional media (TV, newspapers), are seen by many businesses as another place where they can display their promotional messages, through an Instagram or Snapchat account, on a Facebook page or a Twitter feed.

Emotional branding

In some ways all branding is attempting to create some kind of emotional response from consumers to the brand. However, some branding is more overtly emotional than others; think about the sense of fun created by Ben and Jerry's. With the advent of digital media, especially social media, the relationship between a brand and a consumer can reach new emotional levels, with consumers following certain brands for daily updates from their brand of choice.

Now test yourself

TESTED

6 State two forms of promotion that may provide a short-term boost in sales but undermine a firm's brand image.
7 Give one disadvantage that can arise from creating a corporate brand.
8 List three methods that can be used effectively to build a brand.
9 Explain why viral marketing has become more significant in recent years.

Answers online

Pricing strategies

When making decisions on how to decide price for a product, a business is likely to devise a general approach to pricing, such as Apple pricing high to 'confirm' the brand's superiority and to complement other aspects of the marketing mix. Short-term changes in price may occasionally be prompted by external events, but in the medium to long term a company's pricing strategy shapes decisions on the actual price to charge.

Answers and quick quizzes at **www.hoddereducation.co.uk/myrevisionnotes**

Flat

A flat structure has fewer levels within the hierarchy, but wider spans of control. This forces increased delegation by managers who are unable to closely supervise far higher numbers of subordinates. Of course, this can result in more mistakes. It can also lead to far greater motivation from staff, who are expected to use their own initiative. A flat structure also has the benefit of reducing the number of layers between the top of the structure and the very lowest level. This may make it easier for senior managers to develop an understanding of the real day-to-day challenges faced by staff dealing with customers, for example. This can increase the ability of the firm to respond to changes in customers' tastes, boosting competitiveness.

Matrix

A matrix structure differs from traditional structures in one very significant way. Instead of only having one line manager, staff may have two, or even more. Though a traditional functional structure is likely to exist, cross-functional project teams are formed, with staff from different departments working together on a project, under the leadership of the project leader.

Table 5.6 Advantages and disadvantages of a matrix structure

Advantages of a matrix structure	Disadvantages of a matrix structure
Working together allows expertise from each department to be immediately available, preventing possible delays in projects	Each project team member will have at least two bosses
The focus of the project team should be on success of the project, rather than making their functional department more important than others	Two bosses means it can be unclear whose orders should take priority
Learning from the views of colleagues in other departments helps to develop each team member	Getting staff from different functional areas to agree can be difficult

Impact of structure on motivation and efficiency

REVISED

It is remarkable how many ways structure can affect efficiency and motivation and therefore costs and profit. Effects on efficiency and therefore unit costs include:
- poor communication leading to mistakes
- duplication of tasks
- tasks being overlooked and not done
- departments failing to work together effectively.

Meanwhile, structure can affect motivation by encouraging or preventing the following key issues:
- Scope to show initiative
- Extent of delegation
- Responsibility
- Receiving all information required to perform a job
- Opportunities for promotion

Exam tip

Whenever relevant, look to build chains of logic that interweave organisational structure, motivation theory, productivity (efficiency) and unit costs.

Now test yourself

9   In what type of structure may staff have more than one line manager?
10 Why does a flat structure encourage delegation?
11 How does a tall structure offer more scope for promotion?
12 Who makes major decisions in a centralised structure?
13 Look ahead to the next section which deals with motivation in theory. Link up each of the five bullet points above to the work of at least one theorist to understand how you can use motivation theory alongside organisational structure when building a chain of argument in an exam answer.

Answers online

Motivation in theory

The desire to understand what motivates people to work is driven by the commercial need to fully use the human resources at the firm's disposal. For over a century, academics have been trying to put together viable theories that help to explain what motivates people to work. The four key theorists are explained below.

F.W. Taylor (scientific management)

Taylor's approach to motivation can be summarised simply as 'money motivates'. His theory suggests that people only work in order to maximise their own income. This means that to get people to work harder, money should be used as an incentive (or removal of money as a threat). This approach to motivation was accompanied by Taylor's beliefs as to how work as a whole should be organised, summarised below:
● Break the task down into small, simple repetitive parts.
● Design a payment system that rewards each worker each time they complete their task.

F.W. Taylor's work is still visible in many jobs today, where commission or piece rate pay is used to incentivise more work being completed. However, Taylor's ideas of how a business should be organised became extremely unpopular with workers. They felt treated like pieces of machinery and denied the opportunity to use their minds at work. They were also resentful of the level of control that the work process and payment method gave employers.

Elton Mayo (human relations theory)

Mayo's work stemmed from a range of experiments he conducted into the effectiveness of 'Taylorism'. Mayo discovered that there were more factors affecting workplace performance than money. Mayo's findings centred on the importance of interpersonal relations as a factor affecting productivity, thus the name 'human relations theory'. The factors Mayo identified are summarised below:
● Workers gain satisfaction from a certain level of freedom and control over their working environment.
● Workers who feel they belong to a team tend to work more effectively.
● Group norms (what people in a team expect of each other) tend to have a strong influence over workers' behaviour and productivity.
● Managers taking an active personal interest in their employees has a beneficial impact on workers' performance.

Maslow (hierarchy of needs)

Figure 5.3 Maslow's hierarchy of needs

Maslow's hierarchy of needs, shown in Figure 5.3, summarises his beliefs about what explains human behaviour, both in general and in the workplace. He believed that all humans have five sets of needs. These can be arranged in a hierarchy, with the most basic needs for life at the bottom and the higher-level needs at the top. Meeting each level of needs is a priority until they are met, when a person will focus on the next unsatisfied level of needs. Table 5.7 shows how each level of need has workplace implications.

Table 5.7 Maslow's hierarchy of needs: implications for business

Maslow's level of human need	Business implications
Physical needs, e.g. food, shelter, warmth	Pay levels and working conditions
Safety needs, e.g. security, a safe structured environment, stability, freedom from anxiety	Job security, a clear job role/description, clear lines of accountability (only one boss)
Social needs, e.g. belonging, friendship, contact	Team working, communications, social facilities
Esteem needs, e.g. strength, self-respect, confidence, status and recognition	Status, recognition for achievement, power, trust
Self-actualisation, e.g. self-fulfilment; 'to become everything that one is capable of becoming', wrote Maslow	Scope to develop new skills and meet new challenges, and to develop one's full potential

Frederick Herzberg (two-factor theory)

Herzberg's theory relies on accepting his definition of motivation – of doing something because you want to do it. He distinguished this from *movement*, which he defined as doing something to get a reward or avoid a punishment. Herzberg was clear – motivated workers give you their best performance all the time, are willing to embrace change and are great at solving problems.

Professor Herzberg's two-factor theory suggests that factors affecting people at work can be grouped into 'motivators' and 'hygiene factors'. He identifies five common features of instances when workers are genuinely motivated. Providing the opportunity for staff to experience these can lead to job satisfaction. Herzberg's motivators are:

- achievement
- recognition for achievement
- meaningful, interesting work
- responsibility
- advancement – a sense of growth as a person.

> **Typical mistake**
>
> Suggesting that Herzberg claimed that pay and bonuses motivate staff is wrong. Herzberg was clear that money is a hygiene factor and while offering bonuses can generate movement (better than average work), it does not motivate.

The other set of needs all relate to the context, or environment, in which you expect an employee to do their job. These needs, which Herzberg called hygiene factors, must be met to prevent an employee feeling dissatisfied.

- Company policy and administration (the rules and paperwork involved in working for the business)
- Supervision
- Pay
- Interpersonal relations (with peers, bosses or subordinates)
- Working conditions

These hygiene needs do not motivate staff, however they must be satisfied to prevent dissatisfaction. Herzberg argued it is impossible to motivate a dissatisfied worker. Three possible scenarios are explained in Table 5.8.

> Herzberg used the term **job enrichment** to describe designing jobs that include the motivators. Possible methods include: a complete unit of work, direct feedback on performance and the ability to communicate directly with any other member of staff.

Table 5.8 Three scenarios under Herzberg's two-factor theory

Hygiene needs met, no motivators	Worker will give movement (not their best – only enough to gain reward or avoid threat)
Motivators met, but hygiene not satisfied	Employee will be resentful of their job and, no matter how interesting the work is, will perform poorly – and look for another job
Hygiene needs and motivators met	Employees can focus on their job and will do it to the best of their ability

Now test yourself

TESTED

14 Explain how Taylor's belief in why people work ties in with paying people for each unit they produce.
15 Explain how this means a firm should be able to pay staff and make a profit.
16 What did Taylor say was the only thing that motivated people to work?
17 What did Mayo discover also played a part in motivation?
18 List Maslow's five levels of needs.
19 State two examples of Herzberg's hygiene factors and three of his motivators.
20 Explain in your own words the difference between motivation and movement, giving an example from your school/college life.

Answers online

Motivation in practice

Financial rewards

REVISED

- Piecework: Paying each member of staff a set amount of money each time they repeat a task.
  - Advantage: This encourages speed as the quickest staff earn the most money.
  - Disadvantage: It is likely to lead to quality problems as staff rush to complete as many tasks as possible.
- Commission: Paying staff whose role involves selling a certain percentage of the revenue they generate, usually on top of a low basic salary or hourly rate.
  - Advantage: This incentivises staff to sell as much as they can.
  - Disadvantage: It may lead to mis-selling as staff try to sell more expensive products or services to maximise their commission, causing customer dissatisfaction.

- Bonus: Paying a lump sum as an additional reward to members of staff, typically once a year.
  - Advantage: This can provide an excellent way of offering staff a valued extra thank you.
  - Disadvantage: Large bonuses can distort staff behaviour, emphasising the need to reach the bonus target by whatever means possible.
- Profit-sharing: Allocating a certain proportion of annual profits to be shared as a bonus among staff.
  - Advantage: This aligns staff goals with business goals.
  - Disadvantage: Hard-working staff may resent others who receive the same profit share bonus without putting in the same amount of effort.
- Performance-related pay (PRP): This involves rewarding staff whose performance exceeds a certain level where work performance is hard to quantify. The decision whether to award a bonus usually depends on some form of appraisal system.
  - Advantage: This allows individuals' performances to be clearly rewarded financially.
  - Disadvantage: Employees may feel the process used to decide on the award of PRP is unfair or biased against them.

> **Exam tip**
>
> For any financial method, Taylor's theory – that money motivates – can be used to justify why the method should work.

Non-financial techniques

REVISED

> **Delegation** means passing authority down the structure to a subordinate, giving them some decision-making power over how a task is done.
>
> **Empowerment** is a slightly stronger form of delegation in which the subordinate is given some decision-making power over what tasks need to be done, not simply told how to do them.
>
> **Consultation** means asking the views of staff affected as part of a decision-making process, although the manager retains the power to make the decision.
>
> **Job enlargement** is the term used to describe any increase in the scope of a job and this describes both job rotation and job enrichment.

Table 5.9 Non-financial motivation techniques

	Explanation	Why it should motivate	Possible problems
Delegation	Passing decision-making power to staff over how to perform a task	Allows staff to meet Maslow's esteem and self-actualisation needs, as well as being a motivator for Herzberg	Staff must have the skills and experience to make good decisions
Empowerment	Passing even more power to staff, to the extent where they may be given authority to decide what job needs doing	Allows staff to meet Maslow's esteem and self-actualisation needs, as well as being a motivator for Herzberg	The need for appropriate skills and experience is even greater than that needed for successful delegation
Consultation	Seeking staff's opinions before making a decision	May help to meet esteem needs on Maslow's hierarchy	Many decisions will appear to go against the views of many staff – consultation may be seen as a meaningless process
Team-working	Allowing staff to work in a group rather than individually	Allows staff to meet Maslow's social needs, recognises Mayo's belief that human relations are necessary to motivate staff	The performance of more productive individuals may be dragged down to a team average level

	Explanation	Why it should motivate	Possible problems
Flexible working	Allows staff to adjust where and/or when they work to suit their lifestyle	Helps to ensure Maslow's lower-level needs are met, and can be a key factor in meeting Herzberg's hygiene needs	Co-ordinating the workforce can be harder to achieve
Job enrichment	Giving staff added responsibilities and challenge by widening the scope of their job	Meets Herzberg's motivators and Maslow's top two levels of need	Some staff may view extra responsibility as an unwanted burden
Job rotation	Moves staff between different tasks of the same level of complexity	Helps to prevent boredom – little theoretical justification	Prevents the potential productivity benefits that come from specialising in one task

Now test yourself

TESTED

21 State three motivation methods that F.W. Taylor would advocate.
22 State three motivation methods that Herzberg would advise a business to use.
23 What motivation method could be used if workers are struggling to meet their social needs at work?
24 Explain why delegation may need to be accompanied by training.
25 Which motivation methods are designed to align a worker's personal financial rewards with the company's financial success?

Answers online

Leadership

Leaders and managers

REVISED

The roles of **manager** and **leader** are different, although in many businesses, especially smaller firms, the same person may be expected to fulfil both roles. Peter Drucker's quotation 'Managers do things right; leaders do the right thing' sums up the difference nicely.

Table 5.10 Responses of leaders and managers to different circumstances

Circumstances	What managers do	What leaders do
Key staff are leaving	Recruit new staff with care	Rethink the design and responsibilities within the job
An important customer is threatening to go elsewhere	Get staff to smooth things over as best they can	Take personal responsibility for the customer's disappointment and sort the problem out
A downturn means redundancies are necessary	Hire an HR specialist company to handle the whole process	Call a staff meeting, explain what is happening and deal with the whole thing personally
A very promising new product idea has been proposed	Take control of the development and assemble a large project team	Delegate the project to a bright young manager, providing extra resources when needed

A **manager** is a person fulfilling a role whose major job is to oversee putting plans into action, getting the details right and ensuring that the resources allocated are used correctly.

The role of a **leader** is to identify key issues to be addressed, set objectives and decide what should be done to address those issues and who should do it.

Typical mistake

Although some leaders are charismatic characters, with outgoing personalities that subordinates love to follow, many highly successful leaders may go unnoticed – not all great leaders lead by example.

Types of leadership style

Different leaders deal with their staff in different ways. You need to understand four types of leadership style:

- Autocratic: Autocratic leaders issue instructions and expect these to be obeyed. They know exactly what they want done and pay little attention to what workers have to say. Communication will be one-way, top down, with the manager not expecting or responding to feedback.
- Paternalistic: Paternalistic leaders see themselves in the role of a traditional father-figure – the head of the family. They care about the best interests of staff/family and listen to their views. But the leader makes the decisions, albeit decisions believed to be in the best interests of staff.
- Democratic: Democratic managers expect their staff to be involved in decision-making. They will delegate authority to subordinates, believing that this is the best way to get the job done. Some democratic managers will agree clear objectives with staff, then let them get on with doing the job in order to achieve the objectives.
- Laissez-faire: Literally meaning 'leave to do', laissez-faire managers leave staff alone to get on with things, generally without even providing a clear sense of direction. This will often be the result of the manager being either too busy or too lazy to provide focus and structure. However, for a new business needing ideas and creativity, leaving talented creative staff alone can provide a fertile ground for innovation.

Table 5.11 Assumptions and approaches of three types of leader

	Democratic	Paternalistic	Autocratic
Style derived from	Belief in Maslow's higher-order needs or in Herzberg's motivators	Mayo's work on human relations and Maslow's lower- and middle-order needs	A Taylorite view of staff
Approach to staff	Delegation of authority	Consultation with staff	Orders must be obeyed
Approach to staff remuneration	Salary, perhaps plus employee shareholdings	Salary plus extensive fringe benefits	Payment by results, e.g. piece rate
Approach to human resource management	Recruitment and training based on attitudes and teamwork	Emphasis on training and appraisal for personal development	Recruitment and training based on skills; appraisal linked to pay

Now test yourself

26 Name the leadership style being explained:
   (a) The leader seeks and listens to the views of staff, delegating with a clear sense of purpose.
   (b) The manager cares about the welfare of staff and considers this when making decisions.
   (c) The manager expects their instructions to be followed and keeps all decision-making power.
   (d) The manager leaves staff to get on with their work without any clear direction.
27 Explain why the leader and manager are likely to be the same person in a small business.

Answers online

Exam practice

HMRC – the UK organisation responsible for collecting taxes – attracted news headlines in 2016 as a result of its decision to outsource the cleaning of its offices. This meant that cleaners, formerly employed by HMRC, might lose their pension benefits and legal entitlement to sick pay. The company to which the cleaning work was outsourced used staff employed on zero-hours contracts. This shifted the risk involved in employing staff away from HMRC to the subcontractor. In turn, the subcontractor shifts risk to the people they employ. The zero-hours contracts mean the subcontractor does not have to pay staff when there's no work, therefore avoiding unnecessary costs.

Questions

1 What is meant by a zero-hours contract? (2)
2 What is meant by outsourcing? (2)
3 Using a motivation theory of your choice, explain why HMRC's new cleaners, employed by the subcontractor, are likely to do a poorer job than cleaners who were previously employed by HMRC. (6)
4 Assess whether HMRC has made the right decision about how to have its offices cleaned. (10)

Answers and quick quiz 5 online

ONLINE

Summary

- Different employers may view their staff either as a critical asset to the business's success or simply as a cost to be minimised.
- Having a flexible workforce makes it easier to run a business successfully.
- Employer/employee relations can be based on either collective or individual bargaining.
- The need to recruit staff could be triggered by existing staff leaving, growth of the business, or new activities being performed by the business.
- Staff may be recruited internally or externally.
- Selection methods including interviews, testing and profiling, and assessment centres are used to decide which applicants to employ.
- Training staff has both benefits and costs.
- Initial training is called induction training.
- Training can be carried out on the job or off the job.
- Organisational structures can be classified as tall, flat or matrix.
- Key issues affecting the shape of organisational structure are spans of control and levels of hierarchy.

- Organisational structure can have major impacts on efficiency and motivation.
- Methods of motivating staff can fall into two categories: financial and non-financial methods.
- The five financial methods are: piecework, commission, bonus, profit-sharing and performance-related pay.
- Non-financial methods are: delegation, empowerment, consultation, team-working, flexible working, job rotation and job enrichment.
- Clear links can be drawn from the motivation theorists' work to explain why these methods should work.
- The roles of leader and manager are significantly different.
- Different leaders treat their staff in different ways. This is called their leadership style.
- The main leadership styles to focus on are: autocratic, paternalistic, democratic and laissez-faire.

6 Entrepreneurs and leaders

Role of an entrepreneur

Businesses could not exist without entrepreneurs. They are the individuals who spot business opportunities and then act in order to exploit the opportunity. Entrepreneurs must fulfil a number of roles within their businesses, as outlined below.

Creating and setting up a business   REVISED ☐

Generating a business idea

At the very heart of any entrepreneur's success is a good idea, probably based on an understanding of consumers. The main sources of business ideas are:

- Observation: Watching what other businesses are doing or how consumers behave may give an idea that can be copied elsewhere. Or it may suggest an idea that can be adjusted to work even more successfully.
- Thinking ahead: This is spotting trends that will lead to changes in the future that will offer business opportunities, for example noting a government initiative to boost the number of apprenticeships and setting up a website specialising in advertising apprenticeships.
- Personal or business experience: Noticing that certain needs are not met through personal experience or within a workplace.
- Innovations: Scientific breakthroughs or major overhauls of an existing type of product may generate viable business ideas.

Spotting an opportunity

An idea will only become a viable business if a market exists for it. The ability to identify chances to turn ideas into saleable products or services relies on spotting an opportunity. Typical sources of opportunity tend to be centred on changes occurring in the wider world:

- Changes in technology: Increased computing power in mobile handsets broadens the range of possible apps that could be produced to meet a need for consumers to control something on the move.
- Changes in society: Trends in the way people behave, such as increased part-time work opportunities for the semi-retired, can represent an opportunity, such as a recruitment agency for retired workers.
- Changes in the economy: Differing rates of national or regional economic growth may offer opportunities to be exploited.

Running and expanding a business   REVISED ☐

There are four key habits that successful entrepreneurs commonly demonstrate in the way they run their businesses:

- They measure performance in an unbiased way: If there are problems these must be identified rather than ignored.
- They have an eye for detail: It is unlikely that anybody other than the entrepreneur will be as worried about getting the little things right.

- They have the ability to step back from the day-to-day issues: Only by thinking strategically will a new business be able to secure a long-term future.
- They love what they are doing: Without this, the motivation needed to do the three things above will drain away.

Some businesses are not suited to expansion as the idea and opportunities remain small-scale or localised. For other entrepreneurs, expansion may be vital to prevent others from developing an idea more successfully. The three major problems to avoid as an entrepreneur considering expansion are:

- Over-estimating demand: What works in one place may not work elsewhere.
- Failing to raise sufficient finance: It is a lack of cash that ultimately leads to all business failure. Without having made sure that the business has enough finance to support operating on a larger scale, the danger of running out of cash becomes acute.
- Not recruiting enough or the right people: As entrepreneurs expand their business they will find their limited time more stretched, with more to oversee (perhaps causing too much stress). It is therefore vital that when they recruit they get the right staff who understand the business philosophy and have the skills needed.

Innovation within a business

REVISED

If entrepreneurs are loosely defined as those who are able to generate and develop new business ideas, then there is a role for them even in large firms. The kind of creative and disruptive thinking that entrepreneurs can draw on is increasingly being sought by large businesses. They want to nurture innovation within their businesses as a way of maintaining a competitive advantage. Entrepreneurial behaviour within the setting of a large business – **intrapreneurship** – can be seen in many successful large businesses such as Facebook.

> **Intrapreneurship** is the name given to the encouragement of entrepreneurial behaviour within larger businesses.

Barriers to entrepreneurship

REVISED

Funding

Following the financial crash of the last decade, banks in the UK have been less willing to lend to small firms and business start-ups, considering them relatively high risk for relatively low return as they are often believed to be relatively unprofitable. Without institutions willing to lend, entrepreneurship may die back in the UK.

Gender bias

UK entrepreneurs are three times as likely to be male as female. This statistical mismatch between the population/market and the people starting new businesses is likely to mean that much entrepreneurial talent in the UK is going to waste.

Lack of public sector support

Although the image of the entrepreneur has improved significantly in the UK over the past twenty years, some who work in the public sector view entrepreneurs sceptically, suspecting tax avoidance or motives based on greed. This perception in the public sector may lead to an education system that fails to value entrepreneurial skills or other barriers to entrepreneurship.

Anticipating risk and uncertainty in the business environment

Risk and uncertainty characterise the business environment for many firms. This is because of the wide number of external variables that the business cannot control, and may not even be able to influence. The role of the entrepreneur must include understanding the ways that uncertainty affects the business. In some cases the main cause of uncertainty can be reduced, such as introducing new products into the firm's portfolio, thereby reducing the dependence on the sales of one brand.

Now test yourself

1 State two ways that walking around the local town may help to identify a business opportunity.
2 Explain why entrepreneurs may find it harder to secure funding from banks than fifteen years ago.
3 What four habits are important for any entrepreneur to develop if they want to successfully start up their business?

Answers online

Entrepreneurial motives and characteristics

Characteristics and skills

The main characteristics required to become a successful entrepreneur are:
- understanding the market
- determination
- passion
- resilience
- the ability to cope with risk.

Taking sensible risks involves weighing up the risk and rewards that a course of action offers. Risk consists of the likelihood of things going wrong and the size of the consequences of things going wrong. Good entrepreneurs accept risk but will not take on any risk they consider to be too great.

Good entrepreneurs will need to be able to demonstrate a range of common skills:
- Financial skills: This involves understanding key financial documents and, more fundamentally, how finance allows a business to function.
- Persuasive abilities: Good entrepreneurs find a way of persuading many people to do many things that their business needs, from suppliers to staff to customers.
- Problem-solving skills: These are frequently shown by the ability to identify causes of the problem and solve the problem by addressing these causes.
- Networking skills: With a wide range of possible business contacts, entrepreneurs are more likely to find someone who can help when the business needs help.

Reasons why people set up businesses

- Profit maximising: This means to continually seek to get the most profit from every business transaction. Though this may seem the way to get rich, it will often cause long-term problems, with consumers feeling exploited or even cheated with substandard work caused by skimping on materials and workmanship.
- **Profit satisficing**: Long-term success may well be based on satisficing, with the need to accept lower than possible profits in the short term to build a brand or a reputation.
- Independence: Entrepreneurs sometimes set up their own business to avoid the need to take orders from others or fit in with company policy. Research shows the attractions of 'being your own boss' to be a very common motive.
- Home-working: Being able to work at, or from, home can be another form of independence, especially valued by those with family commitments.
- Ethical stance: For those with strong beliefs in how business should be done, their ethical stance may lead them to feel the need to start their own business. They are unwilling to compromise their beliefs by working in a business with whose practices they feel uncomfortable.
- Social entrepreneurship: Although this has a clear cross-over with ethical beliefs, some entrepreneurs will start up a business whose major aim is to make a positive contribution to their community, perhaps by providing a service that benefits people in need. Sadly, some may pretend to be social entrepreneurs while profit remains their real goal.

> **Profit satisficing** means blending a desire for profit with other factors, such as building a good reputation or having a good work–life balance.

> **Exam tip**
>
> An entrepreneur's motives will be a major determining factor behind their decision-making. Decisions taken by an entrepreneur who is seeking to maximise profit will differ greatly from those taken by an entrepreneur driven by an ethical stance.

Now test yourself

4 What are two common financial motives for starting a business?
5 Briefly explain a good entrepreneur's attitude to risk.
6 State three types of people on whom an entrepreneur may need to use their persuasive abilities.
7 Why can profit maximisation damage a firm's long-term chances of success?
8 Why may entrepreneurs who take an ethical stance struggle to make a profit, even in the long term?

Answers online

Business objectives

Business **objectives** are targets set in order to ensure that the whole business is working towards the same goals. Objectives are set by those in charge of the firm, such as the chief executive. Once objectives have been set, a plan for achieving the objectives – a **strategy** – can be devised. The strategy will lay out what each department of the business will need to do in order to enable the business to reach its objectives.

> An **objective** is a specific target set by a business.
>
> The **strategy** is the plan devised by the business to achieve its objectives.

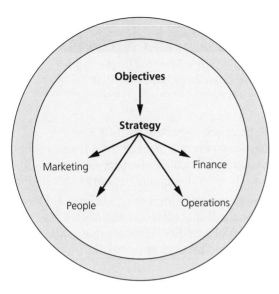

Figure 6.1 **How business works**

SMART objectives

REVISED

To gain most from objectives, they should be SMART:
- Specific
- Measurable
- Achievable
- Realistic
- Time-bound

Common business objectives

REVISED

Common business objectives can be seen in Table 6.1.

Table 6.1 **Common business objectives**

Typical objective	Explanation	Typical circumstances
Survival	Focusing on generating sufficient cash to sustain the business	When starting up, or when a challenging external environment threatens the future of the business, such as a recession or the arrival of a powerful new competitor
Profit maximisation	Earning the most profit possible in a given time period	A common objective for businesses – reflecting the need to generate profit for owners as a primary purpose of business
Sales maximisation	Growing the number of customers, without a major focus on controlling costs	In a rapidly growing market, firms may try to maximise their share of the market, with an expectation of generating profits once the market growth has slowed and competition reduces
Market share	Increasing market share to a dominant level helps to ensure long-term success through greater distribution and preventing new entrants from challenging in the market	Market leaders will often seek to increase their lead and thus power by enhancing market share
Cost efficiency	A focus on seeking to minimise the costs of producing a product or service and the running costs of the business	This objective will be key for firms that are trying to follow a strategy where they will aim to undercut all their rivals on price. If they can keep costs low, they should still be able to make a profit even with a low selling price

Typical objective	Explanation	Typical circumstances
Employee welfare	Looking after staff, by treating them well, and looking to develop them using training and internal recruitment	Where people play a key role in gaining a competitive advantage, whether that be in customer service or through innovation
Customer satisfaction	Prioritising the need to ensure that every customer has a positive interaction with the business	This will be crucial where attracting new customers is costly and losing existing customers is very expensive, such as when providing a regular service such as mobile phone networks or banking
Social objectives	Objectives that relate to the beneficial role a business can play within society	Some businesses see improving society as a key purpose and will therefore set social objectives in a meaningful way. Social enterprises will have social objectives as a top priority

Now test yourself

TESTED

9 Why do businesses set objectives?
10 What does SMART stand for?
11 What are the eight common business objectives?

Answers online

Exam tip

Successful firms choose the right objectives to suit their circumstances. Carefully read the right-hand column of Table 6.1 to ensure you understand when different objectives are most appropriate.

Forms of business

The topic referred to as 'forms of business' refers primarily to the legal status of the organisation. However, later in this topic, 'Other forms of business' covers issues such as licensing the use of a business's name, running a business enterprise to improve society, running a business as part of a lifestyle choice and running a business purely online.

Table 6.2 Different forms of business

Legal forms of business covered in this topic	Other 'forms of business' covered – not specifically relating to legal status
Sole trader	Franchising
Partnership	Social enterprise
Private limited company	Lifestyle businesses
Public limited company	Online businesses

Businesses with unlimited liability

REVISED

Sole trader

A sole trader is a person who starts and runs a business without turning it into a company. This explains why the law sees the business and the owner of the business as the same. As a result, the owner is personally **liable** for any debts built up in running their business. If the business goes bust, the owner has to use personal assets to repay those to whom the business owes money.

Liability refers to the extent to which the owner(s) of the business must repay debts incurred in the running of the business.

Key benefits:
● Owner has full control over decisions
● Owner keeps all profits made
● Minimal paperwork needed to start up

Key drawbacks:
- Owner has unlimited liability for debts
- Hard to raise finance

Partnership

While a sole trader is the single owner of a business, a partnership is perhaps best thought of as a sole trader where several owners are allowed. This helps to raise finance as each partner can bring capital into the business. In addition, the burden of responsibility for running the business can be shared, potentially among people with varied skills and experience. As with a sole trader, partners still have **unlimited liability** for debts incurred in running the business.

Key benefits:
- More owners can allow more finance to be raised
- Partners may bring varied skills and experience
- Shared burden of responsibility among partners

Key drawbacks:
- Partners have unlimited liability
- Potential for disagreement among partners

> **Typical mistake**
>
> Liability for debt only becomes an issue if the business goes bust. The owners' personal assets will only be taken if the business goes under, but still owes money after the assets bought for use in the business have been sold to raise money.

Businesses with limited liability

REVISED

For businesses happy to undergo increased legal formalities, **limited liability** for owners offers a great safety net from which to build a much larger business. Without this protection, far fewer investors would be willing to invest their money into multi-billion pound firms whose debts could run into billions of pounds.

Private limited company

The simpler form of limited company to start is a private limited company with no minimum share capital. Increased legal formalities include having accounts independently audited each year at a probable cost of several thousand pounds.

> **Typical mistake**
>
> Some exam answers wrongly suggest that private limited companies can keep their accounts hidden from public view. In fact, one responsibility for all limited companies is to send a simplified copy of their accounts to Companies House. Anyone can inspect any business's accounts at Companies House or via the Companies House website (for a small fee).

Public limited company

A public limited company is the only type of business that can sell shares via the stock market to the general public. This allows them to raise vast sums of share capital. However, in order to become a public limited company, a business must have a minimum of £50,000 share capital. In addition, there are considerable regulatory requirements involved

> **Typical mistake**
>
> Sole traders can employ staff. Too many exam answers wrongly state that a sole trader has to run the business by themselves, mistakenly believing sole traders are literally one-person businesses. The 'sole' refers to the owner – just one owner. There can be as many staff employed as the owner wishes.

> **Unlimited liability** means that the owners of the business must take personal responsibility for covering debts run up by their business. If the business goes bust, the owner can be forced to sell their own personal assets to repay lenders, suppliers or employees to whom money is owed.

> **Limited liability** is a form of legal protection for business owners which ensures that owners of a limited company can only lose the money they have invested in the business.

> **Typical mistake**
>
> Private limited companies are required to use the letters Ltd as part of their name. The letters PLC are reserved for public limited companies.

in floating the company on the stock market. Continuing to meet the annual requirements of the stock market will cost tens or hundreds of times more than running a private limited company.

Other forms of business

Franchising

Franchising offers the opportunity to start a business using a tried and tested formula. For the **franchisor**, franchising can be a relatively cheap and quick way of expanding their business rapidly. For the **franchisee**, there are both benefits and drawbacks relative to starting entirely independently, as shown below.

Benefits:
● Access to a tried and tested formula for business success
● Support from the franchisor in providing materials and fixtures and fittings
● Advice and training on all business functions
● Possibility of a national advertising campaign from the franchisor
● Easier access to loans as banks recognise the lower risk involved in starting as a franchisee

Drawbacks:
● The franchisee may feel frustrated at being unable to make decisions dictated by the franchisor.
● There is likely to be an initial franchise fee to buy the licence (perhaps several hundred thousand pounds for the most popular franchised brands).
● The franchisor will also expect royalties, a percentage of revenue.

> A **franchise** is a licence to use another business's name and business model in return for payment.
>
> A **franchisor** is a business that sells the right to use its name and logo to other businesses or entrepreneurs.
>
> A **franchisee** is an entrepreneur or company that buys a licence to use another business's name and business model in return for payment.

Social enterprise

Social enterprises place the desire to fix a social problem above the profit motive when making decisions. This is, of course, a terribly broad definition but that is necessary given the wide range of businesses that can be classed as being, in some way, social enterprises.

Lifestyle businesses

Some entrepreneurs start up a business because it suits their desired lifestyle. This may mean that maximising profit is far from the most important issue considered when making decisions for these businesses. For some, running their own business may give flexibility in working hours to fit around family commitments: for example, leaving a highly paid job that requires long periods away from home in order to start up a small computer repair business could allow an entrepreneur to fit work commitments round their children's sports days and Christmas plays.

Online businesses

As the internet has grown over the past 30 years to become a huge part of modern life, business opportunities have grown out of the technology. Most important is the way the internet has enabled businesses to connect with consumers effectively without the need to ever meet face to face. The result is that traditional 'bricks and mortar' businesses now face competition from many online-only companies. In general, online offers two powerful advantages over traditional 'bricks and mortar' businesses:
● Lower costs (with no need to spend on physical premises)
● Higher potential revenues (with the scope to sell worldwide)

12 Which two types of business organisation offer their owners no limited liability?
13 What is the minimum share capital required to form a public limited company?
14 State two benefits of starting a business by buying a franchise.
15 State two drawbacks of buying a franchise rather than starting a business independently.

Answers online

Business choices

Rather than worrying about learning too much in this topic, being aware of **opportunity cost**, choices and trade-offs should help to structure the thought processes needed to write excellent responses to examination questions.

> **Opportunity cost** is the value of the next best option forgone when a business decision is made.

Opportunity cost

REVISED

Too often business decisions are made without a real appreciation of the opportunity cost. In order to genuinely understand the opportunity cost of any decision, it is vital to ensure that all possible options are appropriately quantified. However, this generally needs accurate forecasting, a challenge that most businesses struggle to achieve.

Frequently, decisions may be based on personal preferences of business leaders – leaders in a position to influence the data on which the decision will be made. Though this may sound conspiratorial, it may in fact simply be a reflection of the enthusiasm that the leader has for their 'great idea'. If the best decisions are to be made, cool heads must carefully identify the opportunity costs involved in making a particular business choice.

Identifying opportunity costs requires careful thought and analysis. Figure 6.2 helps to illustrate this.

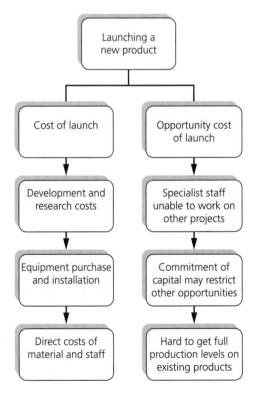

Figure 6.2 Opportunity costs of new product launch

Choices and trade-offs

The choices a business faces are likely to involve some form of compromise – a trade-off between competing objectives – such as minimising costs and maintaining quality standards. Successfully managing these trade-offs will need several attributes on behalf of decision-makers including:

- experience
- understanding of consumer tastes
- a broad understanding of the business's current position
- an understanding of the external issues influencing the decision.

Now test yourself

16 Explain the meaning of the term 'opportunity cost'.
17 Explain the meaning of the term 'trade-off'.

Answers online

Moving from entrepreneur to leader

Once a business start-up has been successful, for those entrepreneurs who are happy to grow their business a number of problems may emerge. Some of these issues will be caused by changes within the business. One of the most common, though, is the challenge for the founder in making the transition from entrepreneur to leader.

Common personal issues when moving from entrepreneur to leader

- Delegating
- Maintaining effective communication
- Co-ordinating far more people
- Keeping an eye on the big issues

Delegating

A successful entrepreneur, used to making all the decisions about the business, can find it hard to let go of authority. But for the delegation to succeed, the subordinate must feel trusted to make decisions without interference from the boss. If the business is to grow, letting go of control can often be the single hardest challenge faced by an entrepreneur.

Maintaining effective communication

Once an organisational structure begins to develop within a growing business, communication is vital, but harder to ensure. The boss will still need to know what customers are saying or what morale is like among shop-floor staff. For this to happen, information must be able to flow upwards through supervisors and managers who may be hesitant to tell the boss about problems.

In addition, if the boss is still going to set the direction for the firm and exert a strong influence over how things get done within the business, top-down communication will be vital. But in a bigger organisation, orders and instructions may get distorted as they pass through several layers of management.

Co-ordinating far more people

In a start-up the boss is likely to know all staff on a personal level. Once the total workforce of a business passes a certain size, the boss may struggle to develop the personal relationships that had marked out their successful start-up. However, all staff (and other business resources) will still need to be heading in the same direction. It is down to the boss to ensure this still takes place, even without the ability to personally work with all members of staff on a regular basis.

Growth requires an entrepreneur to make the change from hands-on boss to leader/manager. As discussed on page 54, these two roles – manager and leader – are different. In order for effective growth to take place, the entrepreneur will have to develop management skills of co-ordination or employ effective managers who can take over this role.

Keeping an eye on the big issues

The role of leader, as explained on page 54, involves being able to understand exactly where the business should be heading and inspiring others with a vision of how the business is going to get there. As a business grows, subtle changes of direction can take place. The entrepreneur-turned-leader will need to keep an eye on the big issues facing the firm, such as what to sell and whom to sell to, while ensuring the management of resources is still taking place efficiently.

Now test yourself

TESTED ☐

18 Why is retained profit unlikely to be a source of finance for the early stages of the growth of a business?
19 In what two ways does a loan result in cash draining out of a business?
20 Why do many entrepreneurs find delegation so hard?

Answers online

Exam practice

After a successful career in banking, Robert Southey had already started one business trading company debt and other financial products. His first business had not been as successful as he had hoped. Robert was disappointed with how little work his partner had been doing, so for his new venture he decided to 'go it alone' with Southey Capital Ltd. Much of the finance was raised with his own personal savings. Robert was keen to avoid loans as banks were not offering attractive rates of interest. With the need to build up his turnover as quickly as possible, in order to build a reputation in the markets he was dealing with, Robert's initial goal was to maximise revenue in the first year of the business. He employed four staff to help manage the office and research the deals he uncovered. However, Robert watched them like a hawk, always with a keen eye for detail and unwilling to let his business suffer from somebody else's mistake. There is no doubt that Robert has that vital skill for an entrepreneur – the ability to cope with risk – but he is not willing to take risks without trying to minimise the chances of failure. His overall strategy, of trying to minimise costs wherever possible in order to enable Southey Capital Ltd to make a profit on deals that competitors would find loss-making, is paying off.

Questions

1 Identify two benefits to Robert of starting his business as a private limited company. (2)
2 Identify two benefits to Southey Capital Ltd of having a clear business objective. (2)
3 Explain the potential opportunity costs to Robert's new business start-up of employing four staff. (6)
4 Assess whether a strategy of minimising costs is always likely to lead to business success? (10)

Answers and quick quiz 6 online

ONLINE

Summary

- Five major sources of business ideas are: observation, brainstorming, thinking ahead, personal or business experience, and innovation.
- Business opportunities may arise as a result of changes in technology, society, the economy, the housing market or the use of market research.
- The market research that precedes business start-ups will almost always be done on a very small budget.
- Common habits for successful entrepreneurs include: measuring performance accurately, stepping back from the day-to-day work, an eye for detail and loving what they do.
- The major characteristics of an entrepreneur include: understanding the market, determination, passion, resilience, the ability to cope with risk.
- The key skills required by an entrepreneur are: financial skills, persuasive abilities, problem-solving skills and networking skills.
- Major motives for starting up your own business are: profit maximisation, profit satisficing, independence, home-working, ethical stance and social entrepreneurship.
- Objectives are targets for a business.
- A strategy must be devised to achieve objectives.
- Objectives provide a clear sense of direction for all parts of the business.
- Common objectives include: survival, profit maximisation, sales maximisation, market share, cost efficiency, employee welfare, customer satisfaction and social objectives.
- Sole traders and partnerships are legal business forms whose owners have unlimited liability.
- Limited companies can be private or public, depending upon whom shares can be sold to.
- Good decision-making requires an understanding of opportunity cost.
- Most business decisions involve trade-offs.
- As small businesses grow they face a range of problems.
- Many problems of growth are personal challenges faced as the role of entrepreneur changes to that of manager/leader.

7 Raising finance

Sources of finance: internal and external

Several circumstances may lead to a business needing to raise finance:
- Starting up
- Growing
- Dealing with a cash flow problem
- Financing extra materials needed when a large order is received

Internal sources of finance

Owner's capital: personal savings

Most likely to be used as a source of start-up finance, an owner's own personal savings, or even redundancy payment, is considered to be an internal **source of finance**. This money could be provided in the form of share capital or lent to the business as a loan.

> Places from which businesses may gain finance are referred to as **sources of finance**.

Retained profit

Once all costs have been covered and dividends paid to shareholders, any profit left is retained in the business and can be used as a source of finance. It is probably the safest and most common form of internal finance for established businesses.

> **Exam tip**
>
> As retained profit must still be available in the form of cash if it is to be used as a source of finance, look on the statement of financial position (balance sheet) for evidence that there is sufficient cash available within the business. Bear in mind that where retained profit appears on a statement of financial position, this is merely an indicator that money has been retained. It does not imply that this money is still available as a source of finance. Look instead under current assets at the cash figure.

Sale of assets

Another internal source, especially available when established businesses are changing strategy, is cash generated by the sale of assets. Especially where a firm has adjusted its strategy, there may be assets that will no longer be needed and can thus be sold in order to generate the cash necessary for other projects.

External sources of finance

Places from which a business can generate finance may also be considered as external to the business itself. These include the following:

Family and friends

In many cases, family and friends provide extra start-up capital necessary for business start-ups. This may be by taking an equity (shareholding) stake in a business set up as a limited company. Alternatively, family and friends may provide loans where banks are unwilling.

Banks

Loans to start-ups are not very common. Banks see start-ups as an extremely risky proposition. Where a loan is provided, banks will insist on some **collateral** as security, either a business asset or a personal asset belonging to an owner.

Collateral is something of value that is used as security when a loan is offered. In the event of the business being unable to pay the loan back, the asset is transferred to the bank and sold in order to generate the money due for repayment.

Peer-to-peer funding

A recent development as a source of finance, peer-to-peer funding relies on websites that can match investors willing to lend to business start-ups with start-ups needing finance. These loans will generally be at a fairly high rate of interest, but provide an option where banks are unwilling to lend.

Business angels

These are extremely rich individuals who provide capital to high-risk, small business ventures or start-ups. The Dragons in BBC's *Dragons' Den* are best thought of as **business angels**, willing to invest in risky business start-ups and become involved in the strategic management of the business in the hope of high returns.

Business angels or angel investors are individuals who invest in the very early stages of a business, taking a significant equity (share) stake.

Crowdfunding

Another source of finance that has risen to prominence thanks to the internet is **crowdfunding**. It allows small investors to find business start-ups in which they are willing to invest through crowdfunding websites. No single investor is likely to be big enough to provide all the finance needed for each business using the site, but the beauty of crowdfunding is that many small investors can be gathered in order to provide all the finance necessary.

Crowdfunding is obtaining external finance from many small investments, usually through a web-based appeal for investors.

Other businesses

Some businesses, especially large firms, actively seek out small businesses either starting up or in their early stages and help them out by providing finance. In return they will take a shareholding. Commonly, this practice occurs in technology-based industries with large tech firms looking to find and cash in on 'the next big thing', even if they did not develop it themselves.

Methods of finance

Loans

Loans can be provided by banks, but could also be provided by friends, family or directors of the business. A loan involves providing a lump sum of cash, which will be repaid over an agreed period of time. In addition, interest payments will also be made over the course of the loan: these represent the 'cost' of the loan. Interest rates may be variable or fixed, decided at the time the loan is taken out. Many lenders, certainly banks, will expect collateral to provide security for the loan.

Share capital

When a private company is formed, the ownership of the business is split into shares. These shares can be sold to investors who become shareholders. When the share is first sold, capital enters the business.

Venture capital

Where selling shares through the stock market or taking out a bank loan are not viable options, especially where a business opportunity is considered high risk, a **venture capital** company may provide finance, generally through a mix of loans and share capital. As the investment is high risk, the loan is likely to be at a relatively high interest rate and the venture capitalist is likely to expect a relatively large shareholding, as well as a meaningful say in decision-making. Venture capital is generally used to fund a significant period of growth for an established small business.

Overdrafts

Overdrafts offer a flexibility that other methods fail to offer. A business using an overdraft only pays interest on the overdraft when it is using the facility; in other words, when the account is negative. Admittedly the interest rate charged is likely to be higher than that on a loan but, as long as the business stays out of its overdraft most of the time, the total cost of this method of finance may not be prohibitive.

Leasing

Leasing is a sensible method of avoiding large chunks of cash outflows each time a major new asset is purchased. Although in the long term leasing will be more expensive than purchasing an asset outright, buying assets can put too great a strain on a business's cash flow.

Trade credit

Trade credit is incredibly common in business to business transactions. On average, two months' credit is offered to customers, acting as a method of financing the purchase of, most frequently, materials used in production. Not all businesses will be able to access trade credit. Start-ups or those with a poor record of payment in the past may be refused credit by suppliers.

Grants

Grants are handouts, usually to small businesses, from local or central government. They are very rare, no matter what politicians claim, amounting to less than 2% of UK start-up finance. The only start-ups that may receive a grant are those likely to create jobs in areas of economic deprivation, or hi-tech firms competing with foreign rivals.

> A **method of finance** is the process through which a source of finance provides money to a business.

> **Typical mistake**
>
> A limited company only receives capital when each share is first sold. If the shareholder subsequently sells that share on, either privately or, for a public limited company, via the stock market, the company receives none of the proceeds of this onward sale.

> **Venture capital** is a method of providing finance in higher-risk investments generally through a combination of loans and shares.

> An **overdraft** is a facility offered by a bank to allow a customer to continue spending money even when their account becomes negative. There will be an agreed limit to the overdraft.

> **Leasing** an asset is an alternative to buying the asset outright. Instead, the asset is rented for a monthly fee for a set period of time.

> **Trade credit** means that goods or services provided by a supplier are not paid for immediately.

Different methods and sources of finance tend to be more or less appropriate in different circumstances. Table 7.1 summarises key issues.

Table 7.1 Methods of finance

Category	Source/method	Appropriateness
Internal sources of finance	Owner's capital/personal savings	Only relevant in a start-up or small business context
	Retained profit	The business must have made a profit and not spent it on anything else. Do not suggest this method for a new business start-up
	Sale of assets	Only for an established business – look especially for those planning to do something new, which may make existing assets redundant, thus available to sell
External sources of finance	Family and friends	Almost certainly limited to small business contexts – most commonly at start-up
	Bank	Most widely applicable source of finance, but many businesses continue to find it hard to get help from banks, certainly at reasonable interest rates
	Peer-to-peer funding	Rare, most likely to be used for a particularly risky start-up
	Business angels	Another rare source, most likely for a start-up or recently started business that may offer high rewards
	Crowdfunding	Another source that tends to be limited to start-ups rather than established businesses
	Other businesses	Rare – only a few businesses are likely to offer this and almost always in hi-tech sectors to new start-ups
Methods of finance	Loans	Note that some collateral will be needed and start-ups may find it hard to negotiate a loan at an affordable rate of interest
	Share capital	Can only be used by a limited company – sole traders and partnerships cannot sell shares without converting
	Venture capital	Only used for higher-risk businesses. They tend to be small businesses looking to achieve a significant spell of growth
	Overdraft	Only to be used infrequently – a business that uses an overdraft as a long-term source of finance will pay a lot of interest. OK for a short-term cash flow problem, not for purchasing new assets
	Leasing	Can only be used for major assets
	Trade credit	Start-ups will struggle to convince suppliers to offer them credit
	Grants	Only likely to be relevant to a business creating jobs in an area of economic deprivation or very high-tech firms trying to compete internationally

Now test yourself

TESTED

1 Identify two methods of finance on which interest must be paid to a bank.
2 Which method of finance is not available to either sole traders or partnerships?
3 Identify four common reasons why businesses need to raise finance.

Answers online

Liability and finance

The concept of limited liability was first explored on page 63. There are major implications to a business of its choice of ownership type with particular reference to the liability of owners for business debts.

Implications of limited and unlimited liability

Table 7.2 Limited and unlimited liability

Unlimited liability	Limited liability
Sole trader	Private limited company (Ltd)
Partnership	Public limited company (PLC)

Those businesses whose owners have unlimited liability (sole traders and partnerships) are unlikely to grow significantly due to the potential downside of business problems. As the owners' liability for business debts is unlimited, they can lose all of their personal assets if the business goes into administration. This is because the businesses/people owed money can chase the owners to settle those debts incurred by their business. This can include customers who have paid in advance and not received the products or services promised, or suppliers who have supplied goods on credit but not been paid.

In many ways, this makes doing business with a sole trader or a partnership less risky because in the event of the business running into problems, customers or suppliers know that they can legally pursue the owners for debts owed.

This, though, means that running a sole trader or partnership can feel riskier as the owners have no protection of their personal assets in the event of things going badly wrong.

Owners of limited companies (shareholders) have the legal protection of limited liability. This means they cannot lose any more than they invest in the business. Without this protection, it is unlikely that businesses would grow to the size of many large businesses today. Individuals would be unwilling to take such large risks if it weren't for the protection of limited liability.

There is a downside to limited liability and that is the ability of unscrupulous individuals to set up limited liability companies, which then rack up debts before the owners place the business into voluntary **liquidation**. If it can be proved that they had fraudulent motives, then limited liability is no protection against a prosecution for fraud. However, business incompetence is not fraudulent, and if a limited company goes into liquidation and still owes money after all its assets have been sold, then those to whom money is owed may lose every penny.

> **Liquidation** occurs when a company's owners close down the company, selling off its assets to generate cash to pay off the debts of the business.

Effect of liability on sources of finance

Sole traders and partnerships are likely to rely on the following sources of finance:
- Owners' capital
- Bank finance (loans and overdraft)
- Leasing
- Trade credit

Private and public limited companies can use:
- Share capital
- Bank finance (loans and overdraft)
- Angel or venture capital investment

- Peer to peer or crowdfunding
- Leasing
- Trade credit

For all established businesses, the most likely and probably the safest form of finance is retained profit.

Now test yourself

4 Which two types of business offer unlimited liability to their owners?
5 What name is given to the owners of a limited company?
6 State two sources of finance that are available to limited companies but not to sole traders or partnerships.
7 Briefly explain why offering credit to a sole trader is less risky than supplying on credit to a limited company.

Answers online

> **Exam tip**
>
> Note that any external provider of finance may be wary of offering funding to a newly created limited company, because of the protection offered to the company's shareholders by limited liability. Often, newly formed limited companies will be refused trade credit in the first months of their existence for this reason.

Planning and cash flow

The business plan

REVISED

A **business plan** is a must for any start-up business or small business looking to grow that needs to attract external finance. Any provider of finance, whether a bank, business angel or other potential shareholder, will expect to see a carefully prepared, logical and viable plan.

Not only will the plan be useful in attracting finance, but preparation of the plan also:
- helps to ensure the entrepreneur has carefully considered potential problems
- has a reference point to maintain a clear sense of direction
- has some quantitative targets to aim for.

> A **business plan** is a document setting out a business idea and how it will be financed, marketed and put into practice.

The main sections of a business plan should include:
1 Executive summary
2 The product/service
3 The market
4 Marketing plan
5 Operational plan
6 Financial plan
7 Conclusion

At the heart of the financial plan should be the cash flow forecast.

Interpreting cash flow forecasts

REVISED

The example of a cash flow forecast in Table 7.3 helps to show the key sections of the document.
- Cash inflow shows the places and timings from which cash flows into the business.
- Cash outflow shows how much cash leaves the business in each month.

Table 7.3 Example of a cash flow forecast

Month £s	March	April	May	June	July	August
Opening balance	0	3,000	(5,500)	(8,500)	(10,000)	(9,500)
Capital invested	30,000					
Cash received from sales			7,000	10,000	13,000	15,000
Cash inflow	30,000	0	7,000	10,000	13,000	15,000
Cash outflow	27,000	8,500	10,000	11,500	12,500	12,500
Monthly balance	3,000	(8,500)	(3,000)	(1,500)	500	2,500
Closing balance	**3,000**	**(5,500)**	**(8,500)**	**(10,000)**	**(9,500)**	**(7,000)**

- Monthly balance, sometimes called net cash flow, shows the net effect of the month on cash flow (cash inflow minus cash outflow).
- Opening balance (usually at the top of the table) shows the amount of cash the business had at the beginning of the month. This will be last month's closing balance.
- Closing balance shows the amount of cash in the business at the end of the month, calculated by adding the monthly balance (net cash flow) to the opening balance.

The main figures to consider when analysing a cash flow forecast are:

- Closing balance: If negative this shows the need for extra finance, quite possibly the need to arrange an overdraft so that the business can continue to spend after its bank balance has fallen to zero.
- Monthly balance (net cash flow): This will indicate how well each month is expected to go for the business.

Negative values for either of these indicate the key benefit of a cash flow forecast, such as the ability to spot problems in advance, in time to do something about them, such as arranging an overdraft or delaying a payment.

> **Exam tip**
>
> Be careful not to over-react to one negative figure on a cash flow forecast. One bad month does not spell the end for a business. However, examiners will really be looking to see whether you can spot upward, or more likely downward, trends on a cash flow forecast. A consistent reduction in monthly balance could spell trouble.

> **Exam tip**
>
> Watch out for the effects of seasonality on a cash flow forecast when you are interpreting it. Think about what type of business is being analysed before deciding whether cash flow looks dangerous. Remember that a toy firm, for which 80% of sales may be made in the run-up to Christmas, may experience poor cash flow during the rest of the year. As long as it is able to maintain a healthy closing balance, there will be enough cash to carry it through to cash-rich months.

Uses of cash flow forecasts

REVISED

The fundamental use of a cash flow forecast is to spot cash problems in advance so that action can be taken in time to prevent a major crisis. Examples of actions that help to improve cash flow include:

- Producing and distributing products as quickly as possible, reducing the time between paying for materials and receiving cash for finished goods
- Chasing customers to pay quickly. This could involve incentivising cash payment with a discount, or more careful credit control, such as chasing credit customers to remind them to settle their payments on time
- Keeping stocks to a minimum, as stock represents cash spent, but not yet converted back as a cash inflow
- Minimising spending on equipment, using leasing or renting as methods of finance, or even postponing investments

Limitations of cash flow forecasts

The forecast is only as good as the estimations that have been made in order to generate the figures. Since most entrepreneurs tend to be fairly optimistic, there can be a great danger that cash inflows are forecast too high, or to arrive too predictably.

A table of figures can give the impression of factual data whereas, in reality, a cash flow forecast remains a best guess of what is likely to occur in the future. If users of the cash flow forecast trust the accuracy of the document too much, they may be lulled into a false sense of security.

Now test yourself

TESTED

8 For whom are most business plans primarily produced?
9 What forms the heart of the financial plan within a business plan?
10 What is cash inflow minus cash outflow called?
11 How can many businesses survive a short time with a negative closing cash balance?

Answers online

Exam practice

Fresh out of school, Phoebe Hart was ready to start her new business, a business she had been planning throughout her time studying Business in the Sixth Form. With no local tanning salon, but a consumer base increasingly 'beauty conscious', Phoebe's suspicions were confirmed when she found secondary research confirming strong growth in the tanning market.

Slightly worryingly, her secondary research had also revealed some major claims for damages from customers of other tanning salons who had suffered injuries and burns following their treatment. However, Phoebe was confident she could avoid these problems and set about planning how to raise the finance she needed to start up.

Her elder sister, who had been saving to buy a flat, was persuaded to lend Phoebe £10,000 at a low rate of interest, while Phoebe's other savings were also ploughed into buying the equipment and lease needed to start up. In addition, Phoebe approached her bank about arranging an overdraft to help her through quieter periods. Phoebe employed a 16-year-old college leaver to help her run the salon as he was willing to work for a low wage.

With her plans firming up, Phoebe produced a thorough business plan, which she showed to the bank. Included was a cash flow forecast. Extracts from the cash flow forecast are shown below.

	Month £s					
	April	May	June	July	August	September
Opening balance	0	(2,000)	(2,200)	(2,000)	(1,800)	d
Capital invested	15,000	0	0	0	0	0
Cash from sales	0	2,500	3,000	3,000	2,500	2,800
Cash inflow	15,000	2,500	3,000	3,000	2,500	2,800
Cash outflow	17,000	2,700	2,800	2,800	c	2,700
Monthly balance	a	(200)	200	200	(200)	100
Closing balance	(2,000)	b	(2,000)	(1,800)	(2,000)	(1,900)

Questions

1 Fill in the gaps on the cash flow, labelled a–d. (2 marks each)
2 Explain two benefits to Phoebe of producing a business plan. (4)
3 Assess whether Phoebe was right to start her business as a sole trader. (10)

Answers and quick quiz 7 online

ONLINE

Summary

- Common situations in which a business needs to raise finance include starting up, growing or trying to solve a cash flow problem.
- Sources of finance can be internal or external.
- Different methods can be used to raise finance.
- Unlimited liability businesses cannot raise finance by selling shares.
- Limited companies have a wider range of sources and methods of finance available.
- Producing a detailed business plan helps attract finance.
- A business plan is also useful to the entrepreneur in planning and running their business.
- Forecasting future cash flows helps to spot problems early enough to take action.
- Several quick calculations can help to analyse what a cash flow forecast is showing about a business's finances.
- Always consider the context of the business when making judgements on what a cash flow forecast shows.

8 Financial planning

Sales forecasting

Sales forecasting forms the basis of almost all future planning. Without plans for the future, businesses would be left to simply react to changes, and fail to deliver effective products and services when consumers want them.

Purpose of sales forecasts

A range of plans will be required within a business to ensure each functional area is able to operate effectively. The sales forecast will be the basis of each of the following:

- HR plan: In order to ensure that, in the medium to long term, the right number of staff with the right skills are employed, and in the short term, the right number of staff are actually at work, the HR department will carefully consider sales forecasts.
- Marketing budgets: In order to decide how to allocate its marketing budget, a business such as Mars uses sales forecasts for each brand, to know whether to boost sales of a star such as Maltesers, or to try to revive the sales of a struggler such as the Mars bar.
- Profit forecasts and budgets: When planning how much the firm is expecting to make in revenue and profit, the basis will be accurate sales forecasts. These will help to shape expectations of spending, as shown in budgets for different departments.
- Production planning: If the business is to satisfy demand for its product or service, it will need to ensure that enough products are made, and before that, that enough raw materials are made. Planning production and inventory levels will take place by working backwards from sales forecasts.

Factors affecting sales forecasts

Consumer **trends** – tastes and habits – change as time passes. Effective sales forecasting must therefore allow for the effect on demand of these changing tastes and habits. Examples of changes in consumer tastes and habits could include:

- increased demand for more convenient foods
- a trend towards healthier eating for some consumers.

Other consumer trends may be based on:

- Demographics: The UK has an ageing population, meaning increased demand for products aimed at the elderly.
- Globalisation: This is an increased willingness to buy products, from food to holidays, which recognise the global nature of today's world.
- Affluence: Despite short-term economic problems, over the past 70 years, UK consumers have become wealthier, thus are more able and willing to spend on luxuries.
- Economic variables: As explained in detail in Chapter 3, pages 23–25, income elasticity is the calculation of the impact on demand for a product of a change in consumers' incomes. Therefore, an economic fluctuation,

> A **trend** is the general path that a variable takes over a period of time.

such as a recession, can have a major impact on sales, especially of income elastic products. Therefore, to forecast sales effectively, a business must pay attention to economic forecasts and use knowledge of its products' income elasticity to help forecast future sales.

In addition to changes in the economic cycle, changes in individual economic variables can affect sales:

- Value of the pound: A decrease in the value of the pound makes imports more expensive and may push consumers to favour UK-produced products.
- Changes in taxation: Taxes on individual items, such as petrol or alcohol, can affect demand, as well as changes in general taxation, such as the rate of VAT.
- Inflation: If inflation is higher than the rate of increase of average incomes, consumers will need to tighten their belts, spending less and damaging sales of some products and services.

Taken together, these issues mean that no sales forecast should be conducted without paying attention to expert economic forecasts. Many economic changes can have a significant effect on sales for a wide range of businesses, especially those with income elastic products and services.

Exam tip

Examiners love to see you combining knowledge from different areas of the specification into one argument. If answering a question about sales forecasting, you are extremely likely to be able to use income, or even price elasticity, within your argument to effectively develop the point you are trying to make.

Actions of competitors

Even harder to predict are the potential actions of competitors and the impact these may have on sales. Key competitors' actions that may affect sales are:

- Changing price: A competitor that begins to undercut our prices is likely, depending on price elasticity, to steal sales, thus rendering our sales forecast overly optimistic. If we respond by cutting prices, although we may still sell the same number of products, sales revenue may be lower than expected, affecting profit and cash flow forecasts.
- Launching new products: A competitor launching a new product, or a new competitor entering our market, can have a dramatic negative effect on forecasted sales.
- Promotional campaigns: Competitors running successful promotional campaigns to try to steal market share from our product can again leave sales forecasts looking overly optimistic.

More than any of the other factors affecting sales forecasts, the actions of competitors are usually likely to have a solely negative impact. Worryingly, they are also harder to predict than economic changes or change in consumer tastes.

Difficulties of sales forecasting

REVISED

Most sales forecasts use a technique called extrapolation, meaning assuming that past trends will continue. However, as explained above, there are many reasons why past trends can change. It is the ability to forecast these changes to past trends that marks out the best sales forecasters. In many ways, great sales forecasting is as much an art as a science, as the ability to spot future changes in trends may be impossible to find in past data.

Now test yourself

1 State three types of plan that rely on a forecast of sales as their basis.
2 List three broad categories of factors where changes may have a major influence on the accuracy of sales forecasts.
3 Explain why forecasts lose accuracy as they look further into the future.

Answers online

Sales, revenue and costs

Calculating sales volume and sales revenue

The two ways to measure how much a business has sold are:
- sales volume
- sales revenue.

Knowing how many products have actually been sold is fairly straightforward, even for a large business, as long as the business has effective internal accounting systems. Calculating the value that those sales have generated is trickier as sales revenue is calculated by multiplying sales volume by selling price. For a business selling a range of products at different prices this adds complication. If a business sells the same product at different prices depending on where or when the product is sold, even more careful recording is needed to generate an accurate figure for sales revenue.

To boost revenue, businesses can either increase their selling price (as long as sales volume is not hit too hard) without having a major impact on sales volume, or look to increase sales volume without reducing their selling price significantly.

The choice here is likely to depend on price elasticity (Chapter 3, pages 23–26).

Table 8.1 Price elasticity

Price elasticity	Change to price	Effect on sales revenue
Price elastic	Increase	Revenue falls
	Decrease	Revenue rises
Price inelastic	Increase	Revenue rises
	Decrease	Revenue falls

Calculating fixed and variable costs

To run a successful business, managers must understand not just how much they are selling but also whether they are receiving more in revenue than it is costing to run their business. No business can survive in the long term if its costs exceed revenues. Recording and monitoring running costs is thus vital.

When calculating the costs of producing a product or providing a service, a common classification for costs is to split them into:
- fixed costs
- variable costs.

When added together, these figures allow a firm to see its total costs for a time period, which can be compared with sales revenue.

Fixed costs

These are costs that do not change as output changes. They are linked to time (e.g. rent per month) rather than to how busy the business is. Fixed costs have to be paid even when a business is not producing. However, they will be the same whether the business had a great month or an awful month in terms of sales volume.

Table 8.2 Examples of fixed costs

Rent	Business rates (local tax)	Management salaries
Interest charges	Advertising spending	Heating and lighting

As these costs won't change as output changes, a rise in sales will spread these fixed costs over more units, meaning the fixed cost per unit is lower. This is especially important for a business for which fixed costs are higher than variable costs.

> **Exam tip**
>
> This concept of spreading fixed costs in directly with the concept of capacity utilisation is explored in Chapter 10, page 97.

Variable costs

These are costs that change in direct proportion to the level of output. So, if a manufacturer doubles the amount produced, the cost of materials will double.

Table 8.3 Examples of variable costs

Raw materials	Piece rate pay
Fuel costs	Packaging

> **Exam tip**
>
> Questions frequently state the variable costs of one unit of output. To calculate the total variable costs it is crucial to remember to multiply this figure by the number of units produced:
>
> **Total variable costs
> = variable cost per unit × number of units produced (output)**

Variable costs may not actually rise in direct proportion to output. The simplest reason is that as a business increases its output, it may be able to negotiate a lower price from material suppliers, meaning that the cost of materials may not quite double as output doubles. However, for the purposes of simple profit calculations and break-even analysis, this effect tends to be ignored.

> **Typical mistake**
>
> Fixed costs *do* change as time goes by, for example the landlord may decide to put up rent next month. They are fixed in relation to the amount produced, not for ever.

> **Typical mistake**
>
> As variable costs are often stated 'per unit', students sometimes get confused because the variable cost per unit does not change. They are variable in the sense that the total amount spent on, say, raw materials will double if the output doubles.

Total costs

Adding together variable costs and fixed costs shows the total costs of running a business for a period of time. This is the figure that is deducted from sales revenue to calculate profit.

Analysing the proportion of total costs that is fixed against the proportion that is variable can help a business to understand the importance of boosting sales volumes. Remember that:
- A business with a high proportion of fixed costs is better off trying to boost sales volumes so that fixed costs are spread over more units of output.
- For a business with relatively low fixed costs but higher variable costs, it is easier to operate at low levels of output, since its fixed outgoings each month will be relatively low.

Now test yourself
TESTED

4 State the two ways in which the sales of a business can be measured.
5 Define fixed costs.
6 Define variable costs.
7 Explain why a business with high fixed costs should seek to maximise sales volumes.

Answers online

Break-even

Knowing the **break-even** point is useful to managers of a business as it allows them to have a minimum target of sales to aim for to ensure that they are not making a loss.

> **Break-even** describes a position where a business is selling just enough to cover its costs without making a profit.

Break-even point
REVISED

To calculate the break-even point, a business needs to know the following:
- selling price
- variable cost per unit
- fixed costs.

Break-even is calculated using the following formula:

$$\text{Break-even} = \frac{\text{fixed costs}}{(\text{selling price} - \text{variable cost per unit})}$$

The bottom line of the formula shows the amount each unit sold contributes towards covering the fixed costs of the business.

Using contribution to calculate break-even
REVISED

Selling price minus variable cost per unit (the bottom line of the break-even formula) is called contribution per unit. This figure can be used to calculate break-even:

Break-even charts
REVISED

It is possible to illustrate the break-even point on a graph, known as a break-even chart. This shows costs, revenues and therefore profit at any possible level of output for a business. On the horizontal axis, all possible levels of output are shown, while the vertical axis shows costs and revenues, measured in pounds.

The example break-even chart in Figure 8.1 shows the break-even point, which occurs at the point where total costs and total revenue are the same.

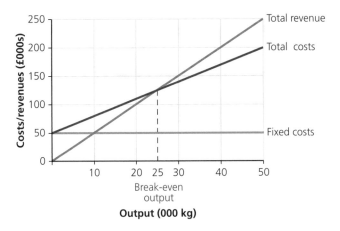

Figure 8.1 Example break-even output chart

Note the following features of the graph:
- The fixed cost line is flat, showing that fixed costs are the same at all levels of output.
- The total cost line shows the effect of adding fixed costs and variable costs together. It therefore starts on the left at the fixed cost line and moves upwards in line with the rate of increase of variable costs.
- The total revenue line begins at point (0,0) since no revenue is generated if nothing is sold.
- The break-even output is identified by dropping a vertical line down from the point at which total revenue and total costs cross to read off the amount of output that needs to be sold to cover costs.

Measuring the vertical gap between total revenue and total costs at any level of output allows the profit to be easily identified. For example, the profit when 50,000 kg is produced is £50,000.

Margin of safety REVISED

The horizontal distance between the actual output of a business and its break-even output is called the margin of safety. This shows how far demand can fall before the firm slips into a loss-making position and can be a vital figure to look out for during difficult trading periods.

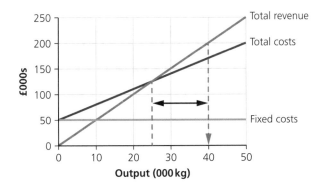

Figure 8.2 Margin of safety

Figure 8.2 shows the margin of safety if the business sells 40,000 kg. The margin of safety is 40,000 kg × 25,000 kg = 15,000 kg.

Interpreting break-even charts

In addition to showing the break-even point and margin of safety, break-even charts also serve useful planning purposes.

Being able to read off profit or loss at any given level of output can help a business plan for success or failure.

The chart can also allow other 'what if' questions to be asked, relating to what would happen to profit, break-even or margin of safety if:
- selling price is reduced or increased
- variable cost per unit reduces or increases
- fixed costs change.

Each of these requires a fresh line to be drawn on the graph, showing the effect of the possible change.

Table 8.4 Effects of change on break-even charts

What could change	What line would need to be redrawn	Direction of change	Effect on break-even point
Variable cost per unit	Total costs	Up	Up
		Down	Down
Fixed costs	Fixed costs AND Total costs	Up	Up
		Down	Down
Selling price	Total revenue	Up	Down
		Down	Up

Typical mistake

A change in sales or output does not change any lines on the graph. The effect would simply be shown by moving along the horizontal axis to read off the new figures at the new level of output.

Limitations of break-even analysis

Break-even analysis relies on certain simplifying assumptions. These may well be false in a real, dynamic business environment:
- Variable costs are assumed to increase constantly. In fact, they may increase more slowly at higher levels of output due to bulk-buying discounts.
- Break-even analysis assumes that the firm sells all its output in the same time period, which may well be untrue.
- Break-even analysis is based on a firm selling only one product at a single price.

Exam tip

Calculating the break-even point for individual products sold by a multi-product firm is quite possible, and very useful. However, this relies on splitting up the firm's **overhead costs** and allocating some to each product.

Overhead costs are those that are incurred by the business as a whole but can be difficult to attribute to a particular section of the business. For example, the costs of running Nestlé's Head Office can be hard to attribute to the actual production of any one of its hundreds of different products.

- Any break-even chart is a static model, showing only the possible situation at one moment in time. The business environment is dynamic, so break-even is not well suited to showing the effects of changing external variables such as consumer tastes or the state of the economy.

> **Exam tip**
>
> Although these assumptions weaken the power of break-even analysis, exam answers should never underestimate just how important this type of, albeit flawed, analysis is to business planning.

Now test yourself

TESTED ☐

8 What formula is used to calculate the break-even point?
9 What is the formula for calculating profit using a break-even chart?
10 What three lines are drawn on a break-even chart?
11 How is margin of safety calculated?
12 If the variable cost per unit of a product decreases, what will be the effect on the break-even point?
13 What would be the effect on a firm's break-even point of deciding to cut the selling price?

Answers online

Budgets

Budgets represent the way in which most medium to large businesses manage their finances. Budgets will be set for both income and expenditure:

- Income budget: This sets a target for the value of sales to be achieved.
- Expenditure budget: This gives budget-holders a limit under which they must keep their department's costs.

> A **budget** is a target for revenue or costs for a future time period.

An example of a simple budget statement is shown in Table 8.5.

Table 8.5 Example of a budget statement

	January	February	March
Income	25,000	28,000	30,000
Variable costs	10,000	12,000	13,000
Fixed costs	10,000	10,000	11,000
Total expenditure	20,000	22,000	24,000
Profit	5,000	6,000	6,000

Note that setting both income and expenditure budgets allows for a budgeted profit figure to be identified in each month.

Purpose of budgets

REVISED ☐

- They focus expenditure on the company's main objectives for a time period.
- Expenditure budgets are set to ensure that no department or individual spends more than the company expects.
- All budgets provide a yardstick against which performance can be measured.
- Expenditure budgets allow spending power to be delegated to local managers, who may understand local conditions better and be better placed to decide how money should be spent at a local level.
- Both income and expenditure budgets can help to motivate staff in a certain department to try to hit targets.

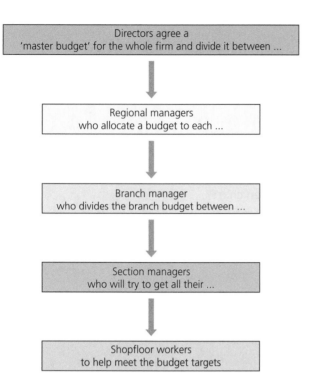

Figure 8.3 Budget holders

Types of budget

The process of setting budgets can take place in two broad ways:
- A historical budget is set using last year's budget as a guide and then making adjustments based on known changes in circumstances for the department, so if 10% more staff have been employed at a branch, that branch's income and expenditure budgets may be increased by 10%.
- Zero-based budgeting involves setting each budget to zero each year and then expects each budget-holder to justify a budget figure that they can work to for the coming year. This is very time-consuming, but can prevent the wastage that occurs if all budgets simply creep upwards year after year under a system of historical budgeting.

In reality, to prevent too much time being wasted, many businesses will use zero-based budgeting every few years before a period of historical budgeting. The result is shown in Figure 8.4.

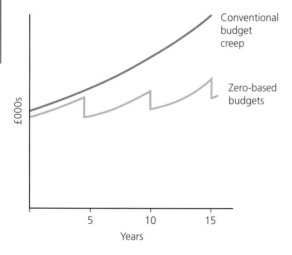

Figure 8.4 The benefits of zero budgeting: keeping costs down

Exam tip

Whichever method of setting budgets is used, perhaps a more important concept is the extent to which budgets are agreed or imposed. Imposing budgets reduces the sense of responsibility that a budget-holder feels compared to their desire to hit targets that they have agreed with their managers.

Variance analysis

Setting budgets is a helpful planning technique. However, the real power of budgets probably comes from **variance analysis**.

Variance analysis, which in most large firms will take place using a spreadsheet system such as Microsoft Excel, allows managers to spot areas where there is a significant difference between the budget and the reality. With an automated system it is possible to flag up variances of a certain size only, so that managers can focus their attention on areas with a significant variance. It is in the analysis of the causes of these variances that successful financial management tends to lie.

Variances can be:
- Adverse: The actual figure was worse than the budgeted figure.
- Favourable: The actual figure was better for the business than the budgeted figure.

> **Variance analysis** involves looking back to calculate the difference between a budgeted figure and the actual figure that occurred.

Table 8.6 Variance analysis

Type of budget	Relationship between budget and actual	Effect on profit	Classification of variance
Income	Actual lower than budget	Lower than expected	Adverse
	Actual higher than budget	Higher than expected	Favourable
Expenditure	Actual lower than budget	Higher than expected	Favourable
	Actual higher than budget	Lower than expected	Adverse

> **Typical mistake**
>
> Budget variances should not be recorded as positive or negative, as an income figure higher than budget is a good thing but an expenditure figure higher than budget has a negative impact on profit. This is why the words 'adverse' and 'favourable' are used.

Budget variances can occur for three underlying reasons. Only one should really result in the budget-holder being blamed:
- The original budget was unrealistic.
- The target was not met due to factors beyond the budget-holder's control.
- The target was not met due to factors within the budget-holder's control.

Holding a manager to account for either failing to meet an unrealistic target or missing a target as a result of issues over which they had no control will only demotivate that manager and probably others within the business. Senior managers should therefore take care over investigating the causes of budget variances before taking action as a result of those variances.

> **Typical mistake**
>
> Whenever calculating a budget variance it is vital to note whether the variance is adverse or favourable. The answer to a question asking you to calculate a variance should be the actual size of the variance and the word 'adverse' or 'favourable'.

Difficulties of budgeting

Problems with budgeting systems can occur in several key areas:
- Setting budgets: It can be hard to ensure targets are set realistically, but also to avoid budgets creeping upwards over time.
- Agreeing or imposing budgets: Imposing budgets is far less motivating and effective than giving budget-holders a genuine say in setting their own targets, in agreement with senior managers.
- Failing to understand the causes of a budget variance: Blaming a budget-holder for failing to meet a target that turned out to be impossible is a sure-fire way of demotivating that manager.
- The costs of the system outweighing the benefits: In small businesses, there is less need for financial control to be delegated as a single boss may be able to keep an eye on all the finances without taking the time to set up a system of budgets.

Now test yourself

14 State three purposes of budgets.

15 What are the two main methods of setting budgets?

16 If actual income is lower than the budgeted figure, will the variance be adverse or favourable?

17 If actual expenditure is lower than the budgeted figure, will the budget variance be adverse or favourable?

Answers online

Exam practice

Andy Hemmings plans to set up a small firm manufacturing specialist signalling devices for use in vehicles. As an experienced entrepreneur, he has taken care to produce an accurate sales forecast. He has also carefully planned his finances, in order to identify his break-even point. In addition, he has set budgets as a way of checking the success of the business as he goes along. A range of information about his business is provided below:

Sales forecast for first three months:

> January – 1,600 units

> February – 2,400 units

> March – 3,000 units

Selling price = £20

Variable cost per unit = £8

Fixed costs = £24,000 per month

Questions

1 Using the information provided, calculate Andy's:
  (a) Break-even point   (3)
  (b) Profit or loss in January   (3)
  (c) Margin of safety in March   (3)
2 Explain two factors that may cause Andy's sales forecasts to be inaccurate.   (4)
3 Assess how useful break-even analysis will be to Andy in starting up and running his new business.   (10)

Answers and quick quiz 8 online

Summary

- Sales forecasts are at the heart of most business planning.
- Sales forecasts begin by assuming past trends will continue.
- The art of successful sales forecasting lies in being able to spot when the future will not reflect the past.
- Sales can be measured by volume or value (revenue).
- Costs of production can be split into variable costs and fixed costs.
- Total costs are calculated by adding total variable costs to fixed costs for a time period.

- The break-even point is a useful piece of information for managers.
- Break-even charts show profit or loss at any possible level of output.
- Contribution can be used to calculate profit.
- Break-even analysis has several limitations.
- Break-even analysis allows a business to ask 'what if' questions.
- Budgets are used to manage a firm's finances.
- Variance calculations allow performance to be measured against budgeted targets.
- Budget variances can be adverse or favourable.

Profit

Profit is a simple concept. What can make it less clear is when businesses report on different kinds of profit. This is done so that businesses can identify where things are doing well or badly for them, by analysing the differences between the different types of profit.

> **Profit** is the difference between the revenue of a business and the costs generated by the business during a period of time.

Calculating different types of profit

REVISED

Each type of profit is calculated after allowing for different types of cost.

Gross profit

This is a raw measure of profit that deducts the **cost of sales** from total revenue to show what is left after taking away the costs directly involved in making a product or providing a service.

> **Gross profit = total revenue – cost of sales**

> **Cost of sales** is the collective name given to the costs directly associated with making a product, such as materials, and costs of running the factory.

Operating profit

Fixed overheads are deducted from gross profit to calculate operating profit. This is perhaps the clearest indicator of just how well a business has been run during a year. As the name suggests, this is the profit generated by the normal operating activities of the business.

> **Operating profit = gross profit – fixed overheads**

> **Fixed overheads** are the costs that have to be paid no matter how well the business is performing, such as management salaries and rent on the head office.

Profit for the year (net profit)

The final measure of profit on your specification shows profit net of all costs except for corporation (profit) tax, which is usually charged at 20%.

> **Profit for the year (net profit) = operating profit – (net financing cost and corporation tax)**

> **Net financing cost** is the income from interest on bank deposits minus the interest charges from overdrafts and loans. It will usually be a negative number.

Ways to improve profit

REVISED

Improving profit can sound simple. There are only three basic routes:
- Increase revenue
- Reduce costs
- Do a combination of the two

Unfortunately, each choice tends to involve a trade-off. Increasing revenue can be achieved by spending more on advertising, but that pushes up costs. Reducing costs may involve making sacrifices on quality or customer service, which could damage revenue too. Put simply, this is why running a business is hard.

Statement of comprehensive income

All public limited companies are required to produce and publish a financial document known as the **statement of comprehensive income**. Most people refer to this as the profit and loss account. This is the document on which the different types of profit can be found. In addition, comparing this document with previous years allows judgements to be made about the performance of the business for the current financial year.

> A **statement of comprehensive income** is a document produced by public limited companies that shows revenue, a break-down of different types of cost and different types of profit for a year.

Measuring profitability

While profit is an absolute number of pounds, each different profit figure can only tell us so much about the performance of a business. More powerful than figures for profit are figures that show **profitability**. Profitability allows us to make meaningful comparisons between firms of different sizes in order to judge who has been more successful.

> **Profitability** states profit as a percentage of sales revenue.

Gross profit margin

This shows gross profit as a percentage of sales revenue:

$$\text{Gross profit margin} = \frac{\text{gross profit}}{\text{sales revenue}} \times 100$$

A business that is able to take relatively cheap raw materials and turn them into highly priced products would have a high gross profit margin. A good example is a coffee shop.

> **Typical mistake**
>
> Do not confuse profit (measured as a number of pounds) with profitability (measured as a percentage).

Operating profit margin

This is the main focus for the analysis of overall company performance. It shows operating profit as a percentage of sales, and therefore includes the impact that deducting fixed overheads has on profitability.

$$\text{Operating profit margin} = \frac{\text{operating profit}}{\text{sales revenue}} \times 100$$

> **Exam tip**
>
> For all profit margins, the higher the better.

Profit for the year (net profit) margin

The profit for the year (net profit) margin shows profitability after allowing for all business costs (apart from tax).

$$\text{Profit for the year (net profit) margin} = \frac{\text{profit for the year (net profit)}}{\text{sales revenue}} \times 100$$

Ways to improve profitability

In order to increase profit margins, a business faces two simple options:
- Increase selling price
- Cut costs

Increasing the selling price will increase profit margin but may decrease overall profit. This is because an increase in price may lead to a drastic fall in sales volume. The wisdom of increasing price hinges on price elasticity. For a price inelastic product, the fall in demand that results from a price rise may be so small as to be outweighed by the increased revenue per unit. However, for a price elastic product, increasing price is almost certain to reduce profits.

As explained above, cutting costs is rarely simple. Using cheaper materials or employing fewer staff can damage a company's reputation and thus revenue. Only where genuine waste can be identified and painlessly removed from the business is cost reduction likely to lead to a straightforward increase in profitability.

Exam tip

Look for the trade-offs involved in cutting costs as a way of boosting profitability. This helps you to identify a two-sided argument, perhaps arguing about whether to buy cheaper materials and whether consumers will stop buying your brand. This offers opportunities to display the skill of evaluation by offering and justifying your judgement as to which option is best for the business.

Distinction between cash and profit

REVISED

Profit is not the same as net cash flow. The reasons are two-fold:

● Sales revenue does not equal cash inflows.
● Costs do not equal cash outflows.

The simplest way to illustrate is to consider a business that offers credit to its customers and receives credit from a supplier. Sales revenue is recorded when a product changes hands, so selling an item on 60 days' credit generates sales revenue, but will not lead to a cash inflow for at least 60 days. Likewise, when the business buys materials on credit, the cost is incurred when the materials are delivered. However, no cash flows out until the supplier is actually paid, 30 days later.

Table 9.1 helps to illustrate this and other differences for a number of typical business transactions.

Table 9.1 **Differences between cash inflows and revenue**

Financial item	Cash inflow	Revenue
Cash sales made to customers	✓	✓
Credit sales made to customers	✗	✓
Capital raised from share sales	✓	✗
Charge rent on flat upstairs	✓	✓
Take out a £20,000 bank loan	✓	✗
Carry out a sale and leaseback	✓	✗

It is this difference between cash flow and profit that explains why profitable businesses can go bust when they run out of cash. Selling on credit especially can be very dangerous. As long as the bank manager believes credit customers will pay, an overdraft will still be available. However, a bank may withdraw the overdraft facility, leaving the business with no cash to pay its bills on a day-to-day basis.

Exam tip

Examiners will be impressed if you can show an understanding of the difference between cash flow and profit (as this is something so few students seem to grasp). Explaining how boosting sales can boost profit, but that doing so by offering more credit could damage cash flow, would score well.

Typical mistake

Never use the word 'profit' when explaining what a cash flow forecast shows. Likewise, do not state that cash flow must be good if a business makes a profit. The distinction should be clear.

Now test yourself

1 What are the three most commonly quoted types of profit?
2 What is the difference between profit and profitability?
3 What financial document shows different types of profit for a public limited company?
4 Give an example to illustrate why cash flow and profit are different.

Answers online

Liquidity

Statement of financial position (balance sheet)

Every year, all limited companies are required to send a statement of financial position, commonly known as a balance sheet, to Companies House. This shows what the business owns, as well as what it owes and where it got its money from.

For the AS part of your specification, the key question answered by a statement of financial position is: Does the firm have enough cash to pay its bills? This question means testing the firm's **liquidity**.

> **Liquidity** is the ability of a business to find the cash it needs to pay its bills. The cash must be readily available either in the bank account or in the form of a payment from a customer that is due very soon.

Measuring liquidity

A balance sheet shows more information than is needed to measure liquidity. If looking at a whole balance sheet, the section to be concerned with is just above halfway up – the section that shows **current assets** and **current liabilities**.

Measuring liquidity involves comparing the value of current assets against the current liabilities that will need to be paid. This can be done in two ways.

> **Current assets** are items the business owns that are in the form of cash or can be easily turned into cash quickly without a major loss in their value. There are three current assets: cash, money owed by customers (receivables/debtors) and stock.

> **Current liabilities** are debts owed by the business that are due to be paid within the next 12 months. The two main current liabilities are trade creditors and overdrafts.

Calculating current ratio

The current ratio is a calculation that enables a simple judgement to be made about a firm's liquidity. Accountants tend to state that the ideal current ratio is 1.5:1. The formula used to calculate the ratio is:

$$\text{Current ratio} = \frac{\text{current assets}}{\text{current liabilities}}$$

This therefore means that if a company has a current ratio of 1.5:1, it will have £1.50 of current assets for each £1 of short-term debt it has. If the ratio is significantly lower than 1.5:1, this could mean that it will face problems settling its short-term debts. If the ratio is significantly higher than 1.5:1, the business could be criticised for having too much of its resources tied up in non-productive current assets.

Calculating acid test ratio

Often referred to as a tougher test of liquidity, the acid test ratio does not count inventories (or stock) as a liquid asset that can be set against current liabilities. The formula is therefore:

$$\text{Acid test ratio} = \frac{(\text{total current assets} - \text{inventories})}{\text{current liabilities}}$$

The ideal value for the acid test ratio is 1:1. This would mean that a firm has £1 of cash or money owed by customers for every £1 of short-term debt, so liquidity is sound. If the acid test falls far below 1:1, that really could spell trouble for a business trying to find the cash to pay its bills.

Some firms can trade on surprisingly low acid test ratios, notably Tesco, which rarely has an acid test of more than 0.5:1. This is less of a problem for a business that can generate millions of pounds through its tills every day or one that is large enough to be likely to access bank finance fairly easily when needed.

> **Exam tip**
>
> Notice that inventories form the difference between the two liquidity ratios. A company with a high current ratio but low acid test is likely to have high stock levels, which could cause a problem. The size of the problem will depend upon how quickly it can turn its stocks into cash.

Improving liquidity

REVISED

Improving liquidity relies upon bringing extra cash onto the balance sheet. This could involve one or more of the following:
● Selling under-used **fixed assets** such as equipment or machinery
● Raising more share capital
● Increasing long-term borrowing through loans
● Postponing planned investments

> **Fixed assets** are items owned by the business which it intends to use over and over to generate profit. Examples include property and machinery.

Managing working capital

REVISED

Figure 9.1 The working capital cycle

Figure 9.1 shows the different stages through which **working capital** passes as a business buys, produces and sells products or services. Managing this cycle, to ensure that there is always enough working capital in the system to prevent blockages or delays, is crucial to successful financial management. Actively managing the working capital cycle involves:
● ensuring there is enough money in the system altogether
● making sure cash moves through the cycle as quickly as possible.

> **Working capital** is the money that is available for the day-to-day running of the business.

If these two requirements are to be met financial managers are likely to consider the following actions:
● Control cash used. This involves keeping the amount of cash used as low as possible, by reducing stock levels, controlling credit periods

offered to customers and gaining as much credit as possible from suppliers, and getting products on sale as quickly as possible.

● Minimise spending on fixed assets. This can be helped by leasing rather than buying new assets, which prevents large outflows of cash draining working capital from the system.

● Plan ahead to estimate carefully the amount of cash that will be needed in the next few months. This will ensure that adjustments to the cycle can be made in good time.

Now test yourself

TESTED

5 On which financial document can the information to test liquidity be found?

6 (a) What two ratios can be calculated to test liquidity?
   (b) What is the ideal value for each?

7 State three methods for improving liquidity.

8 Why is working capital management crucial for a firm's survival?

Answers online

Business failure

Ultimately, any business that fails will do so because it does not have enough cash to pay the bills. However, the reasons why businesses run out of cash can be complex. Not all, or even many, of these are caused by financial issues. It is other causes that lead to the financial problems that bring down the business. Major issues tend to focus on marketing or strategic problems such as:

● not really understanding consumers
● failing to differentiate from rivals
● failing to communicate what is special about your business to consumers
● poor leadership
● not being able to find enough ways to generate revenue.

Internal causes of business failure

REVISED

Marketing failure

Problems understanding changes in the marketplace, or even what consumers are really looking for, will lead to a shortage of revenue. Poor decisions relating to the marketing mix can often result from this.

Financial failure

Managers need to manage finances actively, planning ahead and making adjustments when necessary. Failing companies sometimes stumble into cash flow crises without seeing them coming.

Systems or operations failure

If IT systems simply do not provide the right people within the business with the information they need, things start to go wrong. If physical systems break down, such as manufacturing or ordering stock, the business will find itself unable to satisfy demand for its product and will rapidly lose customers.

External causes of business failure

Shifts in the external environment within which a business is operating can lead to business failure. In these cases, it is perhaps easier to find sympathy for business managers brought down by factors that are outside their direct control. However, really good leaders are adept at anticipating and adapting to external changes.

Change in technology

A major technological advancement can destroy a company's sales very rapidly. As its product struggles to compete against a better product, price cutting is almost assured and, ultimately, the company may fail to operate at its break-even point.

New competitor

A new rival entering a market that is able to operate far more efficiently, perhaps as a result of innovative processes or distribution channels, may cause such a large effect as to drive existing businesses out of the market and out of business.

Economic change

In times of economic downturn, orders for luxury goods tend to dry up. If economic growth does not recover quickly, some businesses will find it hard to continue operating above their break-even point – those with insufficient cash will fail.

Behaviour of banks

The banks have a vital role to play in providing finance to business:
● To fund long-term investments designed to raise competitiveness
● To provide short-term finance to help working capital management

A failure to supply credit to businesses, or forcing businesses to accept unreasonably high interest rates, can both lead to business failure. This helps to explain why banking is a crucial but controversial sector of the UK's economy.

Now test yourself

TESTED

9 How can marketing mistakes lead to business failure?
10 Why are consistent stock control problems likely to lead to business failure?
11 State three external causes of business failure.

Answers online

Exam practice

Hickmet and Hickmet Ltd was a trading firm that imported speciality foodstuffs from Turkey for the UK market. In early 2017, the business failed. Analysts suggested that the failure was down to external causes. The directors were convinced there was nothing they could have done to tackle the twin external factors of:
● declining value of the pound from late 2015 onwards; and
● the arrival, in 2014, of a larger new competitor that had previously focused on importing similar products from Greece.

However, analysis of extracts from the company's accounts suggested that the directors could have seen problems coming.

Edexcel A-level Business 95

Extracts from statement of comprehensive income

	2014 (£m)	2015 (£m)	2016 (£m)
Revenue	4.5	4.4	4.0
Gross profit	1.4	1.0	0.5
Operating profit	0.2	0.1	(0.7)
Profit for the year	0.1	0	(2)

Extracts from statement of financial position (balance sheet)

	2014 (£m)	2015 (£m)	2016 (£m)
Total current assets	0.8	0.6	0.5
Inventories	0.5	0.4	0.4
Current liabilities	0.3	0.4	1.0

Questions

1 For each of the three years shown, calculate:
  (a) Gross profit margin (4)
  (b) Operating profit margin (4)
  (c) Profit for the year (net) margin (4)
2 Use these results to comment on trends in the firm's profitability. (4)
3 For each of the three years shown, calculate:
  (a) Current ratio (4)
  (b) Acid test ratio (4)
4 Use these results to comment on the firm's liquidity. (4)
5 Assess the directors' view that the failure of the business was entirely due to external factors. (10)

Answers and quick quiz 9 online

ONLINE

Summary

- There are three main types of profit.
- Profit and profitability show different things.
- Cash flow and profit are not the same.
- Liquidity measures the availability of cash to meet short-term debts.
- Liquidity can be measured using the current and acid test ratios.
- Successful working capital management is the key to ensuring healthy liquidity.

- Internal causes of business failure could include poor marketing, poor financial management or systems failure.
- External causes of business failure may include technological change, the arrival of a new competitor, economic problems or the behaviour of banks.
- Ultimately most business failures are the result of the business running out of cash.

10 Resource management

Production, productivity and efficiency

The process of creating a product or delivering a service can be a crucial source of competitive advantage. Choosing how to organise production and ensuring it is efficient are vital in making sure business resources are managed effectively.

Methods of production

REVISED

How to organise production tends to be a trade-off between uniformity and speed on one hand against the ability to adapt a product to meet individual customers' needs on the other.

Job production

Job production, making tailor-made products to suit customer tastes, brings benefits and drawbacks.

> **Job production** involves making one-off items to suit each customer's individual requirements.

Table 10.1 Benefits and drawbacks of job production

Benefits of job production	Drawbacks of job production
Can charge a higher price as products can be tailored to meet exact specifications	Cost per unit is very high, due to high level of skill and low rates of production
Work should be more interesting for staff	Finding staff with sufficient skill can be hard and pay will have to be high

Batch production

Batch production is really a kind of compromise between job production and flow production (see below).

> **Batch production** makes a group of products to one specification at a time, allowing some variation in products, yet some specialisation.

Table 10.2 Benefits and drawbacks of batch production

Benefits of batch production	Drawbacks of batch production
Allows variation in the product being made	More costly to set up than job production as some specialist machinery will be needed
Speedier than job production as making a batch of identical products speeds up production	Cost per unit will still be higher than flow production as machinery will need to be adjusted between batches

Flow production

Flow production allows huge volumes of output to be produced extremely quickly and cost effectively. It is likely to rely heavily on **automation**.

> **Flow production** refers to continuous production of a single, standardised product.
>
> **Automation** means using machines to complete tasks within a process.

Table 10.3 Benefits and drawbacks of flow production

Benefits of flow production	Drawbacks of flow production
Unit labour costs are extremely low	High initial costs of installing production machinery
Huge volumes allow huge demand in mass markets to be met	Products need to be identical – no tailoring to suit different tastes

Cell production

Cell production, with its roots in the Japanese philosophy of lean production, harnesses the power of group working to increase productivity, yet maintains the scope to tailor-make different variations on a product within the cell.

> **Cell production** involves organising workers into small groups or cells that can produce a range of different products more quickly than job production allows.

Table 10.4 Benefits and drawbacks of cell production

Benefits of cell production	Drawbacks of cell production
Group working allows ideas to be generated within the cell for improvements to processes	As it is still heavily reliant on people rather than automation, costs are relatively high
The small highly skilled cell can adjust products to suit customers' needs	Production volumes will not be as high as flow production

Due to the benefits and drawbacks of each, different methods are suited to different circumstances, as shown in Table 10.5.

Table 10.5 Circumstances when each production methods is at its most effective

Job	Batch	Flow	Cell
When every customer wants something unique, e.g. a wedding dress	When production has to be split into chunks, e.g. shoes in different sizes and colours	When there is consistent, high demand for a single product, e.g. the *Sun* newspaper	When there is a need for flexibility but also high production volumes, i.e. lean production
When labour costs are low, e.g. suits tailor-made in Bangkok	When labour costs are high enough to mean job production is too costly	When labour costs are high, e.g. in France or Sweden	When labour has a lot to contribute to ideas and improved efficiency
When tailor-making something adds real value, e.g. shoes for a marathon runner	When a firm wants to limit the availability of an item, e.g. Hermès with its 'Birkin' bag	When efficiency allows prices low enough to boost sales on everyday items, e.g. baked beans	When a degree of uniqueness adds value for the customer

Productivity

REVISED

Productivity generally refers to output per worker. It is the speed at which an employee completes their task. It is calculated using the formula:

$$\text{Productivity} = \frac{\text{total output}}{\text{number of workers}}$$

> **Productivity** is a measure of the efficiency of the production process. It is usually measured as output per worker per time period.

Typical mistake

Productivity is not the same as production or output. Output can be increased by simply employing more staff, working at the same rate. To increase productivity, the output produced by each worker must be improved.

Factors influencing productivity

Many factors influence productivity. The speed at which workers can produce units of output may depend on the workers or on the environment in which they are working. Key factors affecting productivity include:

● quality and age of machinery
● skills and experience of workers
● level of employee motivation.

Link between productivity and competitiveness

Higher levels of productivity lead to lower unit costs. This is because the labour cost involved in making each unit falls as workers work faster. If a worker is paid £10 per hour and makes £10 of units each hour, the labour cost of each unit is £1. If that worker's productivity doubles, the labour cost per unit would only be 50p (£10/20 units). Lower unit costs allow businesses to cut prices while maintaining the same profit margin.

Efficiency

REVISED

Efficiency differs from productivity in that it considers waste. A process may have a high rate of productivity, but generate a lot of waste. Therefore, it is not efficient. Wasted time, which is reduced as productivity rises, is certainly a factor, but a highly productive system may come with a cost in terms of quality, meaning many of the items produced are faulty and must be thrown away.

> **Efficiency** measures the extent to which the resources used in a process generate output without wastage.

Factors influencing efficiency

The factors that determine efficiency are the same as those affecting productivity. It is only the measurement that differs.

Table 10.6 Factors affecting production and efficiency

Factor affecting production	Affects productivity because	Also affects efficiency because
Quality and age of machinery	Newer machinery may work faster, and break down less	Fewer breakdowns mean fewer faults and newer machinery may produce with less variation
Skills and experience of workers	Highly skilled staff can produce things faster, while experience brings knowledge of how to complete tasks with high efficiency and quality	Skilled staff are likely to make fewer mistakes, while experience can mean staff spot the problems that lead to faults before they occur
Level of employee motivation	Motivated staff are likely to focus on the task without distraction and to work as quickly as they can	Motivation brings pride in work, so motivated staff will be careful not to make errors, and to lose concentration less

Labour intensive versus capital intensive production

The trade-off faced by firms considering how to produce their products often boils down to the extent to which they wish to rely on machines versus relying on people.

Key issues relating to **labour intensive production**:
● Labour costs will form a high proportion of total costs.
● Managing labour cost becomes critical, perhaps forcing a firm to move abroad to lower-wage countries or spend heavily on motivational methods.

> **Labour intensive production** means that a production process relies heavily on human input with little use of automation.

- Labour intensive production offers far greater scope for tailoring products to suit customers' needs, thus adding value and allowing a higher selling price.

Key issues relating to **capital intensive production**:
- Initial costs will be very high, with the need to invest in a lot of specialist machinery.
- Running costs will be relatively low.
- It may offer little flexibility in terms of product variations.

> **Capital intensive production** uses high levels of automation, reducing the role of humans as much as possible, replacing them with machines.

Now test yourself

TESTED

1 Is job production likely to be labour or capital intensive?
2 What is the key difference between productivity and efficiency?
3 State three key factors that affect productivity.
4 What formula is used to calculate productivity?

Answers online

Capacity utilisation

Having unused assets sitting around in a business producing no profit is inefficient. Therefore, businesses continually aim to operate close to full **capacity** to avoid waste and boost profitability.

> **Capacity** is the term used to describe the maximum possible output of a business.

Calculating capacity utilisation

REVISED

The formula used to calculate **capacity utilisation** is:

$$\text{Capacity utilisation} = \frac{\text{current output}}{\text{maximum possible output}} \times 100$$

A firm's capacity utilisation is expressed as a percentage figure.

> **Capacity utilisation** is the proportion of maximum capacity being used by the business.

Implications of under-utilisation of capacity

REVISED

The major negative implication of under-used capacity is that fixed costs per unit will be higher. The following worked example illustrates this:

Maximum capacity = 5,000 units per month

Total fixed costs = £10,000 per month

When capacity utilisation is 100%, fixed costs per unit
= £10,000/5,000 = £2 per unit.

When capacity utilisation is only 50%, fixed costs per unit
= £10,000/2,500 = £4 per unit.

That means that with under-used capacity, a greater amount of the revenue generated by each product must be used to cover fixed costs. This reduces operating margins significantly.

In addition, under-utilisation of capacity can:
- lead to fears for job security among staff, damaging motivation
- cause poor morale among managers
- contribute to a poor reputation for the business, especially in the service sector; imagine a restaurant that usually has many tables empty even during busy periods.

> **Typical mistake**
>
> Given the implications of capacity utilisation for fixed cost per unit, some students falsely believe that all businesses should try to reach 100% capacity utilisation at all times. There are problems associated with this, as shown by the implications of over-utilisation of capacity (below).

Answers and quick quizzes at **www.hoddereducation.co.uk/myrevisionnotes**

Implications of over-utilisation of capacity

If capacity utilisation stays close to 100% over a long period, two potential problems arise:
- The firm may be unable to accept any new orders, potentially turning away new customers to rivals.
- There will be little or no time to carry out maintenance on machines or train staff.

The ideal level of capacity utilisation is therefore close to 100%, without ever staying at 100% for a long period.

Ways of improving capacity utilisation

There are two basic ways to boost the proportion of maximum output being used:
- Increase current output: This is likely to be accomplished using marketing methods to boost the volume of sales made by the business, perhaps through advertising or cutting the selling price. Alternatively, the business could use its capacity to make products for other businesses looking to subcontract work.
- Reduce maximum capacity: This will involve selling off assets or laying off staff. Although redundancies can be costly in the short term, reducing maximum capacity reduces fixed costs.

Now test yourself

5 What formula is used to calculate capacity utilisation?
6 How does a high capacity utilisation help to boost profitability?
7 State two reasons why 100% capacity utilisation can be a problem.
8 What are the two basic solutions to under-utilisation of capacity?
9 If a business has monthly fixed costs of £120,000, a maximum monthly output of 1,000 units, and a contribution per unit of £250, calculate profit when:
 (a) The firm is operating at 100% capacity utilisation
 (b) The firm is operating at 60% capacity utilisation
 Assume all output is sold.

Answers online

> **Exam tip**
>
> If the causes of under-used capacity are short term, for example poor weather, it would be foolish to reduce maximum capacity. Instead, the solution is likely to lie in boosting current demand using marketing methods. If, however, the causes are long term, such as a change in consumer lifestyles, a longer-term solution – such as reducing maximum capacity – would be more appropriate.

Stock control

> **Stock** or **inventory** is the name given to the materials, partially made products and finished goods owned by a business, which have not been sold.

Stock or inventory is often viewed as a necessary evil in business. Holding stock costs money and ties up cash, but with no stock, production can grind to a halt or customers may be disappointed.

Interpreting stock control diagrams

One method used to help control stock levels is a stock control diagram. A typical stock control chart is shown in Figure 10.1.

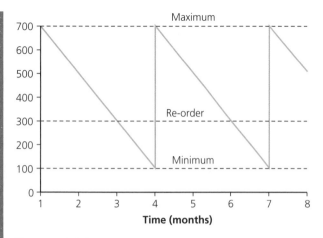

Figure 10.1 Stock control diagram

Key features of the diagram include:
- The maximum stock level set by the business, strongly affected by the amount of space available and the firm's stock-holding policy.
- The minimum or buffer stock level, i.e. the amount of stock of that item that the business aims to always have available.
- The re-order level, which is the amount at which a new order for stock is triggered.
- The re-order quantity, which is the vertical jump upwards in stock level that occurs at the start of months 4 and 7 on the diagram. This is the amount of stock that is ordered each time an order is placed.
- The lead time, or delivery time, which is the horizontal gap between a re-order being placed and the delivery of stock arriving – in this case, one month as stock is re-ordered at the start of months 3 and 6 and arrives at the start of months 4 and 7.

> **Exam tip**
>
> On a stock control diagram, any vertical gaps or changes refer to the quantity of stock. Any horizontal distances are times.

Buffer stocks

Most businesses aim to keep minimum stock levels of raw materials used in production and also, in many cases, finished goods at all times. The reasons for this are shown in Table 10.7.

Table 10.7 Reasons for keeping buffer stocks

Reasons for keeping buffer stock of raw materials	Reasons for keeping buffer stock of finished goods
If deliveries are delayed, buffer stock allows production to continue	Helps to ensure that the business can always supply customers when they need a product, with the right size or colour
If a batch of supplies is found to be faulty, the buffer stock can be used to continue production	Allows the firm to accept rush orders from customers

Implications of poor stock control

Effective stock control is focused on always maintaining the 'right' level of stock. The 'right' level, however, varies from business to business. Get it wrong and the business can end up with too much or too little stock. Each causes a number of problems.

Too much stock leads to the following problems:
- Opportunity cost: This ties up capital, as stock prevents that money from being used in other ways.
- Cash flow problems: Stock represents cash that has been converted into stock but not yet converted back into cash. Hold too much stock and there is a danger the firm will run short of actual cash.
- Increased storage costs: Keeping stock costs money; it needs space, perhaps security, or even refrigeration costs.
- Increased financing costs: If stock has been purchased using any form of borrowing, the business will experience extra interest costs.
- Increased wastage: Too much stock may lead to stock 'going off', or becoming obsolete.

Too little stock could cause the following problems:
- Lost customers: If an order or customer arrives expecting to receive their products immediately and there is none in stock, that customer or order may be lost to competitors.
- Delays in production: If there are no materials to process, machinery and workers may be left standing idle until the next delivery arrives.
- Loss of reputation: This may occur if word gets around that the business struggles to maintain enough stock to meet customer needs promptly.

Just-in-time stock management

REVISED

Just-in-time stock management, with no buffer stock, relies entirely on frequent, small deliveries of materials from suppliers being delivered without delay and without any quality problems. This brings many benefits, eliminating costs involved in stock-holding, but increases the danger of production halting due to a lack of materials.

> **Just-in-time stock management** is a Japanese-rooted approach to stock management that aims to eliminate buffer stock completely.

Key issues to consider for a firm using just-in-time stock management:
- Suppliers must be willing to deliver frequently (often several times a day).
- Deliveries must be absolutely reliable; missed deliveries leave the firm without stock.
- Suppliers may need to relocate close to the company using just-in-time.
- Will smaller, more frequent deliveries lead to a loss of bulk-buying discounts?
- Will frequent deliveries lead to increased congestion and pollution from lorries?

Exam tip

Overall, the introduction of just-in-time stock management increases the importance of the relationship between a business and its suppliers. Look for evidence in any case study of how well a company gets on with its suppliers to help decide whether a switch to just-in-time would work well.

Waste minimisation

REVISED

Waste minimisation is a just-in-time approach that helps to reduce waste in several ways:
- Less stock is held, meaning there is far less likelihood of stock wastage.
- Cash is not tied up in stock, effectively wasting it.
- Removing buffer stocks helps to highlight bottlenecks and problems in production processes. These can be ironed out by adjusting the production system.

> **Waste minimisation** is the aspect of lean production that to focuses on reducing waste in any business process, such as wasted time, labour on materials.

Competitive advantage from lean production

Lean production, featuring just-in-time stock management, continuous improvement linked with total quality management, as well as cell production, can improve how businesses are run in a number of ways:
- More input from staff
- A focus on quality
- Fewer wasted resources through just-in-time and total quality management
- A focus on reducing wasted time, so speed can become a source of competitive advantage

These features lead to the following sources of competitive advantage:
- Higher levels of productivity, reducing labour cost per unit
- Less space used to hold lower stock levels, reducing fixed costs
- Higher quality, leading to reputational advantages and greater repeat custom
- Faster development of new products, allowing the firm to be first to market with new ideas

> **Lean production** is a collective term for a range of Japanese techniques designed to eliminate waste from business processes.

Now test yourself

10 What name is given to the minimum level of stock a business aims to keep at all times?
11 How does a stock control diagram show the time taken to deliver by suppliers?
12 State three problems of having too much stock.
13 State two problems of having too little stock.
14 Briefly explain how introducing just-in-time stock management increases a firm's reliance on suppliers.
15 How would an increase in the level of production for a short time show up on a stock control diagram?

Answers online

Quality management

When consumers buy a product or service, they expect it to be of a certain quality. At a minimum level, customers expect the product to be fit to perform the purpose for which it was bought. Some businesses use quality as a point of differentiation.

There are three main methods of managing quality.

Managing quality

Quality control (QC)

This system involves checking output to find any faults in a production system. It is the traditional method used and relies on inspecting output, with inspection carried out by a person not involved in working on or making the products.

Quality assurance (QA)

This system focuses on producing methods to prevent quality problems arising. These methods are checklists or procedures that form a part of company policy. If employees follow these procedures, the systems are designed to prevent any quality problems.

> **Typical mistake**
>
> Too many students suggest that quality assurance ensures top-quality products. In reality, quality may simply be okay; what will be excellent are the systems of paperwork designed to try to manage quality.

Total quality management (TQM)

This is less of a system and more a way of encouraging all staff to think about the business. In order for this to work, everyone in the organisation has to understand and 'buy into' the idea of getting things 'right first time'. Quality becomes a part of everybody's job, not just production workers, but designers, accountants and sales people.

Table 10.8 Pros and cons of TQM, QC and QA

	TQM	Quality control (QC)	Quality assurance (QA)
Pros	• Should become deeply rooted into the company culture, e.g. product safety at a producer of baby car seats • Once all staff think about quality, it should show through from design to manufacture and after-sales service, e.g. at Lexus or BMW	• Can be used to guarantee that no defective item will leave the factory • Requires little staff training; therefore suits a business with unskilled or temporary staff (as ordinary workers don't need to worry about quality)	• Makes sure the company has a quality system for every stage in the production process • Some customers like the reassurance provided by keeping records about quality checks at every stage in production; they believe they will get a higher-quality service and may be willing to pay more
Cons	• Especially at first, staff sceptical of management initiatives may treat TQM as 'hot air'; it lacks the clear concrete programme of QC or QA • To get TQM into the culture of a business may be expensive, as it requires extensive training among all staff, e.g. all British Airways staff flying economy from Heathrow to New York	• Leaving quality for the inspectors to sort out may mean poor quality is built in to the product, e.g. clothes with seams that soon unpick • QC can be trusted when 100% of output is tested, but not when it is based on sampling; Ford used to test just one in seven of its new cars – that led to quality problems	• QA does not promise a high-quality product, only a high-quality, reliable process; this process may churn out 'okay' products reliably • QA may encourage complacency; it suggests quality has been sorted, whereas rising customer requirements mean quality should keep moving ahead

Quality circles

The people involved in doing a job tend to have real expertise in getting that job done. This expertise includes understanding how they could get the job done even better. Giving staff a formal system for discussing these improvements in their working area – a **quality circle** – encourages an approach of continuous improvement throughout the business.

> A **quality circle** is a group of staff who meet regularly to find quality improvements.

Exam tip

Involving staff in quality circles can be highly motivating. Look to tie in answers about this effect with the work of either Maslow or Herzberg.

Continuous improvement (kaizen)

REVISED

Whereas automation is an attempt to get a big leap forward in productivity, continuous improvement encourages staff to put forward a stream of small ideas on how to do things better. Empowering staff to make changes to their working systems brings quality and productivity improvements.

Based on cell production, each small group of employees becomes expert in their area and best placed to find improvements.

Key aspects of continuous improvement are:
- cell production
- quality circles
- small but frequent changes
- regular suggestions
- quality and productivity improvements.

Competitive advantage from quality management

Spending money on quality management systems to ensure high-quality production and service delivery brings rewards:
- It allows a price premium to be charged (often greater than the extra cost of producing high quality).
- It helps to gain distribution, with retailers confident they will not need to deal with product returns and refunds.
- It creates brand loyalty and repeat purchase.
- It can help to build a brand reputation that spreads to other products within a firm's portfolio.

Now test yourself

16 Who is responsible for ensuring quality in a quality control system?
17 What type of production is ideally suited to a system of continuous improvement?
18 What name is given to the meetings where small groups of staff discuss possible improvements within their area?
19 What is the main source of ideas for improvement in a kaizen system?
20 How can each of the four benefit, of quality management listed above lead to increased profits?

Answers online

Exam practice

Evaluate the likely impact on a UK-based manufacturer of high-quality, branded clothing of introducing a system of lean production.

(20)

Answers and quick quiz 10 online

Summary

- Job, batch, flow and cell production all have pros and cons, meaning each is best suited to different circumstances.
- Increasing productivity leads to lower costs per unit.
- Efficiency differs from productivity in that it measures wastage as well as speed.
- Firms face a choice between labour or capital intensive production methods.
- Capacity utilisation has major impact on fixed cost per unit and thus profit margins.
- Increasing capacity utilisation can be done through increasing current output and sales or reducing maximum capacity.

- Stock control diagrams can be used to help manage stock and show a range of different features of stock management.
- Firms can face problems from having either too much or too little stock.
- Just-in-time stock management aims to eliminate buffer stock.
- Lean production is an approach to production that includes JIT, TQM, cell production and continuous improvement.
- Quality management systems include quality control, quality assurance and total quality management.
- Good quality management can bring competitive advantage.

11 External influences

Economic influences

Effects on the business of economic changes

The economic environment within which businesses operate can have a major impact on both revenues and costs. It is therefore a vital determinant of profit. Changes in several key economic variables influence business performance in different ways.

Inflation

If prices are rising throughout an economy, the costs paid by a business for raw materials, property and labour (wages) will be rising. However, if consumers are used to prices rising, firms may be able to increase their selling prices in order to protect profit margins. The circumstances in which **inflation** has a major effect are:

- when rates of inflation are significantly above 2%
- when prices are rising faster than average earnings
- when UK inflation is higher than that in most other countries.

> **Inflation** is the percentage rate at which average prices rise during a year within the whole UK economy.

> **Typical mistake**
>
> If the rate of inflation is falling, say from 2% to 1%, prices are not going down. They are simply rising more slowly. Deflation – a situation where average prices are falling – is rare in the UK and would be shown by a negative rate of inflation, e.g. –1.5%.

> **Typical mistake**
>
> Too many student answers to questions on inflation simply consider the effect of inflation on costs, ignoring the fact that firms may well be able to increase their selling prices to protect profit margins.

Effects of inflation on businesses

- A firm with a long-term fixed price contract may find that if costs rise rapidly while the contract is being completed, the fixed price does not even cover its higher level of costs, damaging profitability.
- Firms with substantial long-term borrowings will find the real value of the money they repay will be lower following a period of high inflation, as inflation has the effect of reducing the real value of money.
- If inflation in the UK is higher than in other countries, UK businesses may lose competitiveness against foreign rivals whose costs are likely to be rising more slowly. This would allow foreign firms to charge lower prices.

> **Exam tip**
>
> Look for evidence of a company's revenues and costs being affected differently by inflation to show whether profits would be harmed or not. If many resources are imported from countries with low inflation, costs may be rising more slowly than the business can push up domestic selling prices, meaning profit margins may actually rise due to inflation.

Exchange rates

It is changes in the **exchange rate** of the pound that will affect UK businesses. Most directly affected will be UK businesses that export their products and services, and UK businesses that buy materials or other supplies from abroad.

> An **exchange rate** is the value of one currency expressed in terms of another.

Effects of exchange rates on businesses

Table 11.1 Summary of effects of exchange rate changes

	Example	Impact on exports	Impact on imports
£ appreciates	£1 was $1.60 but now buys $1.80	UK exports get pricier, so sales volumes slip	Imports to UK get cheaper, making it harder for UK firms to compete
£ depreciates	£1 was at €1.30 but now slips to €1.15	UK exports get cheaper, so sales volumes rise	Imports to UK get more expensive, so UK firms can compete more effectively

A handy way to remember the effect of a stronger pound is the word SPICED:

- **S**trong
- **P**ound
- **I**mports
- **C**heaper
- **E**xports
- **D**earer

Interest rates

Although different lenders will charge different **rates of interest**, most will adjust their rates in line with those charged by the Bank of England. This is why the Bank of England's base rate is such an important economic variable.

> A **rate of interest** is the amount charged by a lender per year for borrowing money. This is expressed as a percentage of the amount of money outstanding.

Effects of interest rates on businesses

An increase in interest rates tends to have negative effects on businesses in four ways:

- Consumers are likely to have less money to spend as payments on mortgages or other borrowings will increase. This is likely to reduce demand.
- The amount paid in interest on any borrowing by the business will rise, pushing up costs.
- Consumers are less likely to 'borrow to buy', so products that are often bought on credit, such as cars or sofas, will see demand fall, as the credit will cost more.
- Businesses are less likely to invest as the opportunity cost of investment (keeping the money in the bank to earn interest with no risk) will be greater.

Reducing interest rates is likely to have the same effects in reverse, being mainly beneficial to businesses.

Taxation and government spending

In the UK, government spending (on the NHS, defence, education, etc.) accounts for roughly 40% of all spending in the economy. So government decisions on spending and how to raise the money to spend (taxation) have a major impact on businesses.

Many private sector businesses are largely dependent upon the state for their income, such as:

- publishers of textbooks
- road–building firms

- pharmaceutical firms (producers of medicines)
- railway companies (given government subsidies).

Companies in general tend to press governments to cut their spending (and taxes), but many are heavily dependent on that government money.

Effects of taxation and government spending on businesses

Governments change levels of taxation and government spending to try to manage the economy. Their goal is to create stable economic growth. Table 11.2 shows government aims combined with the effects of changes in taxation and government spending.

Table 11.2 The impact of a change in taxation and government spending

	Government spending up	Government spending down	Government puts taxes up	Government puts taxes down
To help reduce the level of unemployment	Extra spending on road-building, health and other services with big workforces			Reduce income tax to enable families to keep and spend more of the money they earn
To cut the growth rate when it is rising too fast		Cut the spending on health, education and defence, to take a bit of spending from the economy	Increase income tax to force people to think harder and more carefully about what they buy	
To improve the competitiveness of British firms	Extra spending on education			Cut company taxation (corporation tax)
To cut the rate of imports, especially of consumer goods		Cut benefits, e.g. state pension, to reduce people's ability to buy exports	Increase VAT on all goods other than food and drink	

The business cycle

Economic growth does not tend to follow a stable path. At times, economies grow quickly; at other times, growth is slower, or economies even shrink from year to year. The pattern of economic growth in the UK tends to follow a pattern where strong growth (boom) is followed by periods of recession, where the economy actually contracts.

Effects of the business cycle on businesses

The key impact that the business cycle has on businesses is primarily related to demand for products. If the economy slows, consumers will, on average, reduce their spending, while in a boom period, consumer demand rises rapidly. Changes in consumers' incomes are the result of changes in wages or even changes in the level of unemployment.

The effect of the business cycle on businesses is therefore mainly dependent on one thing:
- income elasticity of demand.

This was covered in depth in Chapter 3, pages 25–27. Table 3.5 summarises the effect of the changes in income brought on by economic boom and economic recession, according to the income elasticity of the product being sold.

Effect of economic uncertainty

Predicting the economy is a little like trying to predict sales for every business in the UK. In Chapter 8, pages 80–82, we explored why forecasting sales of just one product is difficult. It is therefore vital to remember that forecasting the economy is an inexact science.

Business decision-makers love certainty. When devising plans for investment over the next five to ten years, directors want to be sure that the money they spend will be recovered and generate a profit. Uncertainty means they cannot be sure. In Chapter 2, page 11, we explored the reasons for uncertainty. Featuring high on the list of reasons for uncertainty in business, along with the reasons why sales forecasting is difficult, is economic change.

No business decision-makers will make any long-term decisions without thinking first about the likely state of the economy in the future. Therefore, business leaders prefer economic stability to the uncertainty that comes with cyclical economic growth.

Now test yourself

1 Briefly explain what is happening to prices when the rate of inflation falls from 2% to 1%.
2 Why can many businesses maintain profit margins during times of inflation when their costs are rising?
3 Which word is helpful in remembering the effects on UK businesses of a stronger pound?
4 Identify three ways in which an increase in interest rates has a negative effect on businesses.
5 What type of products find sales particularly hard hit during a recession?

Answers online

Legislation

Laws passed by parliament are needed to ensure that businesses behave in what is generally considered to be an acceptable way. Although many specialist areas of the law exist covering business activities, the five main areas in which legislation affects business are explained below.

Effects of consumer protection laws on business

The main goal of consumer protection legislation is to ensure that businesses actually deliver on what they promise the consumer.

Aspects of this include:
● Does the product do what it claims to do?
● Is the product correctly labelled?
● Is the product sold in the correct weight or measure?
● The rights of consumers to refunds or to exchange faulty products.

The driving force behind consumer protection legislation is to ensure that no business can gain an unfair advantage over its rivals through deceitfulness. Ultimately, competition should be based on the product and price at which it is sold, not claims that bend the truth.

Two major Acts of Parliament covering consumer protection are:
● the Sale of Goods Act
● the Trade Descriptions Act.

> **Exam tip**
>
> Many argue that businesses that mistreat customers will ultimately gain a poor reputation and lose business, making consumer protection legislation unnecessary. However, too many examples exist of 'cowboys' who mistreat customers, then set up under another name to rip people off again, to suggest that these laws are unnecessary.

Effects of employee protection on business

Employee protection law aims to state and uphold minimum standards of treatment that employees can expect from their employer. Major issues covered include:

- fair pay
- sick leave
- maternity and paternity leave
- employment contracts
- relationships with trade unions
- the ability of businesses to get rid of staff
- the responsibilities of businesses to employees who are made redundant.

Almost all businesses would prefer less protection for staff, since this gives them greater flexibility in terms of their human resources. Businesses tend to argue against increased rights for workers, claiming that increased costs will result and this will make it harder for them to compete with international rivals. A summary of the effects on businesses of employee protection legislation is shown in Table 11.3.

Table 11.3 Implications of employment legislation

Key area of employment law	Possible implications for firms
Minimum wage	Increased labour costs, which may lead to increased automation in the longer term and increased unemployment; on the plus side, employees may be more motivated by a fair wage satisfying basic needs
Right to a contract of employment	Meets employees' security needs but can reduce employers' flexibility in how they use their staff
Increased right to sick, maternity and paternity leave	Increased cost of paying for cover for these staff; however, staff may feel more valued as they feel well treated by employers, reducing staff turnover levels, which saves the costs of recruiting new staff
Redundancy	Reducing capacity becomes expensive due to statutory payments to staff made redundant; this can mean that closing a factory or office has a negative impact on cash flow in the short term
Trade union rights	Employers can be forced to deal with a trade union if enough staff are members; this does bring benefits as well as drawbacks

Effects of environmental protection on business

Given the broadly accepted need to regulate the effect of business on the environment, a range of legislation now governs how businesses treat the natural environment. Major areas include:

- materials that firms must use for certain products
- processes firms are allowed to use to make certain products
- the need to use recyclable materials for certain products
- landfill tax
- the need to carry out environmental risk assessments for different parts of a business's activities.

Once again, businesses tend to resist new, tougher legislation, claiming it will increase their costs in a way that foreign rivals will not have to cope with.

Much of the recent legislation on the environment came from the European Union. Now that Britain has voted to leave the EU, the UK government will have to replace many of the EU laws that governed the way UK businesses had to treat the environment. Businesses and many others will be interested to see what decisions are taken.

Effects of competition policy on business

When businesses compete with one another, they tend to keep prices at a sensibly low level, provide a good service and generate new innovative products and services. With no competition, prices can be pushed high, service standards can slip and innovation can dry up. Therefore, governments seek, through legislation, to ensure that there is competition in all markets. The key legislation is the creation in 2014 of a government-funded body called the Competition and Markets Authority (CMA). The CMA is responsible for:

- investigating proposed takeovers and mergers
- investigating allegations of anti-competitive practices
- taking legal action against those who collude to maintain high prices within a market, such as **cartels**.

> A **cartel** is a group of companies operating in the same market who make agreements to control supply and thus prices.

Figure 11.1 Functions of the CMA

The work of the CMA should, indirectly or directly, ensure that:

- companies have to set competitive prices
- companies do not collude with others in their market to the detriment of consumers
- mergers and takeovers that will create overly powerful firms are prevented.

Effects of health and safety on business

Health and safety law is designed to protect employees and customers in the workplace. The major piece of legislation – the Health and Safety at Work Act 1974 – places the burden on employers. Key aspects of this burden are:

- safe physical conditions
- precautions that firms are required to take when planning their work
- the way in which hazardous substances should be treated in the workplace.

Complying with health and safety legislation has both positive and negative effects on businesses as shown in Table 11.4.

Table 11.4 Positive and negative effects of health and safety legislation on businesses

Positive effects on businesses	Negative effects on businesses
Should prevent incidents that create negative publicity	Extra paperwork
Should help to motivate employees, who feel safe	Need to pay for extra safety equipment
Accidents can delay or halt production – these should be avoided	Need to pay to adjust physical work conditions

Exam tip

In spite of the fact that legislation exists to prevent unscrupulous firms stealing an advantage, illegal practice still occurs. Although some may argue that consumers will avoid these firms, forcing them out of business, virtually no businesses are forced to close as a result of breaking the laws that govern business. It can be argued that the penalties for breaking the law are simply not strong enough.

The role of the publicly funded body, the Health and Safety Executive, is to find and prosecute companies guilty of major breaches of this legislation.

TESTED ☐

Now test yourself

6 State two potential impacts on a business of complying with new, tougher environmental legislation.
7 What is the name of the organisation responsible for enforcing health and safety legislation?
8 Whose responsibility is it to ensure employees work in a safe environment?
9 State two areas the Competition and Markets Authority can investigate.

Answers online

The competitive environment

The number of businesses supplying products or services in a market can have a major effect on how businesses operate. From monopoly markets with only one dominant supplier to fiercely competitive markets with many businesses fighting one another for consumers, business behaviour can vary dramatically.

> The **competitive environment** experienced by a business refers not just to how many competitors it faces, but to how directly other firms' products are in competition and how fierce rivalries are.

Exam tip

The best exam answers recognise the level of competition within the market, suggesting courses of action appropriate to the level of competition found in the market being examined.

Competition

REVISED ☐

One dominant business

A market dominated by a single business, described as a **monopoly**, is bad for consumers because:
- Consumers have little choice.
- Prices tend to be high.
- There is little incentive for the dominant firm to innovate or provide great customer service.

> A **monopoly** is a single business that dominates supply in a given market.

As described on page 112, governments generally try to prevent monopolies occurring to prevent consumers suffering.

However, companies strive to become an effective monopoly. A key focus of this activity is trying to build barriers to entry that prevent new firms entering the market. Examples of possible barriers to entry include:
- patents and technological breakthroughs
- incredibly strong brands and high advertising budgets
- heavy spending on infrastructure (such as mobile phone network masts).

Competition between a few giants

In an **oligopoly** market, rivalries are intense, as it is clear that in most cases one firm can only gain market share by directly taking it from one of just a handful of rivals.

> An **oligopoly** is the name given to a market dominated by just a few major suppliers.

Given the intense rivalries, it may appear odd that companies in an oligopoly rarely compete on price. The reason is that they fear a price war would start, leading to lower profit margins for all in the industry. Instead, non-price competition exists, focusing on aspects such as:
● branding
● product features
● product design
● advertising
● technical innovations.

The fiercely competitive market

These markets tend to be characterised by many small businesses competing with one another, often on the basis of price. This keeps profit margins low and ensures consumers usually get a bargain. However, a business that is able to find an effective method of differentiation within a fiercely competitive market will stand a far better chance of success.

Many of these markets tend to be for commodity products which, by definition, are hard to differentiate. For businesses selling these, there may be little choice of strategy other than keeping costs as low as possible in the hope of undercutting rivals' prices and still making some profit.

Market size

REVISED

Big markets

Larger markets, even those with a few fairly dominant firms, offer scope for new competition, usually through carving out a niche. Therefore in a large market there is likely to be a fair degree of competition. This is likely to keep even dominant producers from becoming complacent, as they recognise the need to offer good service to avoid opening an opportunity to a rival.

Small markets

In a smaller market, with fewer customers and lower total sales, it may be easier to build up barriers to entry, carving up the market between just a few businesses.

Markets whose size is changing

Markets tend to grow or shrink in size over time. Predictably, the direction of this change in size will affect the level of competition:
● Growing markets … attract new entrants … seeking higher profits on offer.
● Shrinking markets … see established firms exiting … as profitability tends to be low and thus unattractive.

Business responses to a tougher competitive environment

REVISED

When new competitors arrive, or the intensity with which an existing rival is fighting increases, businesses face a choice of how to respond.

Price cutting

Attracting new customers, or hanging on to existing customers, could be achieved by cutting the selling price. Unless this is accompanied by cutting the costs of production, profit margins will fall. This is why price cutting is rarely a successful long-term answer.

Increased product differentiation

Finding or stressing new ways to show that our product is different to those of our existing or new rivals is likely to be the key to success in a tougher environment. Methods of product differentiation could include:
- branding
- product features
- product design
- advertising
- technical innovations.

Collusion

Through desperation or deliberate cunning, companies trying to survive in a really tough competitive environment may be tempted to behave illegally. It is easy to understand why a desperate business may be willing to break the law in this way. It is harder to see it as a sensible choice, given the strength of anti-**collusion** legislation in the UK.

> **Collusion** occurs when two or more rival businesses agree to fix supply or prices within their market. This is illegal.

TESTED

Now test yourself

10 What name is given to a market dominated by just a few large companies?
11 State two reasons why monopolies tend to be bad for consumers.
12 List three methods of non-price competition.
13 What is meant by a barrier to entry?

Answers online

Exam practice

Evaluate whether uncertainties in the current external environment in the UK mean that business success is, more than ever, down to luck rather than good decision-making. (20)

Answers and quick quiz 11 online

ONLINE

Summary

- The major economic changes that can affect businesses are: the business cycle; government spending and taxation; inflation; exchange rates; interest rates.
- Economic change is a source of great uncertainty for business decision-makers.
- There are five main areas in which the law can affect businesses: consumer protection; employee protection; environmental protection; competition law; health and safety.
- Most changes to the law lead to an increase in costs for a business.
- The competitive environment faced by a business will affect its strategy.
- The number of firms in a market affects the degree of competition.
- The size and growth rate of a market affect the degree of competition.
- Firms can compete on price and non-price aspects, including branding, advertising, product features, design and innovation.

Corporate objectives

A sense of direction or a clear target provides focus for any activity. Productivity and co-ordination can be enhanced if staff know how their jobs will help the firm achieve its goals. All businesses are likely to have **corporate objectives**. These may be specifically stated and measurable targets or, more likely for small businesses, implicit from the entrepreneur's behaviour and priorities.

> **Corporate objectives** are targets set for the whole firm to reach in a given time period.

Corporate aims

REVISED

An aim provides a general sense of what is to be achieved. The key benefit to having a clear aim is the sense of purpose and drive that the aim can bring to day-to-day tasks. If everyone in a business is aware of what the firm is trying to achieve, they will be more driven to achieve their part of that whole. Typical corporate aims could include:

- growth
- maximising profit
- entering new markets
- surviving the first two years of being in business
- improving the communities in which we operate.

Focusing on any one of these would help employees to understand what factors should be prioritised when making decisions. This should allow decisions to be made quickly, without the need for lengthy consultation with senior management.

> **Exam tip**
>
> Corporate aims can help to explain unethical business behaviour. An employee who has understood that the business's primary aim is to maximise profit may persuade a customer to buy a product or service she or he doesn't really need, in order to boost profit. Many low-grade savings products have been sold in this way.

Mission statements

REVISED

If employees can be convinced to 'buy into' a business's **mission**, they are likely to find sufficient motivation from trying to achieve this purpose, without the need for extra motivational techniques. Staff working in the NHS will often put up with dreadful working conditions and poor pay, yet still remain driven in their jobs, because they believe in the mission of the NHS: to provide high quality medical care to all.

Mission can be thought of as the reason why a business exists, exemplified by Google's mission to 'organise the world's information and make it universally available'. This is a noble goal that can give staff a genuine sense of purpose, explaining without the need for extra management input, why they are doing their job and why their job is worthwhile.

Though mission can be a woolly concept within an organisation, many businesses will attempt to produce a short statement that summarises their mission: a **mission statement**. This can be communicated widely within the business, and even shared with other stakeholder groups, notably customers.

> **Mission** is the underpinning purpose behind the existence of a business.
>
> A **mission statement** is a catchy summary of the reason why a business exists.

Influences on business mission

Major factors affecting the actual sense of mission created within a business are:

- Purpose: Why the business exists — likely to be rooted in the founder's beliefs.
- Values: What the business believes in doing and guiding principles behind how it should be done.
- Standards and behaviours: The way that people in the business actually act, both towards others in the business and towards stakeholders. Behaviours of managers are likely to have a very strong influence over the behaviours exhibited by their staff.

Now test yourself

TESTED

1 Explain the difference between corporate aims and mission.
2 State four factors that may influence a firm's mission.
3 Briefly explain why a sense of mission can be a powerful advantage to any business.

Answers online

Corporate strategy

Strategy can be thought of as the plan for achieving objectives. So, a **corporate strategy** refers to the overall plan that a business chooses to follow in order to reach its overall objectives. Strategic decisions are large in scale and hard to reverse, so a corporate strategy will address major issues for a firm for the medium- to long-term, perhaps most significantly, what to sell and who to sell to.

Strategy should not be devised in a vacuum. A successful strategy should consider two broad sets of influences, as shown in Figure 12.1.

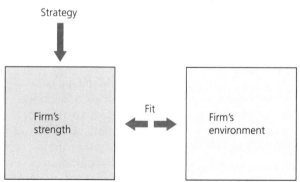

Figure 12.1 If a strategy is to achieve the objectives set, it must match the firm's strengths to its competitive environment

A successful strategy must find a way to use the firm's strength(s) to meet the conditions presented by the external environment faced by the business over the coming years.

Porter's (Generic) Strategy Matrix

REVISED

Michael Porter's Generic Strategy Matrix provides advice to any business on the potential routes to choosing a successful corporate strategy. Porter sees this as a crucial element in achieving a long-term competitive advantage.

Exam tip

Standards and behaviours in particular can be the root cause of a business acting in a way that does not seem to reflect its founding purpose or stated values. If staff copy managers behaving in a way that seems to follow some other goal, such as maximising profit, what the business actually does may seem very different to its stated mission. In some schools, teachers are placed under such pressure for results that they may feel expected to abuse regulations relating to coursework or controlled assessment.

A **corporate strategy** is a medium- to long-term plan for achieving the corporate objectives.

Typical mistake

Student responses to answers asking for advice on 'the best strategy' can fall victim to ignoring one or both of these major influences on strategy. The best strategic recommendations will always make clear how the strategy plays to a firm's strengths and addresses the external environmental conditions faced by the business.

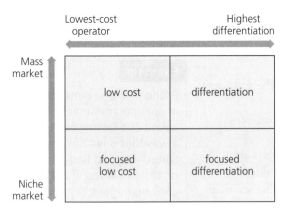

Figure 12.2 Porter's (Generic) Strategy Matrix

The matrix shows the four major strategic choices that Porter suggests can lead to long-term success. The key issues to consider when analysing a company's strategy are whether it is selling to a mass or a niche market and how it makes itself stand out from its rivals — either through being the lowest cost operator or having a significant **point of differentiation**.

Porter's low-cost strategy

Being sufficiently efficient in its operations allows a business to be able to undercut rivals on price and still make a profit. The key to successful cost leadership is likely to lie in harnessing an operational advantage, such as better economies of scale than rivals, or higher productivity in factories than anyone else can manage. To be effective in the long-term, the low-cost strategy must be based on an advantage that rivals cannot easily copy, so outsourcing to China may not prove the heart of a successful low-cost strategy, as that is relatively easily copied.

Porter's differentiation strategy

Differentiation works. The challenge is to find a way to differentiate the product which is:

- Cost effective: Adding features that cost more to add than a consumer is willing to pay is not profitable.
- Sustainable: A method of differentiation that lasts is the key: doing something to a product that rivals can quickly copy will not provide long-term success.

Although branding and image building marketing methods can provide successful, protectable sources of differentiation, these are not the only methods. Great design or amazing customer service can differentiate a business just as effectively through the work of the operations management function.

Focused low cost

A strategy that focuses on a niche market and succeeds in being the lowest cost provider within that niche can also bring success. Here, the key is less likely to be cost reduction through economies of scale and more likely to be based on operational efficiencies and high productivity levels.

Focused differentiation

Successful differentiation within a niche market can also lead to long-term success, generally with a very high margin, relatively low volume business model.

Product differentiation describes a business's attempts to make its product stand out from those of rivals, perhaps through marketing, design or quality.

Typical mistake

Low cost does not necessarily mean lowest price. Having the lowest costs in an industry does give firms the chance to charge a lower price than rivals while remaining profitable. But a low-cost strategy may be a success because a firm can charge average market prices with higher profit margins than any rivals.

Exam tip

When considering a case study featuring a business trying to use a strategy of differentiation, consider carefully whether their point of differentiation is something that will appeal to consumers and whether it is hard for competitors to adapt this, destroying their differentiation.

Competitive advantage through distinctive capabilities

A business that is clear on its core strengths has the beginning of a successful route to long-term strategic advantage. If core strengths, such as innovative R&D departments, hugely committed staff or creative marketing departments can be used to provide a competitive edge over rivals, then these can be the basis of long-term success.

> **Exam tip**
>
> A distinctive capability need not be quite so obviously related to a business function as those listed above. A business that has a proven track record of reacting quickly to changes in the market, or one that has shown it learns well from mistakes, can build a competitive advantage around these attributes. Look for evidence of 'softer' capabilities such as these when analysing a business case study.

Now test yourself

TESTED

4 Distinguish between corporate strategy and corporate objectives.
5 State three methods of differentiating a product.
6 Briefly explain why a company choosing a low-cost strategy may earn high margins, when rivals struggle to break even.

Answers online

Ansoff's Matrix

Strategic direction

REVISED

Few decisions are more fundamental in business strategy than:
● What products do we sell?
● Which markets should we target?

Making these decisions sets a firm's course for the medium to long term and adjusting these choices is likely to take a long time and affect the whole of the business. Therefore these are considered to be the major choices made in choosing the strategic direction a firm will follow with its corporate strategy.

Strategic direction and Ansoff's Matrix

REVISED

Business academic Igor Ansoff devised his Strategic Matrix to show the major choices open to a business considering its strategic direction, and highlight the level of risk involved in each choice.

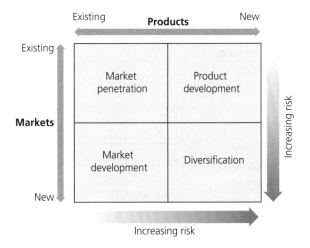

Figure 12.3 **Ansoff's Matrix and risk**

The level of risk is lowest in the top left-hand corner of the matrix, rising as a company's choices move further away, with the highest level of risk associated with the bottom right corner of the matrix, representing extreme diversification.

Market penetration

The commonest and lowest risk strategy involves boosting market share through selling more of the same product to the same target market. Methods to do this include:

- finding new customers within the target market
- taking new customers from competitors
- increasing usage of the product among existing customers.

Risks are low as the company is still operating on familiar ground with tried and tested products.

Market development

While still selling existing products, the business now aims the products at new markets. This can be done most obviously by looking for new geographical markets, often breaking into foreign markets, or by repositioning the product to aim at a different type of customer, as Land Rover has done, moving from targeting farmers to wealthy city dwellers.

The major risk factor here is that the company may not understand consumer behaviours in the new market they are entering. Although market research can help to reduce this risk, even thorough research is unlikely to equip a firm with the depth of understanding of consumer behaviour possessed by established rivals in these new markets.

Product development

The new feature here is the product. A business choosing product development as their strategic direction will still be selling to current markets, so is likely to have a sound understanding of customers' needs, wants and preferences. However, the plan will be to sell new products to these customers. Developing new products successfully is tough; there are so many reasons why new product launches can fail, from design problems to manufacturing issues to, most commonly, a failure to actually meet customers' needs. New products can either be:

- changes made to an existing product
- developing and launching brand new products.

The first option may be slightly lower risk, although adding new features or ingredients can still backfire. Developing and launching brand new products presents more hurdles and thus involves greater risk.

Diversification

Ansoff's Matrix highlights the dangers involved in attempts to diversify. A business choosing this strategic direction faces the problems of product development and market development combined. Selling new products to customers whose tastes you have no experience of is likely to be very tough to do successfully.

Diversification can, however, bring exceptionally high rewards. As is normally found in business, higher risks are associated with the potential to achieve higher rewards if the risks can be successfully managed.

> **Exam tip**
>
> When using Ansoff's Matrix to analyse a company's strategic choice, focus your argument on the level of risk associated with the choice and explain carefully why the risk is relatively high or low.

> **Diversification**, as defined by Ansoff, means selling new products to new markets.

Table 12.1 Risks and rewards in different strategies

	Risks	Rewards
Market penetration	• Few risks should arise, other than decline in the product life cycle • Lack of ambition may make your best staff look for more challenge elsewhere	• You know the customers and the competitors, so should make error-free decisions • Returns on extra investment will be predictable
Market development	• Subtle cultural differences add hugely to risk, e.g. many UK retailers have flopped in the US • Practical differences matter too, such as distribution channels, consumer legislation and differences in managing staff	• There are huge potential economies of scale if your product succeeds elsewhere, e.g. Fever-Tree • If you take the time to understand the cultural differences, you may be able to localise your product range effectively, as McDonald's does
Product development	• Most new products fail (at a rate of about 6/7 in the UK) so the risk level is very high • Because new product success is tough, companies put their best people on it; this can mean too little brainpower devoted to ordinary brands (or, in Tesco's case, its UK supermarket heartland)	• As shown by Apple, nothing adds value and creates differentiation more than innovative product development • Continuous, successful product development should mean the organisation lives forever
Diversification	• Not knowing the market and having a brand new product means the risk level is multiplied by two • Therefore it is vital to plan for the operational risk of diversifying by making sure your financial position is especially secure	• When diversification works, it can transform the size of and opportunities for the business, e.g. Apple in the era since the iPod breakthrough • Radical diversification (Google making cars) can be hugely exciting for the workforce, helping you recruit the best

Now test yourself

TESTED ☐

7 Draw a properly labelled diagram of Ansoff's Matrix (remember to label the axes).
8 What are the main dangers of:
   a) market development
   b) product development?
9 Briefly explain how Ansoff's Matrix illustrates the risk involved in different choices of strategic direction.

Answers online

> **Typical mistake**
>
> Just as many failed leaders have done in the past, defining the market in which a business operates is key to using Ansoff's Matrix successfully. Assumptions about products being similar or markets being similar to existing ones lead to a failure to understand the risks involved in straying from existing products and existing markets.

SWOT analysis

Purpose

REVISED ☐

If a good corporate strategy involves matching a business's strengths to the external environment within which it is operating, an analytical framework that picks these out has to be a helpful strategic tool. A **SWOT analysis** sets out to gain a full understanding of what a firm does well and badly and what major issues it must address in the future. It is therefore a framework used to help begin the process of strategic planning.

> **SWOT analysis** identifies a business's strengths and weaknesses along with the opportunities and threats it faces.

How to conduct a SWOT analysis

Top down approach

This method tends to use external management consultants working directly with the boss of the business.

Benefits include:

- A dispassionate approach to identifying strengths and especially weaknesses.
- Detachment from the company culture may allow aspects of the business to be seen in a new light.

Drawbacks include:

- Managers may fail to share all necessary information with those conducting the SWOT in an attempt to present their area of responsibility in a more favourable light.

Consultative approach

A boss who takes the opportunity to travel around the business, engaging in conversations with those who understand each aspect best, can conduct, albeit perhaps more slowly than consultants, a more thorough analysis, really beginning to understand what works well and less well within the business.

Benefits include:
- Greater insight from a wider range of contributors.
- The chance for the boss to gain first-hand understanding of the whole business.

Drawbacks:
- Staff may be even less willing to point out problems if they feel this will reflect badly on the leadership of the person they are talking to.

> **Exam tip**
>
> Consider how the SWOT analysis has been conducted before assessing just how reliable its results are. If a case study suggests a top down approach has been taken, it is worth considering whether the SWOT will have really revealed all of the internal problems.

Internal considerations: strengths and weaknesses

The skill in identifying strengths and weaknesses for a business is in picking out the areas that really matter to the business's performance. This is something of an art form as many managers who focus simply on financial data may miss a 'softer strength' on which a future strategy may be based. However, a key part of ensuring a robust identification of strengths and weaknesses is to focus the analysis on a few **Key Performance Indicators** (**KPIs**). Examples of commonly used KPIs include:

- like for like sales
- market share
- capacity utilisation
- unit cost
- brand recognition
- staff turnover.

If compared with industry rivals and/or previous years' figures these KPIs can offer clear statements of strengths or weaknesses.

> **Key Performance Indicators (KPIs)** are quantifiable measures of aspects of a business's performance that the business considers to be the main determinants of its commercial success.

> **Typical mistake**
>
> Be careful not to consider external factors, such as a growing market, as a strength. Strengths and weaknesses are internally controllable factors. Operating in a market which is growing simply represents an opportunity to boost sales in an existing market.

External considerations: opportunities and threats

The external environment in which a business operates is subject to significant changes. Few changes leave a firm unaffected. Therefore, in order to understand the situation in which they are operating it is vital to include an assessment of the external environment. This is done by assessing the opportunities and threats brought about by the environment. Key areas to consider when looking for opportunities and threats include the following.

Demography

Changes to the population, especially in its structure, could be relevant. Britain's increasingly ageing population offers opportunities to sell to more retired people, while the effects of immigration have opened up new market niches for some UK businesses. These issues can simultaneously represent threats to businesses that fail to find a way to turn these changes to their advantage.

New laws and regulations

Changes in laws and regulations can open up opportunities or make existing products obsolete overnight. The introduction of a sugar tax on soft drinks has had a significant impact on manufacturers. Perhaps even bigger still will be changes to UK law necessitated by Britain's decision to leave the EU.

Technological factors

A further source of both opportunity and threat is changes in technology. For those who drive technological change, the factor tends to be an opportunity seized, but for some businesses, a change in technology can destroy sales of now outdated products within a matter of months.

Economic factors

Changes in the whole range of economic variables will affect a business's operations. Depending on the direction of the change and the business being considered, changes in variables such as:

- economic growth
- inflation
- exchange rates
- unemployment
- interest rates
- government taxation and spending could represent either an opportunity or a threat.

For more detail on this see Chapter 12 of the AS revision guide.

> **Exam tip**
>
> When assessing the effects of economic changes on a business's external environment, don't forget to use tools learned in the first year of your course to help understand the impact, notably income elasticity.

Now test yourself

10 State three common KPIs used by businesses to assess strengths and weaknesses.
11 State three common areas of external environmental change that may represent opportunities or threats to a business.
12 What are two broad ways in which a business may carry out a SWOT analysis?

Answers online

Impact of external influences

In order for a firm to better understand the external environment within which it is operating, it may carry out a PESTLE analysis. This acronym sets out the six main areas of external influences:

- **P**olitical
- **E**conomic
- **S**ocial
- **T**echnological
- **L**egal
- **E**nvironmental.

This structure can be a helpful way to ensure that no opportunities or threats are overlooked when compiling the SWOT analysis.

Political factors

Decisions made in the political arena can affect businesses' fortunes. Government policies encouraging investment in infrastructure or exports can represent significant opportunities to some firms. However, without a doubt, the most significant political factor that affects, and will continue to affect, UK businesses for the foreseeable future is the decision to leave the European Union. The impacts of this decision will be many and various and could include factor such as:

- harder to access EU markets
- harder to fill lower paid job vacancies without free movement of labour
- more expensive imported materials due to the reduction in the value of the pound
- less foreign direct investment to the UK from foreign multinationals
- EU laws will need to be replaced, which may allow the UK Parliament to relax legal responsibilities placed on firms in areas such as employment protection or environmental standards
- a weaker pound may make exporting to non-EU markets easier for businesses that have previously only traded domestically
- UK businesses will find it easier to compete on price with more expensive foreign imports due to the exchange rate shift.

The media are likely to be reporting on the effects of Brexit on a daily basis over the next few years. It is important to stay abreast of current developments.

> **Exam tip**
>
> Be careful to ensure that you support arguments relating to Brexit with data and evidence: such a hotly debated political issue tends to encourage assertions with no justification from case study material provided.

Economic factors

Perhaps the most widely significant external environmental factor faced by businesses is the state of the economy. The link between economic growth and average incomes does tend to have an impact on sales of most products, dependent upon their income elasticity. However, it is important to remember that while economic gloom may be a threat for many businesses, for others it can represent a significant opportunity to grow. Discount stores such as Poundland and supermarkets Aldi and Lidl have seen significant growth in the last few years as average incomes in the UK stagnate and consumers become more price sensitive.

Other economic factors to be assessed include:

- The exchange rate: This impacts not only on exporters, but also on businesses that sell imported products, or use imported components or materials. Meanwhile, for those who compete against these firms without using imported supplies, exchange rate movements will also have an indirect effect.

- The rate of inflation: As it rises this tends to cause uncertainty and lead to reductions in investment and decisions to expand.
- The rate of unemployment: An increase will reduce average incomes but make it easier to recruit staff without needing to offer high wages.

Social factors

REVISED

Changes in social attitudes and behaviour frequently relate to lifestyle. Trends such as:
- greater awareness of the need to eat healthily
- changed attitudes to smoking
- an increased desire for convenience and speed of service
- an ageing population

can represent both opportunity and threat to different firms. While some will find their products becoming less desirable as society changes its attitudes, others will see the chance to cater to new lifestyle choices. Of course, a business that sees a change damaging sales of one product may be able to launch new products specifically designed to cater for new tastes — if it is practising effective strategic planning.

Technological factors

REVISED

Changes in technology (not just information technology, but new scientific endeavours in any field) can affect businesses in a range of ways.

Technological changes can allow new ways of making existing products, lowering costs, improving quality, reliability, durability or recyclability. They can also enable the development of brand new products, similar to existing ones, such as electric cars, or the launch of really new product concepts, such as fitness trackers like the Fitbit watch.

Generally, businesses that develop these new technologies, or harness them early, will be able to see technological change as an opportunity. For those without access to the technology, or whose competitors introduce the technologies earlier, these changes are likely to represent a threat.

Legal factors

REVISED

Passing new laws can, once more, disrupt existing industries, forcing businesses to change the way they make products, the materials they use, or even banning certain products. Firms directly affected by such legal changes will face a strategic challenge as to how to turn what appears to be a threat into an opportunity.

Environmental factors

REVISED

Environmental pressures, applied to businesses to ensure that their operations do not have a harmful impact on the natural environment, are generally seen as a threat since mostly businesses are encouraged to change their methods of operating. However, many businesses see improving their environmental impact in the light of environmental pressures as an opportunity. This can be brought about by adopting more efficient methods that also reduce costs or through using their environmental record as a point of differentiation from rivals.

Typical mistake

Do not always consider that tightening environmental regulations and legislation represent a threat to all businesses. They could lead to certain niche markets growing, thereby offering an opportunity.

What to do about external influences

● Make the most of favourable external factors while they last: An external change that works in a business's favour should be capitalised upon, giving the business time and money to help prepare contingency plans in the event that the factor moves against it.
● Minimise the impact of unfavourable external influences: This can be through adjustments to controllable aspects of the business's performance, so cope with a negative exchange rate movement by considering shifting factory location, for example.

Now test yourself

TESTED

13 What does PESTLE stand for?
14 State two possible positive and two possible negative effects of Brexit for British firms.
15 Which aspects of a SWOT analysis does PESTLE help to develop?

Answers online

The competitive environment

The importance of the structure and nature of competition within a business's market was introduced in Chapter 45 of the AS book. In the context of studying corporate strategy, this theme is developed by considering a framework commonly used for analysing the attractiveness of the competitive environment for businesses.

Porter's Five Forces

Michael Porter (the same one famed for his Generic Strategy Matrix) offered a structure for conducting analysis of a business's competitive environment. The matrix identifies five key aspects of the competitive environment that affect a firm's likelihood of long-term success. Once a business has assessed how favourable each force is in the particular market in which it operates (or plans to enter), it should be better placed to decide just how attractive that market really is.

Figure 12.4 Rivalry among existing competitors (Source: Michael E Porter, 'The Five Competitive Forces That Shape Strategy', *Harvard Business Review*, January 2008)

Rivalry among existing competitors

REVISED

At the heart of Porter's Five Forces is the intensity of rivalry between competitors in the industry. Profitability is more likely where rivalry is less intense.

Table 12.2 Characteristics of markets where rivalry is low and high

Where intensity of rivalry is low	Where intensity of rivalry is high
● A few companies dominate the market ● Branding is very important to consumers ● Booming market gives opportunities for all ● Little spare capacity ● High barriers to entry, e.g. a new Chinese aeroplane facing consumer credibility issues ● No direct competition from abroad, e.g. 'bricks' retailing such as retail petrol	● Many competitors of roughly equal size ● Products are relatively undifferentiated ● Market growth is slow ● Capacity utilisation is low ● Low barriers to entry, so it is cheap and easy to enter the market ● Directly faces overseas competition, e.g. manufactured goods and some services

Where the intensity of rivalry is high, pressure to maintain a low price and thus keep costs low enough to still make a profit is great. Those companies which are unable to keep their costs under control are likely to disappear. Where rivalry among competitors is less intense, non-price competition on marketing, branding or innovation is more likely — offering scope for some firms to survive without necessarily going through the pain of continually looking for the efficiency gains that bring cost reductions.

Threat of new entrants

REVISED

The danger of new companies entering the market, thus creating extra competition, is largely dependent on the existence of **barriers to entry**.

Typical barriers to entry include:
● patents and technical knowhow of staff
● strong brand identity and customer loyalty
● high costs to customers of switching supplier
● substantial network infrastructure (such as physically building the masts and cabling needed to construct a mobile phone network).

Barriers to entry are factors in a market that can make it hard for new companies to break into the market.

If the threat of new entrants is low, companies in the market may be able to keep prices relatively high, enjoying strong margins, without the need to worry about new rivals entering the market and undercutting them.

Changes in the buying power of customers

REVISED

When the power in any bargaining between a business and its customers shifts in the customers' direction, this can be unfavourable to the business. A company that sells its product to many individual customers is likely to find this force favourable. However, for businesses that sell their product to just a few large customers, a threat from one of them to stop buying unless they are offered a discount may be too grave to ignore. If customers merge, or take over other customers, this will shift this force against the business.

Customer power is reduced significantly in contexts where a business's product is complex or such a major investment that customers may not be able to afford to change the firm they buy from.

Changes in the selling power of suppliers

REVISED

At the other end of the business lies its relative power when dealing with suppliers. If the power in this relationship shifts towards suppliers, this is bad news for the business and its future profitability. Factors affecting supplier power include:
● number of alternative suppliers available
● uniqueness of supplier's product or service
● reliance of the business on technical support from its supplier.

Threat of substitutes

REVISED

Whereas Porter's threat of new entrants considers the risk of a new firm entering our market, the threat of substitutes considers the chances that a product or service in another market may become seen by customers as a viable substitute for our product. So while airlines offering domestic UK flights from London to Manchester or Scotland may enjoy a time advantage over other forms of transport, building a high speed rail link to speed up train times on longer domestic journeys may transform rail travel into a viable substitute considered by those needing to make rapid domestic journeys within the UK.

> **Typical mistake**
>
> Do not confuse this force with the threat of new entrants. The threat of substitutes considers the threat posed by indirect competitors, rather than companies selling exactly the same type of product or service.

How the five forces shape strategy

REVISED

The use of Porter's Five Forces model may identify changes in the balance of one or more forces against the business. In these cases, the business can look to produce a strategy that addresses this issue before it causes the firm major problems. For example, if a company considers that the power of suppliers is increasing, it may be tempted to take over a supplier, to shift that force right back into its favour.

Above all, Five Forces analysis should be seen as another model to be used to help to analyse a business's situation. Using the Five Forces should help to ensure that strategic decision-making is wiser, and more effective.

Now test yourself

TESTED

16 Briefly explain why Porter's Five Forces model should be used on a regular, perhaps annual, basis by sensible firms.
17 State three typical barriers to entry that may reduce the threat of new entrants.
18 If a business is to be profitable, state which forces it would like to be high and which it would prefer to be low.

Answers online

Exam practice

1 To what extent are methods of analysing a company's position, such as SWOT, PESTLE or Porter's Five Forces, of limited value due to the increased speed of change in markets such as mobile phone handsets and other consumer electronics products? (20)

N and N Ltd have experienced great success since launching a new range of remote control toys ten years ago. Priced a little above the market average, these toys used recycled materials and completely recycled packaging. This is allied to the company's mission 'to enrich the lives of children while improving the environment'. N and N Ltd have taken the decision to pursue an objective of growth. The strategy they are considering is to maintain their point of differentiation as the most environmentally friendly supplier of remote control toys. However, as a result of a range of external factors, including new regulations, stalling economic growth and intense rivalry among existing rivals in the UK market, the decision has been made to launch the product in three European markets: Austria, Germany and Switzerland. With no experience of operating abroad, N and N Ltd plan to conduct thorough market research in these markets.

2 (a) Explain why Ansoff would consider N and N Ltd's strategy as riskier than remaining in the UK. (4)
  (b) Analyse the likely impact on N and N Ltd of stalling economic growth and intense rivalry among existing rivals in the UK. (6)
  (c) Assess the importance to N and N Ltd of maintaining the clear sense of corporate mission that led to their initial success. (10)

Answers and quick quiz 12 online

ONLINE

Summary

- Mission explains primarily to staff why a business exists, creating a shared purpose.
- Corporate aims provide a general statement of direction for a business.
- Corporate strategy is the plan a company devises to achieve its corporate objectives.
- Michael Porter's Generic Strategy Matrix shows four potentially successful strategic choices available to all businesses:
  - Low cost
  - Differentiation
  - Focused low cost
  - Focused differentiation.
- Porter's strategies focus on the need to develop a distinct capability as a long-term source of competitive advantage.
- Ansoff's Matrix clarifies key choices in deciding on strategic direction.
- The matrix highlights the choices of market and product faced by a business.
- SWOT analysis is a framework used to help inform strategic planning.

- SWOT considers both internal strengths/ weaknesses and external opportunities and threats.
- PESTLE is an analytical framework that focuses on a business's external environment, using the following headings:
  - Political
  - Economic
  - Social
  - Technological
  - Legal
  - Environmental.
- Another method of considering a firm's competitive position is Porter's Five Forces Analysis.
- Porter's Five Forces are:
  - Competitive rivalry
  - Threat of new entrants
  - Buying power of customers
  - Selling power of suppliers
  - Threat of substitutes.
- Where all Five Forces are in a business's favour, the business is likely to be highly profitable

Growth

Not all businesses grow, but many aim to do so either through a planned strategy of gradually expanding capacity or, more radically, through taking over other businesses. Some growth can be unplanned, where owners are caught unawares by the success of their product. In all cases, growth can bring benefits, but also presents potential dangers.

Reasons why firms grow

REVISED

To increase profitability

Growth is likely to mean more customers. More customers can bring more revenue. Increased revenue, where each new customer spends more than the costs of servicing them, means more profit. In cases where a business can grow revenues faster than their fixed costs rise, profit margins are likely to increase too.

To achieve economies of scale

Growth should bring benefits in terms of lower running costs for the firm. Typical **economies of scale** include:

- Purchasing economies of scale: This is where firms are able to negotiate a cheaper unit cost for supplies they buy as they buy in greater bulk following an increase in the scale of their operations.
- Managerial economies of scale: Growing businesses are more likely to be able to hire specialist managers to handle particular areas within the business, so instead of having one HR manager, a business that has grown may be able to justify employing a specialist training manager and a specialist recruitment manager. Specialists are likely to bring greater expertise to their role, thus reducing unit costs.
- Technical economies of scale: This is where growth allows a firm to afford to buy in specialised machinery and equipment, so reduced unit costs may follow.

In addition, as a whole industry grows, there can be 'external' economies of scale. Benefits may emerge such as local colleges offering specialist training courses to improve the relevant skill levels of the local workforce. In addition, other specialist services such as waste disposal or specialist component suppliers are more likely to open in an area where an industry has grown.

> **Economies of scale** are reductions in unit cost caused by the growth of a business.

> **Typical mistake**
>
> Too often any reduction in unit costs is referred to by weaker students as an economy of scale. Unit costs may fall for many reasons. Economies of scale only come into play if the reduction in unit costs is a direct result of an increase in total capacity.

Increased market power over customers and suppliers

Growth in size is likely to boost the power that a business has over both customers and suppliers. This is a clear reference to two of Michael Porter's Five Forces. As Porter suggests, the ability to influence factors in its favour is likely to boost a company's overall long-term profitability.

Power over suppliers would be increased by growth, as a firm that has grown would be likely to have become a more significant customer as it increases the quantity of supplies purchased. Meanwhile, power over customers increases as one business's growth may well have led to a reduction in choice available to customers.

Increased market share and brand recognition

Growth that boosts market share will, by definition, involve taking share from rivals. This will help to boost power over customers as explained above. Growth will also lead to wider recognition of a company's brand. The benefits of this are twofold:

- Customers tend to buy brands they recognise, thus increased recognition can lead to a further boost in sales as consumers start choosing its, more recognisable, brand.
- As brand recognition increases, it is possible to make cuts to marketing budgets if awareness-boosting advertising is no longer necessary. This reduces the firm's overall operating expenses.

Problems arising from growth

REVISED

Though undoubted benefits can flow from growth of a business, there are also problems involved in growth. These can be managed and their effects lessened. However, these help to explain why, for some firms, growth can lead to disaster.

Diseconomies of scale

Growth can make organisations harder to manage. A small business that was once efficient, with a massively committed staff, can become a large business which suffers from one or more of the following problems:

> The flipside of economies of scale, **diseconomies of scale**, are the inefficiencies related to growing as a business that can lead to upward pressure on unit costs.

Poor internal communication

Growth can lead to a worsening of communication within an organisation for several reasons:

- Larger organisations tend to rely on more written forms of communication than oral. This can harm the effectiveness of communication.
- Larger organisations need to add more layers of organisational structure to ensure spans of control do not become too wide. This means that messages need to pass through more layers of structure.
- The effectiveness of communication is affected by the motivation levels of sender and receiver. As motivation can suffer in larger businesses (see below), this can have a negative impact on communication.

Poor employee motivation

As a business grows and personal contact is reduced between staff members and managers, employees can feel a growing sense of alienation. They may feel their work goes unnoticed and may struggle to see how their achievements can impact on the success of the business. The result can be falling motivation levels.

Poor managerial co-ordination

Ensuring that everyone is heading in the same direction in a small business can be achieved by the boss maintaining regular contact with everyone and monitoring their progress. As an organisation grows, the boss will struggle to keep an eye on everything. The result may be hiring managers, but these can head off in subtly different directions unless the boss ensures that they meet on a regular basis. These meetings can take up valuable time and become ignored. Controlling more resources will always be tougher in a bigger business. A failure to co-ordinate effectively can cause mistakes that drive up costs.

Exam tip

It is worth noting that economies of scale tend to be easier to measure, or quantify, than diseconomies. For this reason, advocates of growth can often justify their case numerically by calculating the likely cost savings that come from economies of scale. It is less likely that growth projections will manage to quantify the effects of diseconomies of scale.

Overtrading

Organic growth that happens too fast can cause **overtrading**. If a business grows rapidly, its level of cash outflows rises consistently as it expands. As most firms need to wait several weeks or even months between spending money on materials or assets and when those assets generate a return or the materials can be processed and sold, cash inflows only rise to a higher level after that period of time. This can create a situation where a business is trying to fund a large-scale operation with cash inflows from the smaller organisation it was several weeks or months previously. The result can be a cash crisis.

> **Overtrading** occurs when a business experiences cash flow problems as a result of expanding too quickly without sufficient cash in the bank.

Now test yourself

TESTED ☐

1 State three different types of economy of scale.
2 State three different diseconomies of scale.
3 List three possible reasons why a business may choose to grow.

Answers online

Organic growth

Inorganic vs organic growth

REVISED ☐

The difference between these two types of growth concerns whether growth comes from within the business or outside it. **Inorganic growth** involves growing by taking over other businesses. Typically, inorganic growth strategies would be used by businesses fitting one or more of the following criteria:

- a poor record of new product development and innovation
- a need to grow very quickly
- a business looking to eliminate a competitor.

> **Inorganic growth** means growth that occurs as a result of taking over or merging with another business.
>
> **Organic growth** is growth which takes place without any merger or takeover activity.

Typical mistake

Consider the criteria that make inorganic growth a sensible choice. Just because organic growth carries less risk does not always mean it is the best choice for a business.

Organic growth does not involve the purchase of other businesses; instead, the business grows 'from within', expanding its own capacity or opening new branches.

Answers and quick quizzes at **www.hoddereducation.co.uk/myrevisionnotes**

Methods of growing organically

REVISED

Organic growth involves harnessing the power of a business's resources, primarily its staff and its financial resources. Staff, especially the culture developed within a business, if nurtured and successful, can allow the firm to naturally expand its operations following the same blueprint with the same leaders doing things the same way, simply on a larger scale. Meanwhile, organic growth tends to allow a business to finance the growth through retained profits, rather than seeking riskier sources of external finance, such as loans.

> **Exam tip**
>
> When considering growth of a business, how the growth is funded will provide rich material for analysing the wisdom of a growth strategy.

Advantages of organic growth

REVISED

The leader's influence stays strong

Organic growth prevents the need to merge two workforces and replace a leadership team in a business that has been taken over. In these cases, the leader of the predator company will need to assert their leadership and find a way to get new staff to embrace the original company's culture. This is avoided as growth is organic; there is a far greater chance of preserving the original business culture which is likely to be successful as it has put the company in the position to grow.

> **Organisational culture** is the term used to describe acceptable norms of behaviour within a business: 'the way we do things round here'.

Reduction of financial risk

As organic growth will tend to be far slower than inorganic methods, the finance required is likely to be needed in smaller, more steady batches. This suits the use of retained profit as a source, since using the profit generated each year to continually grow the business should enable the firm to grow steadily, without the need to take on debt, with its extra cost of interest and the cash-draining impact of repayments.

Secure career paths

As a business grows over time, the management team who have led the growth may be looking to turn their success into higher powered and higher status jobs. If the business continues to grow, its structure will grow and more senior managerial positions will open up. Internal promotions to fill these will prevent middle and junior managers leaving the business to develop their careers: their skills, talents and experience are retained within the business.

Disadvantages of organic growth

REVISED

Limited speed leading to limited size

By its nature, organic growth tends to be a far slower process than inorganic growth. This may mean that a business sticking to an organic growth strategy may fall behind growing rivals who use takeovers to add significantly to their scale rapidly. The result can be that rivals are able to achieve economies of scale that make competing with them far harder.

Failing to fully exploit a short-lived opportunity

With shortening product life cycles as rates of change in many markets increase, a firm that fails to fully expand its capacity before the product enters the decline phase in the marketplace may have missed out on significant levels of sales as a result of ignoring opportunities to grow inorganically.

Predictability

Organic growth will often (not always) involve doing the same thing in a new place year after year after year. This can prevent staff looking for new and exciting challenges from staying with the business in the long-term, leading to the loss of potentially innovative and entrepreneurial staff.

Now test yourself

TESTED

4 Briefly explain why organic growth may be less risky financially than inorganic growth.
5 Which is generally faster, organic or inorganic growth?
6 State three potential drawbacks of choosing to grow organically.

Answers online

Mergers and takeovers

Growth can be achieved through merging with or taking over another business.

Reasons for mergers and takeovers

REVISED

- Growth: The ability to increase the size of an organisation is the general motive behind any merger or takeover. The specific benefits expected are likely to be one or more of those below:
- Cost synergies: When a business grows through merger or takeover, its increased size is likely to lead to economies of scale, allowing it to reduce their unit costs. Other cost savings can come by eliminating duplicated functions and jobs.
- Diversification: A company that wants to spread the level of risk for its business can do so by using a merger or takeover to enter new markets with new products, reducing its reliance on one market or product in case of problems.
- Market power: When two firms in the same market come together, the combined business is likely to increase their power over customers, perhaps enabling them to raise prices to boost margins, while also benefiting from increased power over suppliers.

> **Synergies** are the benefits of two things coming together that could not exist when they are separate — such as economies of scale resulting from a merger of two businesses.

Distinction between mergers and takeovers

REVISED

Typical mistake

The terms merger and takeover should not be used interchangeably. They are different types of transaction.

A merger occurs when two businesses of roughly the same size agree to come together to create a brand new single business, where the owners of the two businesses will share the ownership of the new firm.

A takeover occurs when one business buys over 50% of another business's shares, thus effectively gaining control.

Exam tip

Mergers may be less successful than takeovers as managers from both the original firms may tussle for a long time in a bid to assert their dominance in the new business, without a dominant partner — a scenario takeovers would avoid.

Types of integration

REVISED

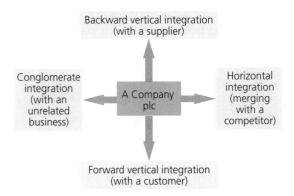

Figure 13.1 Vertical and horizontal integration

Vertical integration

Vertical integration refers to a merger or takeover involving two companies at different stages of the same supply chain. Forward vertical integration, where a company buys a customer, may involve a manufacturer buying a retailer to secure distribution for its products. Backward vertical integration occurs when a company buys a supplier, so a retailer may buy a distributor or a manufacturer.

Horizontal integration

Where a business buys or merges with a rival, in the same industry at the same stage of the supply chain, the deal is called horizontal integration. Economies of scale, reductions in costs as a result of elimination of duplicated roles and one less competitor allowing prices to be increased should all lead to increased profit margins.

Conglomerate integration

Where a merger or takeover involves the coming together of two unrelated businesses, the deal is called conglomerate integration. The main benefit is that the new business is no longer reliant on just one market or product. This is designed to spread risk for the new business. If one product or market suffers, the firm's other product or market is unlikely to be affected.

The key benefits and potential drawbacks of each type of integration are shown in Table 13.1.

Table 13.1 The key benefits and drawbacks of integration

Type of integration	Benefits	Drawbacks
Backward vertical	• Secures supplies • Should lower the cost of supplies	• Can tie the business into a supplier that may not always offer the best option
Forward vertical	• Guaranteed outlet for the business's products	• Consumers may resent the loss of choice — with one firm's products dominating these outlets
Horizontal	• Likely to provide clear economies of scale	• Can lead to diseconomies • Could be confusion over which firm's culture should be adopted in some areas
Conglomerate	• Diversifies the business — spreading risk into different markets	• Potential failure to understand the target company as it will be in an unfamiliar market • May distract management from original business due to unfamiliarity and slowness to integrate

Financial risks and rewards

REVISED

Most takeovers are funded by debt. Borrowing to grow makes sense as long as the rewards from the growth outweigh the cost of the borrowing:

If return on investment from takeover > interest rate on loans required *then* the deal makes sense

This is more likely to be the case when the economy is performing well or interest rates are particularly low. However, if sales dry up due to economic downturn, or the Bank of England pushes interest rates up, the equation could turn. In such circumstances, the funding of takeovers through debt could lead to the demise of a previously sound business.

> **Exam tip**
>
> When assessing the likely success of a takeover, consider the long term as well as the short term. Even a deal that is currently likely to succeed could fail in the longer term as external conditions change.

Problems of rapid growth

REVISED

Inorganic growth, through merger or takeover, sees much more rapid transformation than organic growth. The speed of growth can present significant issues mainly focused on relationships:

- With new management structures in place, staff may find themselves working for a new boss.
- At least one set of staff are likely to need to make adjustments to operate in a new business culture; many will feel uncomfortable.
- Customers and suppliers who may have had a long-standing relationship with their contact in the business may be discomforted by the need to deal with somebody else, or to be dealing with a larger, perhaps less personal organisation.

Now test yourself

TESTED

7 State three possible reasons, other than pure growth, behind a merger or takeover.
8 Describe each of the following transactions using the correct terminology:
 (a) A manufacturer buys one of its customers
 (b) A supplier of car parts buys another supplier of similar car parts
 (c) A coffee manufacturer buys a coffee plantation
 (d) A manufacturer of mobile phone handsets buys a specialist wooden furniture retailer
 (e) Two airlines agree to come together to share costs and routes within their global networks
9 When does borrowing to finance a takeover stop making sense?

Answers online

> **Typical mistake**
>
> Do not assume that all businesses aim to grow as large as possible. As discussed above, there are problems that come with scale. Many large businesses attempt to structure themselves internally to mimic small businesses so they can take advantage of the benefits of being small.

Reasons for staying small

Growth can certainly bring advantages to a business. However, it also brings problems. Some businesses will choose to avoid growth to avoid the associated problems. Many other businesses will stay small because their objectives do not require growth; in fact, growth may directly contradict their objectives.

Survival in competitive markets

REVISED

The ability to cope with rapid change in the marketplace may be the key strength of small businesses. They do not have large, unwieldy decision-making structures. Often, the boss will be able to make rapid and effective decisions to respond to changes in market conditions. In this way, small firms can stay ahead of larger rivals in the hunt for differentiation.

Reasons to stay small

REVISED

Product differentiation and USPs

Porter's Generic Strategy Matrix helps to explain how some small firms can trade successfully in the long term. A strategy of focused differentiation, whereby a business finds a point of differentiation while selling to a niche market, is perhaps easiest for small businesses. Without the need to push for growth by looking for a wider market, or finding other ways to differentiate, a small business can spend all its time protecting and deepening its point of differentiation.

Flexibility in responding to customer needs

With nimble management structures and less need to worry about what the stock market may think, small businesses will have greater speed of response to market changes. In addition, decision-makers are likely to know about changes in the market quicker. With fewer layers between bosses and customer-facing lower level staff, feedback from the shop floor is likely to reach managers quicker, enabling quicker response times than larger businesses.

> **Exam tip**
>
> To gain better analysis marks when explaining a point such as the flexibility of small firms, be sure to spell out why small equals nimble. The ability to show the sequence that leads from small to nimble, i.e. small = fewer layers = decision-makers closer to customers = quicker response to changing tastes, shows good analytical skills.

Customer service

Great customer service will only be delivered by highly motivated staff. Where staff are part of a small, close-knit workforce, they will understand clearly how their performance affects the overall success of the business. This should be highly motivating. Contrasted with staff who work in one of many branches of a large organisation who may feel little loyalty to the business, it is clear to see how small businesses may survive through delivering great customer service.

E-commerce

The magic of e-commerce for small businesses is the ability to reach a global market. The worldwide web is just that: a medium through which the smallest business can reach customers anywhere in the world. It is this that can allow businesses to carve out incredibly specialist niche markets, which would not be large enough to support a business on a national scale. However, a business that specialises only in selling, for example, one brand of second-hand vintage toy can be viable if selling to collectors worldwide.

Now test yourself

TESTED

10 State two business objectives which may be easier for small firms to achieve than for large ones.
11 Which of Porter's generic strategies is ideal for a small business with an unusual idea?
12 Briefly explain why great customer service may be easier to achieve for a small business.

Answers online

Exam practice

1 To what extent is a strategy of growth essential if UK-based plcs are going to continue to offer the continual growth in earnings expected by the stock market? (20)

Wilson Hooper Holdings PLC (WHH Plc) has been manufacturing high quality wooden furniture for the last 30 years. Started in a single workshop, the firm grew slowly, reinvesting profits to expand to operating from a factory, allowing it to service the whole UK market. During this period, the firm enjoyed low levels of labour turnover; a loyal and highly skilled workforce emerged. The fall in the value of the pound, allied to quality problems with the materials delivered, has led the company to decide to buy a timber supplier in Finland. Concerns were raised at the directors' meeting about the potential clash of cultures between the UK business and its proposed Finnish subsidiary. Part of the firm's original success has been founded on the reputation for customer service and on-time delivery, which stem from great internal communication systems. The Chief Executive was confident that the takeover would improve, rather than worsen, this aspect of the business's operations.

2 (a) Explain two benefits that WHH Plc may have received by pursuing organic growth. (4)
  (b) Identify the type of integration that the purchase of the timber supplier would represent. (1)
  (c) How would Ansoff classify this takeover? (1)
  (d) Analyse the likely benefits and problems that the proposed takeover may create for WHH Plc. (14)

Answers and quick quiz 13 online

ONLINE

Summary

- Reasons for growth include: increased profitability, economies of scale and increased power in the market.
- Diseconomies of scale can arise from growth, namely problems with co-ordination, communication and motivation.
- A business that grows too quickly for its capital base to cope with may fall victim to overtrading.
- Organic growth occurs without mergers or takeovers and tends to be a slower but safer option than inorganic growth.
- A merger occurs when two firms agree to come together to form a single business.
- A takeover occurs when one business buys another.
- Types of integration are classified according to the extent to which the two businesses operate in different industries or at different stages of the supply chain.
- Ansoff's Matrix is a useful tool for analysing the risks associated with takeovers.
- Some firms choose to stay small as this brings advantages over bigger rivals, such as faster reaction to change, easier differentiation and potential for better levels of customer service.

Quantitative sales forecasting

Chapter 9 in the AS revision guide introduced the importance of sales forecasting for businesses. Sales forecasting is necessary as it underpins most of the forward planning needed to run a business:

- HR plan
- cash flow forecast
- profit forecasts and budgets
- production planning

In order to forecast sales for an existing business, the commonest method used is to identify past trends. These trends form the basis of the three quantitative sales forecasting techniques you need to understand:

- moving averages
- extrapolation
- correlation

Moving averages

To identify an underlying trend in a set of data with strong seasonal variations or an erratic pattern, a **moving average** is useful. Table 14.1 shows how the moving average is calculated, firstly by adding several months' worth of raw data (the three-month total in column 2), then calculating the average for those months and centring that figure on the middle of the period (the centred three-month average in column three).

> A **moving average** is a quantitative method used to identify underlying trends in a set of raw data.

Table 14.1 Example of a moving average

	Raw data (monthly sales) (£)	Centred three-month total (£)	Centred three-month average (£)
January	48,000		
February	57,000		52,000
March	51,000	156,000	49,000
April	39,000	147,000	47,700
May	53,000	143,000	46,300
June	47,000	138,000	45,300
July	36,000	136,000	44,700
August	51,000	134,000	

The graph in Figure 14.1 shows just how effectively this technique helps to understand the long-term trend, even when the raw data seems erratic.

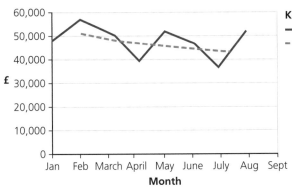

Key
— Raw data (monthly sales)
-- Centred three-month average

> **Typical mistake**
>
> It is vital, when looking for trends in data that have a strong seasonal peak, such as toy sales, that a 12-month or four-quarter average is calculated. This eliminates the effect of seasonal variations, by including one peak period in every average.

Figure 14.1 Underlying sales trends revealed by a three-month moving average

Forecasting sales using extrapolation

Basic human behaviour, and consequently most businesses, predict the future by assuming that past trends will continue: the future will be just like the past. In simple terms, the long-term trend identified in **time series data** is extended into the future, as shown in Figure 14.2.

> **Extrapolation** means predicting by projecting past trends into the future.
>
> **Time series data** is a series of figures covering an extended period of time.

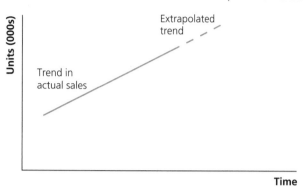

Figure 14.2 An extrapolated sales trend

The challenge in using **extrapolation** comes when the trend is not quite as clear cut. Figure 14.3 illustrates a situation in which the sales forecaster must decide whether the recent downward trend is a blip and the longer-term upward trend will dominate, or whether the recent downward movement is a trend that will continue for the foreseeable future.

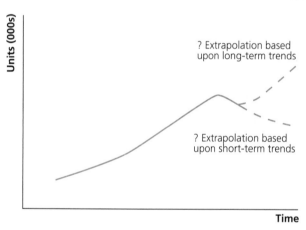

Figure 14.3 Requirement for judgement when extrapolating trends

This indicates the art and skill involved in sales forecasting. Even using quantitative techniques, thought is required to examine and understand underlying causes behind the data being used to extrapolate.

Scatter graphs (correlation)

Plotting the relationship between two variables on a scatter graph can provide great insight relating to the extent to which those variables are linked. Where there is a link between sales and another variable, the relationship can be used to forecast sales if the other variable is controllable or predictable. Such links include:
● sales and advertising expenditure
● sales and temperature
● sales and the number of stores open
● sales and the level of staff bonuses available.

Plotting the data from the past, on advertising expenditure and sales, for example, as shown in Figure 14.4, shows a clear relationship between the two variables.

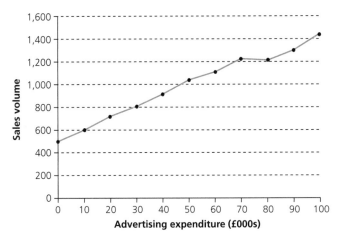

Figure 14.4 Strong positive correlation between advertising expenditure and sales

Clearly, as one variable rises, the other rises in line. This indicates that there *may* be cause and effect at work. Forecasters will then need to decide which variable causes the other; in this case it is likely (though not certain) that changes in advertising expenditure have a strong impact on sales. When a strong **correlation** exists, as shown by a line of best fit that passes close to all the points on the scatter graph, the relationship may be a helpful forecasting tool. Once a business has decided how much it plans to spend on advertising in a given period, it can plot the level of expected sales that is likely to result.

> **Correlation** expresses a relationship between two variables.

> **Typical mistake**
>
> Too often correlation is assumed to imply causality. Relationships can occur by chance; it takes judgement to decide whether one variable causes movements in the other, or vice versa, or whether any correlation is merely down to chance.

> **Exam tip**
>
> When exploring causality, consider all possibilities. Although, in Figure 14.4, it may be assumed that changes in advertising expenditure cause changes in sales, it is also possible that the firm deliberately spends more on advertising in months when it expects to be busy: to capitalise perhaps on seasonal trends.

Limitations of quantitative forecasting techniques

REVISED

There are two major limitations to quantitative forecasting techniques, which help to explain almost all false predictions:

1 The future may not be like the past: Changes in any number of external factors may have a significant impact on sales. Many of these external events may be highly unpredictable, such as changes in tastes and fashion or new entrants to the market.
2 The quality of a forecast is reliant on the ability of the forecaster to interpret the data being used to generate the forecast. Decision-making is needed when forecasting, such as whether a dip in trend growth is likely to continue in the long term or just be a short-term change to trend. In the case of correlation, the challenge is in understanding which variables to pair up, and then exploring the causality, if any, involved in the relationship.

Now test yourself

1 What do moving averages help to identify within a set of data?
2 What is the name of the forecasting technique that predicts the future by assuming past trends will continue?
3 Briefly explain how a clear correlation between the hours worked by sales staff and total sales volume will help to predict next month's sales.

Answers online

Investment appraisal

The three methods of **investment appraisal** are:

● Payback period
● Average rate of return
● Net present value.

All three methods begin with a table or graph showing the forecast cash flows involved in the investment (see Table 14.2).

> **Investment appraisal** is the process of using forecast cash flows to assess the financial attractiveness of an investment decision, linked with a consideration of non-financial factors.

Table 14.2 Example cash flow table (*NOW = the moment the £60,000 is spent; can also be called the initial outlay or the sum invested)

	Cash in	Cash out	Net cash flow	Cumulative cash flow
NOW*		£60,000	(£60,000)	(£60,000)
Year 1	£30,000	£10,000	£20,000	(£40,000)
Year 2	£30,000	£10,000	£20,000	(£20,000)
Year 3	£30,000	£10,000	£20,000	£0
Year 4	£30,000	£10,000	£20,000	£20,000
Year 5	£30,000	£10,000	£20,000	£40,000

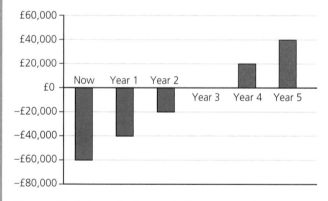

Figure 14.5 Cumulative cash flows on an investment of £60,000

> **Exam tip**
>
> Examiners may only present you with cash inflows and cash outflows. You may need to construct the last two columns yourself.

Payback period

Assessing the period of time a business must wait until its initial investment has been recovered allows a firm to prioritise risk reduction when making investment decisions.

Calculation

Payback occurs when the cumulative cash flow reaches zero. In the example above (Table 14.2), this point is easy to identify as it occurs exactly at the end of year 3. Not all forecasts work out as neatly. If payback occurs part-way through a year, you must calculate how far through the year it occurs. Apply this formula:

$$\frac{\text{outlay outstanding}}{\text{monthly cash flow in year of payback}}$$

In Table 14.2, if year 3's net cash flow was £30,000 instead of £20,000, payback would happen after two years and:

$$\frac{£20,000}{(£30,000/12)} = 8 \text{ months}$$

Interpretation

Payback calculates the length of time that the money invested is 'at risk'. Once payback has occurred, the firm is at least not losing money on its investment. Therefore, a quicker payback is best. However, projects with a quick payback may not turn out to be most profitable in the long term, so ideally, another method of investment appraisal should be considered alongside the payback period.

Average Rate of Return (ARR)

REVISED

This method considers the profit generated by an investment. It involves calculating the average annual profit as a percentage of the initial outlay.

Calculation

There are three steps involved in calculating the ARR:
- Step 1: Calculate the total profit over the lifetime of the project by adding all net cash flows and deducting the initial outlay.
- Step 2: Divide by the number of years the project lasts.
- Step 3: Apply the formula:

$$\frac{\text{average annual profit (from Step 2)}}{\text{initial outlay}} \times 100$$

A simple worked example is shown in Tables 14.3 and 14.4.

Table 14.3

Year	Net cash flow	Cumulative cash flow
0	(£20,000)	(£20,000)
1	+ £5,000	(£15,000)
2	+ £11,000	(4,000)
3	+ £10,000	+ £6,000
4	+ £10,000	+ £16,000

Table 14.4 Applying the three steps

Step 1	Identify lifetime profit	£16,000
Step 2	Divide by number of years (4)	£4,000
Step 3	Calculate annual profit as a percentage of initial outlay	£4,000/£20,000 × 100 = 20%

Exam tip

To contextualise an ARR result it can be compared with the company's overall Return on Capital Employed (ROCE). A project whose ARR is lower than the current ROCE generated by the whole business is unlikely to be attractive, since it would reduce the overall ROCE for the business if accepted.

Interpretation

Simply put, the higher the ARR, the more profitable the investment.

Net Present Value (NPV) using discounted cash flows

Future cash flows may not be worth what they seem. This is not a reference to inaccurate forecasting, but noting that money that is received sooner can be used for other purposes. In other words, money tied up in an investment has an opportunity cost. This can be accounted for by discounting the value of future cash flows to allow for a given percentage return that could be achieved if the money were available now and generated that return.

Considering the likely rate of interest that will be missed out on by tying money up in the investment allows the choice of a discount factor to use, for example a 10% discount factor allows for a return of 10%.

> **Exam tip**
>
> You would never be expected to calculate the discount factors required for an NPV calculation.

Calculation

Each year's net cash flow is multiplied by the relevant discount factor to calculate the present value of the cash flow. These are then totalled to give the overall net present value (NPV) of the project. The example shown in Table 14.5 compares two projects, using 10% discount factors.

Table 14.5 Project Z versus Project Y

	Project Z			Project Y		
Year	Net cash flow	Discount factor	Present value (£s)	Net cash flow	Discount factor	Present value (£s)
0	(£250,000)	1.00	(£250,000)	(£250,000)	1.00	(£250,000)
1	+£50,000	0.91	£45,500	+£200,000	0.91	+£182,000
2	+£100,000	0.83	£83,000	+£100,000	0.83	+£83,000
3	+£200,000	0.75	£150,000	+£50,000	0.75	+£37,500
		NPV =	+£28,500		NPV =	+£52,500

Interpretation

A positive NPV shows that a project generates a greater return on its initial outlay than simply putting the money in the bank at an interest rate equal to the percentage discount factor used. The higher the figure, the more profitable it will be.

> **Short termism** is the tendency to focus on achieving short-term objectives by taking decisions that may preclude better, longer-term options.

Strengths and limitations of quantitative investment appraisal techniques

Table 14.6 Strengths and limitations of quantitative investment appraisal techniques

Investment appraisal method	Strengths of the method	Limitations of the method
Payback	<ul><li>Easy to calculate and understand</li><li>May be more accurate as it ignores longer-term forecasts which may be less accurate</li><li>Takes into account the timing of cash flows</li><li>Very useful for businesses with weak cash flow</li></ul>	<ul><li>Tells us nothing about profitability</li><li>Ignores what happens after payback is achieved</li><li>May encourage a **short-termist** attitude</li></ul>

Answers and quick quizzes at **www.hoddereducation.co.uk/myrevisionnotes**

Investment appraisal method	Strengths of the method	Limitations of the method
Average rate of return	● Clear focus on profitability ● Considers cash flows over the whole project's lifetime ● Easy to compare with other measures of return expressed as percentages, such as interest rates	● Ignores the timing of cash flows ● Therefore values far distant inflows as much as more immediate inflows, which are 'worth' more ● Including forecast data from far in the future may reduce the reliability of the forecasts and therefore results
Net present value	● Takes the opportunity cost of money into account ● Considers both amount and timing of cash flows to indicate profitability	● Complex to calculate and communicate ● Meaning is often misunderstood ● Only comparable between different projects if the initial outlay is the same

Other factors affecting investment decisions

Non-financial factors

Even if all the numbers (the results of calculations of quantitative measures of investment appraisal) point one way, sensible decision-makers consider other, non-financial factors. These include:

● Corporate objectives: Does the chosen investment focus on achieving the agreed objectives of the business?
● Company finances: Expensive investments that may place the firm's financial health at risk if they require external finance may be better ignored.
● Confidence in the data: It is always worth considering the likely accuracy of the forecasts on which calculations are based: who prepared the forecasts; do they have a record of success in forecasting; do they have some bias that could cause them to over or underestimate cash flows?
● Social responsibilities: If an investment clearly helps to meet a business's social responsibilities, some businesses may be willing to proceed even if the project is not the most financially attractive option.

Investment criteria

These are specific targets that directors may set that any investment is required to reach before it can be approved. They will include targets for one or more of the investment appraisal methods, such as:

● payback within three years
● ARR of at least 15%
● positive NPV using 10% discount factors.

Now test yourself

4 Which investment appraisal method is likely to be favoured by firms looking to reduce the risks involved in their investments?
5 Which investment appraisal method considers both the timing of cash flows and profitability?
6 Calculate the payback period, ARR and NPV for the following investment:

Year	Net cash flow
0	(120,000)
1	50,000
2	50,000
3	50,000

Use 10% discount factors: Year 1 = 0.91, Year 2 = 0.83, Year 3 = 0.75

Answers online

Decision trees

When faced with quantifiable decisions, an analytical approach to setting out the problem and assessing the alternatives is to draw a **decision tree**. These diagrams allow the calculation of expected outcomes of alternative courses of action. This can help to provide a clearly favourable option on numerate grounds — it can help managers to see the wood for the trees!

> A **decision tree** is a diagram showing the options and possible outcomes involved in making a decision along with the probabilities of outcomes occurring.

Step-by-step approach

The basics

A decision tree sets out a decision problem from left to right. At the left is a square, representing the initial decision to be made. Sprouting off to the right are the possible options as branches of the tree. The branches consist of:
- a decision to be made, shown by a square (see Figure 14.6)
- chance events beyond the firm's control, shown by a circle (see Figure 14.7)

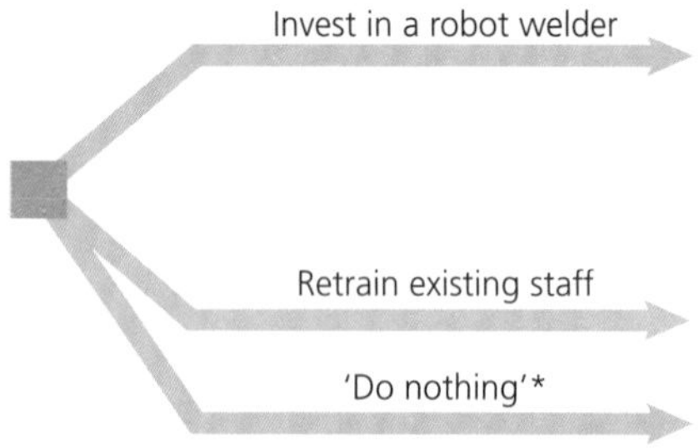

*Note that 'do nothing' is an option for every business decision

Figure 14.6 Decision tree showing a decision to be made

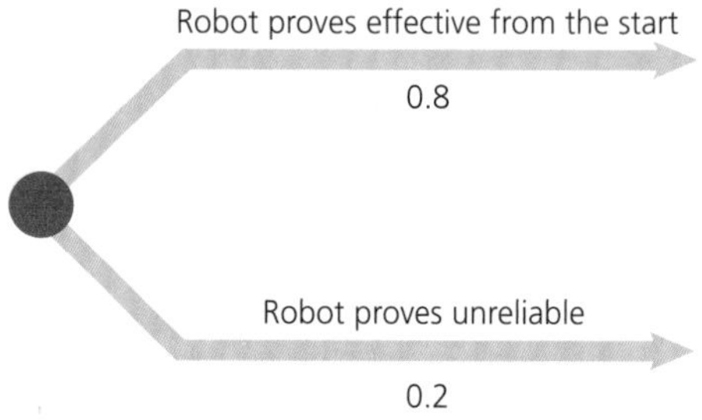

Figure 14.7 Decision tree showing chance events beyond the firm's control

The possible outcomes following chance events must have a probability attached. The probabilities following each chance event must add to 1.

At any square, the business can choose which branch to take. The most profitable option will always be chosen. Figure 14.8 shows the initial decision followed by the chance event that follows the installation of a robot welder.

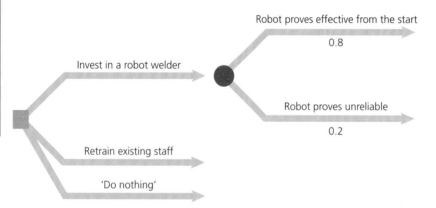

Figure 14.8 Following a decision

Drawing the tree
- Begin drawing the tree from the left with a single square.
- Run a branch from each option out to the right of the square.
- Note the cost (if any) of each option by the line.

Answers and quick quizzes at **www.hoddereducation.co.uk/myrevisionnotes**

- Draw a circle whenever a chance event could occur.
- Run a branch out of the right of each circle to show each possible outcome.
- Record the probability next to each branch.
- Add squares and circles in the order in which they occur as explained within the case study, representing decisions and chance events as required.
- When a branch has no further chance events or decisions to follow, note the expected returns at the end of the branch, as shown in Figure 14.9.

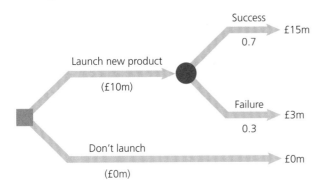

Figure 14.9 A completed decision tree

Making calculations

With the tree drawn, a series of calculations are required to help identify the most attractive option at each decision square. Working from right to left, for each chance event (circle), multiply each expected return by the probability of each possible outcome. So in Figure 14.9, the calculation would be:

$$(£15m × 0.7) + (£3m × 0.3) = £11.4m$$

This is known as the **expected value** attached to a chance event.

Showing decisions

Working from left to right again, once a square is encountered, compare the expected values of each decision option. The business will choose the higher value. Cross through the other options to show these choices would not be taken.

The value of using decision trees

REVISED

Decision trees as a technique to aid decision making can be useful, but it is vital that users are fully aware of their limitations.

Table 14.7 Advantages and disadvantages of using decision trees

Advantages of using decision trees	Limitations of decision trees
The technique allows for uncertainty	Gathering the data required is hard and is likely to involve an element of guesswork
Trees force managers to consider all possible options	New problems mean previous occurrences cannot be used to base estimated probabilities and outcomes on, reducing the reliability of the data still further
Problems are set out clearly, encouraging a logical approach	An element of bias can be introduced by whoever is estimating probabilities and outcomes if they wish to influence the outcome of the decision
Quantification of problems is encouraged by the drawing of the tree and subsequent calculations	Decision trees can lead to a failure to consider qualitative aspects of decisions

Exam tip

If presented with a decision tree in a case study, it is always worth checking where the data came from and whether there may have been any bias generated by the source of the data favouring one option over others.

Expected value is the average outcome expected following a chance event.

Typical mistake

Students and some managers can too often be fooled into believing that decision trees show facts, as they generate a clear numerical result. It is vital to consider the likely accuracy of the numbers that have been put into the tree when assessing the reliability of results it generates.

Now test yourself

7 What shapes are used to represent (a) chance events and (b) decisions on the tree diagram?
8 How is the expected value of a chance event calculated?
9 Using calculations, state whether option A or option B should be chosen based on the decision tree below.

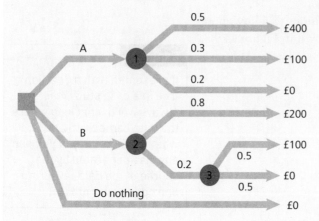

Answers online

Critical path analysis

When a complex project needs to be completed as quickly as possible, **critical path analysis** can help. Time can be crucial in order to:
● get a product to market as quickly as possible
● construct new premises to move into as quickly as possible
● move offices or production facilities to a new location.

> **Critical path analysis** is a technique used in planning the most time-efficient way to complete complex projects.

The technique involves constructing a network diagram which shows:
● the order in which tasks must be undertaken
● an estimated length of each task
● the earliest date when each task can begin.

Drawing critical path analysis diagrams

REVISED

The two key components of a network diagram are:
● lines which represent activities to be completed as part of the overall project
● nodes placed at the start and end of activities.

Five handy rules for drawing network diagrams are:
1 Networks must start and end on a single node.
2 No lines should cross one another.
3 Do not draw the node at the end of an activity until you are sure which activity follows.
4 There must be no lines that do not represent an activity.
5 Nodes should be drawn large (to make room for the figures that must be recorded in them), while lines should be drawn short, to keep the diagram manageable.

Figure 14.10 shows a network diagram drawn to show the tasks involved in running a '3p off' price promotion.

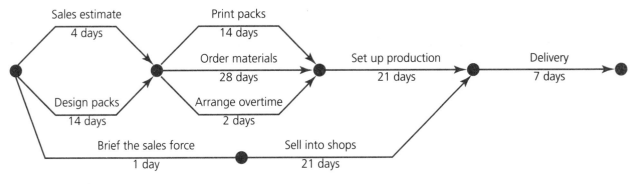

Figure 14.10 '3p off' network

Earliest start times and latest finish times

The power of critical path analysis becomes evident once **earliest start times (ESTs)** and **latest finish times (LFTs)** are added to the diagram.

Figure 14.11 shows the '3p off' promotion network with ESTs and LFTs added and the descriptions of the activities replaced by letters.

The ESTs are shown in the top right-hand corner of the node before each activity. The LFT of an activity can be found in the bottom right-hand corner of the node following the activity.

> The **earliest start time (EST)** of an activity is the earliest possible date on which it is possible to begin the activity.
>
> The **latest finish time (LFT)** for an activity is the last possible date by which it must be complete to avoid delaying the overall project.

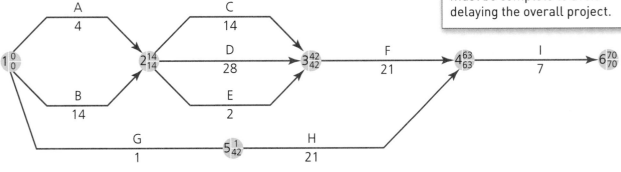

Figure 14.11 '3p off' network with ESTs and LFTs added

The earliest start time shown in the first node is always 0, showing that any activity not dependent on prior activities can start immediately.

Node 2 shows the earliest start time of activities C, D and E, none of which can begin until activities A and B are complete.

Because activity B must be completed, C, D and E cannot begin until day 14, even if activity A was done within 4 days.

ESTs are calculated from left to right, before any LFTs are filled in.

In the final node, the EST represents the shortest possible time in which the entire project can be completed. This becomes the 'deadline' for the whole project and thus the LFT of preceding activities (in this case I).

To calculate earlier LFTs, deduct the duration of the activity from its LFT — in this case 70 − 7 means F and H must be completed by day 63, shown in node 4.

Table 14.8 ESTs and LFTs clarified

ESTs tell you	LFTs tell you
The earliest date resources specially required for an activity may be needed, preventing wasting money on them before they are needed	Deadlines for each activity
The earliest completion date for the whole project	The **float time** (if any for each activity)
	The critical path of the project

> **Float time** describes any slack time available attached to an activity. The LFT minus the duration of the activity minus the EST of the activity shows if there is float time.

The critical path

REVISED

The **critical path** consists of the series of activities that take the longest to complete. Because they take the longest time, they are the ones whose on-time completion is critical in ensuring that the project is not delayed. On the '3p off network' the critical path is B, D, F and I.

> The **critical path** of a project is the sequence of activities on which any delay will delay the whole project: the activities with zero float time.

The simplest way to spot the critical path is to look for activities whose nodes show ESTs and LFTs as equal. The longest activity between these nodes will be the critical path.

Show the critical path on a diagram by drawing two short lines across the critical activities.

Identifying the critical path allows managers to focus their attention on these and their smooth running. Non-critical activities can be delayed by a certain amount (the float time) without delaying the project. A delay on a critical activity will delay the whole project.

Float time

REVISED

Having float time on an activity, such as the 10 days of float time on activity A in our example, shows that some slippage on that activity is available. The formula for calculating the float time on any activity is:

LFT of the activity — duration of the activity — EST of the activity

Remember that activities on the critical path have zero float time.

Benefits and limitations of critical path analysis

REVISED

Benefits

- The careful planning required to work out each activity involved, its likely duration and what activities must be completed before another can begin, forces a thorough planning process.
- Identifying activities that can be carried out simultaneously shortens the overall duration of the project.
- Resources needed for a given activity can be delivered or hired just in time for the activity to begin. This delays cash outflows and avoids having expensive resources sitting around waiting to be used.
- The network diagram shows possible ways of dealing with any unforeseen delays and getting back on track (perhaps by allocating extra resources to subsequent critical activities).

Answers and quick quizzes at **www.hoddereducation.co.uk/myrevisionnotes**

Limitations

- The diagram can lull managers into a false sense of security. It shows what can happen. To hit deadlines work must actually be completed, which will need careful monitoring.
- Diagrams for really complex projects may become unmanageably large.
- Not drawing activity lines to scale could be said to devalue the diagram's visual use.

TESTED ☐

Now test yourself

10 What formula is used to calculate the float time on an activity?
11 How can critical path analysis enable a JIT approach to managing a project?
12 Calculate the critical path on the project shown below:

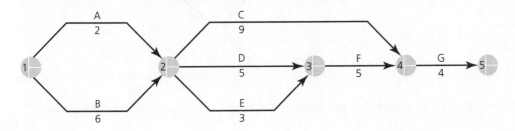

Answers online

Exam practice

1 Given the weaknesses in quantitative techniques such as decision trees and critical path analysis, their value rarely outweighs the costs of conducting the techniques. To what extent do you agree with this statement? (20)
2 Calculate the best course of action shown by the following decision tree. (8)

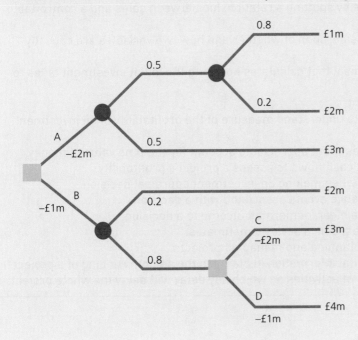

3 Calculate payback, ARR and NPV for the following investments. (12)

	Project A — Net cash flow (£m)	Project B — Net cash flow (£m)
Year 0	(100)	(100)
Year 1	50	80
Year 2	100	80
Year 3	200	200

Use 10% discount factors: Year 1 = 0.91; Year 2 = 0.83; Year 3 = 0.75

4

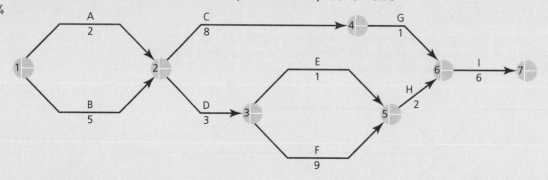

(a) Calculate the minimum time necessary to complete the project shown in the network diagram above. (6)

(b) Identify the critical path. (1)

(c) Calculate the float time available on activities A and E. (2)

Answers and quick quiz 14 online

ONLINE

Summary

- Moving averages, extrapolation and correlation can be used to forecast sales.
- Calculating a moving average allows the identification of an underlying trend in time series data.
- Extrapolation means projecting a past trend into the future as a way of forecasting.
- Correlation can be used to forecast sales by spotting a relationship between sales and a controllable variable, such as advertising spend.
- Using correlation needs very careful consideration of whether and how two variables are causally linked.
- Payback is a method of investment appraisal that calculates how long the initial investment takes to be returned.
- Payback's key weakness is to ignore profit.
- Average rate of return (ARR) is a simple to understand measure of the profitability of an investment.
- ARR ignores the timing of cash flows.
- Discounting future cash flows allows investment appraisal to account for the time value of money.
- Net present value (NPV) uses discounted cash flows to assess a project's profitability.
- Qualitative factors should be considered when making an investment appraisal decision.
- Decision trees set out the options and chance events associated with a decision.
- Calculations allow decision trees to give a clear, numerate outcome to a decision.
- Decision trees are usually constructed based on a series of estimates.
- Critical path analysis is a useful tool for planning and managing projects.
- ESTs and LFTs for each activity provide vital information in planning the smooth running of a project.
- The critical path of a project is the series of activities on which any delay will delay the whole project.

Corporate influences

Fundamental internal factors affecting business decision-making have a tremendous impact on the way a business is run. These corporate influences have such a deep-rooted effect because they are likely to influence most major decisions made within the business.

Corporate timescales

When using data to help make decisions, or considering the targets that are important to decision-makers, some companies find it hard to look beyond next month or this year. Others will be willing to overlook short-term problems, able to look further into the future to assess what effect decisions will have in the long term. They will show patience.

Causes of short-termism

There are four main causes of **short-termism** within the UK:

- The relationship between plcs and financial markets: City investors control far more shares in UK plcs than private investors. The performance of these investors, running pension funds and similar investment vehicles, tends to be judged quarterly. This encourages them to look for companies whose performance is strong now, not in a few years' time.
- The use of short-term performance measures such as earnings per share to award bonuses: If bonuses for plc bosses are based on indicators which can be quickly affected by short-term action, the personal temptation will be to look to enhance bonuses through actions such as buying back shares.
- The threat of takeover: Boosting short-term profit tends to push a company's share price higher. This means that anyone sniffing around with a takeover in mind will find the business more expensive to buy, perhaps dissuading them from bidding.
- The functional background of many UK bosses: Many UK plc bosses have risen through the finance department. Managers from other functional areas, such as engineering or marketing, have a far better understanding of the need for a long-term perspective when making decisions.

> **Short-termism** is when the actions of managers show total prioritisation of immediate issues, ignoring long-term ones.

> **Exam tip**
>
> Look for evidence of one or more of these causes of short-termism when analysing a business case study. If the evidence is there, you can build a chain of logic to explain how these causes can lead to the effects covered below.

Effects of short-termism

As a focus on the short term takes hold in a business, many indicators may arise, which frequently intensify the focus on the short term:

- Inadequate expenditure on research and development
- Accounting adjustments that inflate current earnings
- A bias towards using profit for high dividend payments or to buy back shares, at the expense of investment
- Adopting pay schemes for directors that focus on achieving short-term financial objectives
- A willingness to cut the workforce quickly, leading to high labour turnover and a loss of experience and skills that may be needed in the future

- Ignoring long-term risks with products and services, such as shifts in consumer habits or potential obsolescence
- A focus on takeovers to grow rather than the use of organic growth
- A shortage of investment in image-building advertising
- Minimal training budgets.

Long-term thinking

Companies willing to show more patience will often find themselves in a better position competitively in the long term. However, to do this requires the removal of many of the pressures that lead to short-termism. A great example of long-term thinking can be found in Germany. Major plcs play a far smaller role in the German economy, which is dominated instead by medium-sized private limited companies, often family owned. These companies are collectively referred to as the Mittelstand. Common features of a Mittelstand company are:

- family owned
- family run
- people-centred management
- long-term thinking
- a focus on doing one thing well.

This focus allows a firm to specialise in that one thing: an example of Porter's focused differentiation strategy. The result is that Germany has a disproportionately high number of world market leaders, admittedly in specialised niche markets. However, market leadership offers excellent prospects for long-term profitability.

A comparison of a typical UK plc and a typical Mittelstand company is shown in Table 15.1.

Table 15.1 The short-termist plc vs the long-termist Mittelstand

	Plc	Mittelstand
Typical financial structure	Strong base of share capital with moderate gearing	Strong base of share capital with moderate gearing
Typical ownership structure	Owned by many relatively small shareholders	Family-owned or majority family-owned with some shares listed on the stock market
Typical approach to spending on R&D and trainee staff	Varies, but many will look for a low-spend model with high levels of outsourcing (and low investment in staff)	Desire for very long-term success and a sense of moral duty creates a culture of investment in people and technology
Typical business objectives	Maximise short-term share price to keep the market happy, and to enjoy a big bonus due to the high share price	Maintain a world-leading position to hand over a continually successful business to the next generation

Evidence-based versus subjective decision-making

REVISED

Evidence-based decision-making

Large businesses, with access to sophisticated computer systems, make many routine decisions automatically. A sales forecast, based on recent trends and figures for the same time last year, can automatically generate decisions on issues such as how much stock to order or how many staff need to be at work on a given day. This type of decision-making — evidence-based or scientific decision-making — dates back at least as far as F.W. Taylor, who advocated managers finding the one best way to do tasks. He used time and motion study — a method of experimenting with processes — to identify the best way to complete a task. This approach generated the desire to measure performance and use the data offered by measurement to manage the business.

The weakness of evidence-based decision-making is its basis in extrapolation. The expectation that the future will be similar to the past can prevent revolutionary thinking and decisions. As a result, evidence-based decision-making is less effective when facing strategic decisions, for which limited data may be available.

Subjective decision-making

Subjective decision-making — or the use of intuition by managers — allows human judgement to take precedent over data. It can be thought of as the artistic side of business decision-making, in contrast to the scientific approach. Of course, sometimes intuitive decision-makers have the wrong hunch, but, without demoting the importance of data, many great business decisions would never have been made without hunches. Table 15.2 shows examples of good and bad decisions that would have been made more on the basis of intuition than data.

Table 15.2 Some good and some awful real business decisions

Good business decisions	Bad business decisions
Coca-Cola buys Innocent drinks – giving it a real competitor to PepsiCo's Tropicana. The £200 million deal was completed in 2013	Waterstones bookshop decides to stop selling books online, because 'online will never be more than 10% of the market'
In June 2000, Nick Robertson and Quentin Griffiths launch 'As Seen on Screen'; first year sales are £3.6 million. By 2014 ASOS has sales of £1,000 million	Malcolm Walker, owner of Iceland Frozen Foods, takes the business upmarket – focusing on organic products: it didn't last
Unloved Mondelez (owner of Cadbury) launches Belvita Breakfast Biscuits in 2010. The grocery trade laughed at the idea, but by 2013 Belvita sales had grown to £58 million – that is more than Jaffa Cakes	Rupert Murdoch, media mogul, sells MySpace website for $35 million, having bought it for $580 million six years before
With recession biting, Waitrose launches its Essentials range of lower-priced groceries. By 2015 sales of Essentials exceeded £1 billion a year and Waitrose extended the range to 400 more items	Nestlé relaunches its Willy Wonka chocolate bar range in 2013 (sales were poor when it first launched in 2005); time is no healer and the whole range was discontinued in 2014

Typical mistake

There is not a right or wrong way to make decisions. Although routine decisions are better suited to evidence-based decision-making and strategic decisions may be hard to make in an evidence-based way, much effective decision-making involves elements of both approaches.

Now test yourself TESTED ☐

1 List three main causes of short-termism.
2 State three likely consequences of short-termism.
3 For which type of decisions is evidence-based decision-making most useful?

Answers online

Corporate culture

Easiest thought of as 'the way we do things round here', corporate culture impacts on the way businesses behave, as it strongly influences the way the people working for the business behave. Culture will be determined by several key factors, including:

- the aims or mission of the business
- the behaviour of company directors and senior staff
- the attitude of senior managers to risk and enterprising behaviour
- recruitment and training procedures.

> **Corporate culture** sums up the spirit, attitudes, behaviours and the ethos of an organisation.

Strong and weak cultures

REVISED

Where a clear sense of shared beliefs and behaviours exists, a company can be said to have a strong culture. The difference between a strong and a weak culture can be summarised in the answers to two questions:

- Is there a 'can-do' attitude or a 'must we?' attitude?
- Is there a conviction among staff that the organisation is a force for good, rather than just a money-making machine?

Table 15.3 Strong vs weak corporate culture

Signs of a strong culture	Signs of a weak culture
● Focusing on customers' real needs, allowing staff to make decisions, e.g. refunds	● Staff follow a script when dealing with customers (not trusted to know what is right)
● Staff show a real feeling for the organisation as 'us', as a long-term commitment	● 'Us' tends to be a department, not the business as a whole; there may even be a feeling of them and us
● A united view among staff that the organisation is a force for good, e.g. staff at Greggs taking pride in the company's support for school breakfast clubs	● A cynical view among many staff, doubting the company's supposed principles and ethos; suspecting that there is too much PR spin; too little commitment
● Sticking together and working together at a time of crisis	● When things look bad, better qualified staff look to find another job

Handy's classification of cultures

REVISED

Charles Handy classified business culture into four types. Identifying the underlying cultural type of a business can help to explain its actions.

Power culture

A power culture will occur when there is one or a small group of extremely powerful people leading an organisation. Characteristics include:

- Everything goes through the boss.
- Few rules or procedures are laid down.
- Communication is through personal contact.
- Decision-making is likely to be governed by the desire to please the boss.
- The leadership style is autocratic.

Power cultures can work effectively under great leaders, but too often can lead to unethical behaviour as the desire to please the boss drives staff to make poor decisions.

> **Exam tip**
>
> If you can use case study information to decide what type of culture is evident within a business, you can use Handy's cultural types to explain how culture affects issues such as speed of decision-making, responsiveness to change and motivation.

Role culture

This is likely to exist in an established organisation dominated by rules and procedures. Characteristics include:

- Power depends on the position held within the organisational structure.
- All employees are expected to follow the rules.
- Career progress will be predictable and based on who follows procedure best.
- The culture is **bureaucratic**, focused on avoiding mistakes.
- The organisation will struggle to cope with rapid change, especially problematic if there is rapid change in the market.
- Leadership style is likely to be autocratic or paternalistic.

Role culture can be an effective culture for maintaining a company's current position but really struggles in dynamic environments.

> In a **bureaucratic organisation** initiative is stifled by paperwork and checking and re-checking of actions.

Task culture

In a task culture, the project being worked on is the central focus. Senior managers allocate projects to teams of employees from different functional areas. Project teams become the normal working environment for staff.

Characteristics of a task culture include:

- Each project team is formed for a single project, then disbanded once the project is complete.
- An individual's power depends on their expertise rather than status within the organisational structure.
- Employees become used to working with staff from other departments — helping employees to understand the different perspectives of each functional area.

This culture works when dealing with rapid change. However, a potential drawback is the chance of project teams developing their own objectives rather than sticking to the corporate objectives.

Person culture

Operating in organisations with highly skilled, professional staff, a person culture sees individuals form groups in which they share their knowledge and expertise. In this way individuals can develop new skills and knowledge. Characteristics include:

- Staff are well paid and treated.
- Leadership style is democratic.
- Staff feel a sense of personal development which is likely to be highly motivating.

How corporate culture is formed

REVISED

Several factors will affect the formation of a company's culture:

- Leadership style: Organisations formed by an entrepreneur with a strong character who is still in charge, or who led the organisation for a long time, may reflect that leader's personality, such as Richard Branson's unfailing entrepreneurial urge at Virgin.

- Type of ownership: Plcs are likely to place the need to satisfy stock markets above all else. This can create a culture where short-term returns are encouraged, unlike privately owned family firms where a longer-term perspective can emerge.
- Recruitment policies: Where recruitment policies end up appointing 'identikit' versions of existing senior staff, a workforce can begin to lack diversity. Even worse is when this creates a workforce that is dissimilar to customers. Policies and procedures can develop which actively harm a business's success in the market.

Difficulties in changing corporate culture

REVISED

Most humans have an aversion to changing firmly established routines and therefore changing the way people do things is not easy. The problem of organisational change in general is detailed in Topic 23 (see A-level textbook, p. 166). Reasons why people will resist attempts to change culture include:

- self-interest
- low tolerance to change
- misunderstanding of the proposed change
- different assessments of the need to change.

Cultural change, if it is to be successful, needs a combination of several key factors:

- a clear purpose
- education and training
- consistency of communication methods and messages
- effective communication that change is going to happen.

> **Typical mistake**
>
> Students looking to explain that a company needs to change the way it operates can too often throw in the phrase 'change the corporate culture' without fully acknowledging just how difficult cultural change is to achieve. References to changing culture should always be accompanied by an explanation of the difficulties in so doing.

Now test yourself

TESTED

4 State three factors that will influence the formation of corporate culture.
5 List Handy's four cultural types.
6 State three reasons why changing culture may be hard to achieve.

Answers online

Shareholders versus stakeholders

Stakeholders are dealt with by businesses on a daily basis. Customers, suppliers and staff are all affected by and have an effect on businesses. It therefore seems sensible, when making decisions, to try to meet the needs of all stakeholder groups, in order to ensure their continued positive relationship with the business. This approach to running a business is known as the stakeholder approach.

In contrast, some believe that the sole, or at least dominant, responsibility a business has is to its shareholders: the owners of the business. This philosophy — the shareholder approach — places increasing shareholder value, through increased profit and share price, above all other responsibilities. Under the shareholder approach, other stakeholder groups can have their interests ignored.

> **Stakeholders** are groups that are influenced by and influence the operations of a business.

Internal and external stakeholders

Typical mistake

Small shareholders, especially in large plcs, have little real influence over the business and take no major part in its day-to-day decision-making. They should therefore be considered as external stakeholders. Where a major shareholder is actively involved in the business as its owner, they should be considered as an internal stakeholder.

A business is more likely to keep stakeholders happy if they draw them towards the category of internal stakeholders, since these groups are more likely to feel a part of the business.

An example here is franchisees of a business such as Subway, where if the organisation makes franchisees feel valued as internal stakeholders, they will be much more co-operative and the franchises are far more likely to be run along the lines the franchisor wants.

Stakeholder objectives

Each stakeholder group is likely to have its own objectives that members want the firm to achieve, which will suit their own interests. Several stakeholder groups with their main objectives are:

- Staff: Growth (preferably organic), new technology products, not processes, introduced and rising profit (if profit sharing takes place)
- Managers/directors: Growth (organic or inorganic), new products and processes, rising profits (especially if bonuses are paid)
- Shareholders: Rising profits in the short and long term
- Suppliers: Growth
- Customers: Quality of product/service, innovative new products
- Bankers: Stable profits
- Local residents: Clean, green production with few deliveries or dispatches.

Stakeholder and shareholder influences

Where stakeholder views are listened to and acted upon, a business can operate as a force for good for most stakeholders most of the time. Some businesses, such as John Lewis, recognise that treating all stakeholders well has benefits for the whole business, including its owners. Committed suppliers, loyal customers, motivated staff and positive local residents are more likely to add up to long-term, sustained profitability.

However, where shareholder influence dominates, businesses may be forced into actions that prioritise the short-term needs of shareholders to the detriment of the business's long-term success. Treating suppliers poorly may boost the immediate cash flow or profitability situation but does not create a relationship where suppliers will be willing to go out of their way to make emergency deliveries when stocks are running low.

Conflict between shareholder and stakeholder objectives

By their nature, different stakeholder groups have different priorities when it comes to what they want from a business. It is therefore no surprise that conflict exists between shareholder objectives and those of other stakeholder groups. Some businesses manage to balance the needs of these groups effectively in certain situations. For others, conflict can result in poor performance. Examples of shared and conflicting stakeholder objectives are shown in Table 15.4.

> **Exam tip**
>
> When considering which stakeholder group is likely to win out in a situation of conflicting objectives, look for evidence elsewhere within the case study as to whether the business seems to follow the stakeholder or shareholder approach.

Table 15.4 Stakeholder needs in different business circumstances

Situation	Shared interests/needs between stakeholders	Conflicting stakeholder interests/needs
Productivity advance — perhaps coming from a staff suggestion scheme	Shareholders, managers and customers	Managers and employees (threats of redundancy)
Fashion or weather turns in the business's favour	Shareholders, managers, suppliers and employees	Green campaigners may object to increased resource use
Consumer demand switches from shops to e- and m-commerce	Shareholders and customers	Managers and employees
High and rising inflation	Shareholders and managers	Employees, suppliers and customers

Now test yourself

7 State three internal stakeholders and three external stakeholders of a plc.
8 Briefly explain how satisfying stakeholder needs helps a business.
9 Give two examples of business decisions where shareholders' needs may conflict with those of staff.

Answers online

Business ethics

> **Business ethics** are the moral principles that underpin decision-making.

What are business ethics?

Making an ethical decision means taking a course of action which is morally right. The extent to which business decisions consider the moral dimension will be determined by two key aspects:

1 The personal moral beliefs of the individual making the decision — what they consider to be morally justifiable
2 The corporate culture, which will influence the beliefs of the decision-maker as to what would be considered morally acceptable by the company as a whole.

Ethical considerations can be found throughout the operations of a business. A few examples include:

● dealing fairly and honestly with customers and suppliers
● protecting the natural environment

- dealing effectively with bullying, harassment and discrimination in the workplace
- providing accurate and transparent financial information
- anticompetitive actions
- testing products on animals
- whistleblowing of unethical actions by members of staff.

The ethics of strategic decisions

REVISED

Given the importance of strategic decisions — defined as decisions that affect the whole firm and are hard to reverse — the morality of these decisions should be carefully considered.

Two key aspects of ethics in strategic decision-making arise regularly:
1 Whether the moral aspects of a decision have been fully considered. Some simple decisions such as selling off part of a business to a new owner may seem logical financially, but have the owners thought through the effect on their soon-to-be former employees and the communities that rely on their incomes, if the division may be quickly closed down by its new owners?
2 The level of risk and who bears the risk. In the scenario above, where part of a business is sold to new owners, the new owners may be confident that they can close the division, sell its assets and fully cover the costs of the purchase. In this case, the deal carries little risk to the new owners. The risk is borne by the staff and their dependents — if the deal does not work well, they will have lost their jobs. In many cases, those that stand to profit from business decisions bear only a small part of the consequences of any possible downside. This is morally wrong.

Trade-offs between ethics and profit

REVISED

Perhaps the truest test of ethical behaviour from a business is their willingness to sacrifice profit in order to do what is right. In the short term at least, ethical behaviour often means paying a little more or making a little less on a business transaction. Alternatively, ethical behaviour may involve spending money on workers' conditions without expecting any financial return. There is almost always a clear trade-off between what is morally right and what is most profitable.

That is not to suggest that profit is unethical. Without profit, businesses would fail, creating redundancies and financial hardship. The grey area tends to be how much profit is made. Firms that behave unethically do so in order to maximise the possible profit they can receive. Ethically run businesses aim to behave well in making a level of profit that represents a satisfactory return on the risks they take.

Typical mistake

Confusing a company that paints itself as being 'ethically concerned' merely as a marketing ploy to try to add value or differentiate its products with one that considers the morality of its decisions is wrong. It is rare to find that genuine ethical behaviour has a positive effect on profit. It is not unheard of, but it certainly doesn't happen as often as companies launch 'ethically branded' products or services.

Pay and rewards

REVISED

The major ethical issue related to pay and rewards is the disparity between the pay of bosses and workers. When CEOs of plcs total up the value of their salary, pension contributions, share options and bonuses, these will be many times higher than the pay received by those who work for their business and allow it to keep functioning. Of course, executives probably should be paid more given the level of responsibility, need for

Edexcel A-level Business 161

major decision-making and the likely rarity of the skills and experience they need to get the job done.

John Lewis's constitution — the rules of how the business is run — limits the chief executive's pay to no more than 75 times the average salary. Although that sounds a lot, there is general acceptance that this is a fair pay multiple; if the average worker gets £20,000 a year, the boss should not be paid more than £1.5 million. If that sounds a lot, a study of the pay of other CEOs would reveal much higher pay multiples. The question is whether the extra pay offered to top bosses has outstripped the extra risk involved in doing their jobs.

Corporate Social Responsibility

CSR could be a phenomenal way of self-regulating business activity. If businesses commit to behaving responsibly so that their actions contribute positively to the societies in which they operate, perhaps our world would be better. However, although some businesses take their social responsibilities seriously, some will use the CSR label merely as a marketing tool without fully committing to behaving in a socially responsible manner.

> **Corporate Social Responsibility (CSR)** describes the desire to run a business in a morally correct way, attempting to balance the needs of all stakeholder groups.

Table 15.5 Advantages and disadvantages of CSR

Reasons for Corporate Social Responsibility (CSR)	Reasons for doubting CSR
Companies that behave, or seem to behave, in a responsible way towards their stakeholders can gain from doing so:	Shareholders and other stakeholders reject the usefulness of CSR for reasons that include:
Marketing advantages: Consumers who have enough disposable income will often pay a premium so that they can buy with a clear conscience from businesses that behave in a socially responsible way. CSR can be a point of differentiation for some businesses.	Reduced profitability: Genuinely embracing CSR is likely to mean higher costs and perhaps lower revenues, with suppliers paid a fair price and selling prices set at a reasonable rather than a rip-off level.
	Reduced growth prospects: Some business opportunities may need to be turned down if they involve compromising the morality needed to be socially responsible.
Positive effects on the workforce: Recruiting high-flying staff may be easier if they do not wish to work for a morally corrupt enterprise. Meanwhile, staff motivation may be enhanced as they feel happier working for a socially responsible business with a clear sense of moral purpose.	Rejection of CSR as a PR tool: There is plenty of evidence to suggest that CSR is often treated as a marketing tool rather than an inherent shift in corporate culture, in which case, it serves no valid purpose.
	If social responsibility means hiking up the price of food that low-income consumers need to eat healthily, perhaps it is better to sacrifice the needs of suppliers to ensure that even those on low incomes can access fresh fruit and vegetables.

Now test yourself

10 What two key factors will influence the ethics of any business decision?
11 In strategic decision-making, unethical decisions may be taken if what two features are unfairly shared by different stakeholder groups?
12 What is the major ethical issue relating to executive pay?

Answers online

Exam practice

The John Lewis partnership, consisting of John Lewis department stores and the Waitrose supermarket chain, is frequently held up as an embodiment of socially responsible business practice. What makes the partnership unusual is its ownership type. The group is owned by its staff, so there are no shareholders expecting dividends and no shares in the business whose price must be monitored closely.

Retiring Chief Executive of the department stores Andy Street has pointed out that the CEOs of his competitors, such as Debenhams, are paid far more than him, but John Lewis's constitution limits his pay to 75 times the pay of the average John Lewis employee. However, whenever interviewed, his commitment to the organisation was clear and he clearly enjoyed running a business with a difference.

Once a year, the staff wait with eager anticipation to discover what bonus they will receive. Once the annual profit is calculated and some retained for further investment within the partnership, the rest of the profit is shared among the partners: the owners of the business.

1 (a) Analyse the likely reasons for the John Lewis partnership's reputation for ethical behaviour. (8)

(b) Explain why John Lewis is likely to take a long-term approach to decision-making. (8)

(c) To what extent is the limit to the John Lewis CEO's pay likely to damage the business's ability to compete with its rivals? (20)

2 'Creating the right corporate culture is the single most important part of a leader's job.' Assess the validity of this statement. (20)

Answers and quick quiz 15 online

ONLINE

Summary

- Key influences on decision-making within organisations include:
  - the timescales considered when making decisions: short-termism versus long-term thinking
  - whether decisions are made in an evidence-based or intuitive or subjective manner.
- Strategic decisions tend to involve more subjectivity while routine decisions are better suited to evidence-based decision-making.
- Plcs are naturally more likely to consider the short-term effects of decisions. Long-term thinking is more likely to be found in private limited companies.
- Corporate culture affects every aspect of business activity.
- Handy proposed four common types of corporate culture to explain how most businesses do things.
- Key influences on corporate culture include:
  - ownership type
  - the founder's personal philosophy
  - recruitment procedures.
- Corporate culture is hard to change.
- The stakeholder approach and the shareholder approach represent differing attitudes as to whom a business is responsible.
- Different stakeholder groups have different objectives.
- The objectives of different stakeholder groups are likely to conflict.
- Business ethics are the moral principles underpinning business decision-making.
- There is usually a trade-off between ethics and profits.

16 Assessing competitiveness

Interpretation of financial statements

Accounts are produced to provide information on the finances of a business to its stakeholders. Shareholders, managers, bankers and suppliers will all be interested to know one or more of the following about the business they are dealing with:

- The amount of cash available to the business
- How that cash compares with the amount of short-term debt owed by the business
- How much of the firm's long-term finance is borrowed
- How profitable the business is.

The two major documents that all companies are required, by law, to publish each year can provide this information. They are:

- The statement of comprehensive income, usually called the **profit and loss account**. This shows the revenue generated by the business this year and the costs that were incurred in generating that revenue.
- The statement of financial position, usually called the **balance sheet**. This details what the business owns, owes and where the money came from.

> A **balance sheet** is a financial document showing a business's assets and liabilities at a point in time.
>
> A **profit and loss account** shows a firm's revenue for a time period along with all the costs associated with generating that revenue.

Balance sheets (statement of financial position)

REVISED

Balance sheets show how wealthy a business is. They do this by listing everything the business owns.

In addition, a balance sheet lists the money owed by the business — its liabilities. The final part of a balance sheet details the shareholders' contribution to the business — the capital they have provided.

Table 16.1 **An example of a simplified balance sheet**

Simplified balance sheet	
	£
Long-term (non-current) assets	300,000
Short-term (current) assets	100,000
Total assets	400,000
Balancing with: Total capital	400,000

Types of asset

Long-term (non-current) **assets** are used over and over again by a business to generate profit. Examples include:

- land and buildings
- machinery and equipment
- vehicles
- patents or copyright.

> An **asset** is any item owned by a business.

Answers and quick quizzes at **www.hoddereducation.co.uk/myrevisionnotes**

Current assets are short-term assets that change regularly. There are three main types:

- Inventories: This is the value of any stocks of raw materials, partially finished goods or finished products owned by the business.
- Receivables: This is money owed to the business, usually by customers who have bought on credit.
- Cash: This is money available in the bank that can be immediately accessed along with physical cash.

Capital on the balance sheet

There are three sources of capital shown on a balance sheet:

- Banks: Loans from banks carry interest payments and must be repaid.
- Shareholders: When the company sells shares, it receives share capital in return. This is theoretically owed to shareholders but is very rarely ever repaid.
- Profits: The reserves figure on a balance sheet shows the total amount of retained profit that has been kept in the business as a source of finance.

A final version of a balance sheet is shown in Table 16.2. Note that the column to the right shows sub-totals from figures in the other column.

> **Liquidity** is the term used to describe a firm's ability to pay its bills and finance short-term spending.

> **Typical mistake**
>
> Note that reserves are not money that the firm has available to spend. This simply shows where money has come from; it is likely that most has already been spent on assets, shown on the top part of the balance sheet.

Table 16.2 An example of the final version of a balance sheet

Balance sheet for 31 December last year		
	£	£
Property	180,000	
Machinery and vehicles	120,000	300,000
Inventories	80,000	
Receivables and cash	60,000	
Current liabilities	(40,000)	
Total assets less current liabilities		400,000
Loan capital	(250,000)	
Net assets		150,000
Share capital	50,000	
Reserves	100,000	
Total equity		150,000

Key information: assessing financial performance using a balance sheet

REVISED

Typically, a business's financial performance is measured by profit, as shown on the profit and loss account. However, longer-term performance can be assessed using the balance sheet by seeing the movements in reserves over time. Reserves build up over time (for a successful firm) because any profit the firm makes after tax that is not paid out in dividends is retained in the business. This annual retained profit is added to the reserves figure on the balance sheet. If the firm makes a loss for the year, this figure is deducted from reserves on the balance sheet. This means that if the reserves figure is consistently rising over time, the firm has been consistently profitable.

Stakeholder interest in balance sheets

Published accounts exist in order to ensure that stakeholders have access to the information that helps them make informed dealings with a business.

Table 16.3 Different interests in the balance sheet

Stakeholder	Interest in the balance sheet
Bankers	Keen to understand a business's reliance on debt for its long-term finance, bankers will study the relationship between long-term borrowings and total equity.
Suppliers	More interested in the short-term financial health of the business, suppliers considering offering credit will want to see the relationship between the company's available cash and its existing short-term debt.
Staff	May be looking at reserves to assess whether the 'wealth' of the business has gone up or down over time, perhaps wondering whether they are receiving a fair reward for their efforts if reserves have rocketed.

Profit and loss accounts (statement of comprehensive income)

The profit and loss account is the record of how well a firm has done, financially, in a given period of time. The financial measure of performance is profit, therefore the profit and loss account shows a variety of different types of profit to help stakeholders studying the account understand the business's performance.

How a P&L account shows profit or loss

In simple terms, a profit and loss account starts with annual revenue, then deducts different costs and expenses to calculate different types of profit. A basic profit and loss account is shown in Table 16.4.

Table 16.4 The basic structure of a profit and loss account

		£m
	Revenue	**26.0**
Less	Cost of sales	(17.0)
Gives	Gross profit	9.0
Less	Overheads	(4.0)
Gives	Operating profit	5.0
Less	Financing costs	1.5*
Gives	Profit before taxation	6.5
Less	Tax	(2.0)
Gives	Profit after taxation for the year	4.5
*In this case more interest was earned than was paid out		

Gross profit

Gross profit is a raw measure of basic trading profit. It shows what is left from revenue once the cost of making or buying the goods sold (**cost of sales**) has been deducted.

Revenue – cost of sales = gross profit

> **Cost of sales** is the cost of buying or making the products sold to generate the revenue for the year.

Operating profit

To move from gross to operating profit, **overhead expenses** are deducted.

Gross profit – expenses = operating profit

Expenses include items such as wages and salaries, rent and rates, heat and light and distribution and marketing costs. Therefore, operating profit shows the amount of profit left after deducting the normal costs of operating the business for the year.

Profit before and after tax

Beneath operating profit, the profit and loss account deals with issues such as the cost of financing the business, taxation and how profits are used. First, an entry is made for net financing costs. This is simply:

Interest earned on money held by the business – interest on money borrowed by the business

A negative figure is typical as many businesses borrow greater sums than they keep at any time in the bank (and interest rates on loans will be higher than those paid out on money in the bank). This figure is deducted from operating profit to calculate the profit before tax is deducted. With corporation tax taken away, the business is left with profit after tax — also referred to as net profit for the year. This is the profit that 'belongs' to the shareholders.

Table 16.5 shows the profit and loss account for SuperGroup plc for the year ending 31 March 2015, with equivalent 2014 figures also shown.

Table 16.5 Summarised profit and loss account for SuperGroup plc (year ended 31 March 2015)

	2015 (£m)	2014 (3m)
Revenue (sales excluding VAT)	486	431
Cost of sales	(190)	(174)
Gross profit	**296**	**257**
Administrative and other expenses	(236)	(212)
Operating profit	**60**	**45**
Net finance expense	(0.5)	–
Profit before tax	**59.9**	**45**
Taxation	(13.5)	(17.5)
Net profit for the year	**46**	**27.5**

Using profit

Shareholders are left with a simple choice: should they withdraw profit after tax for their own benefit, or leave that money in the business to finance extra spending by the firm? It is directors who will recommend the balance between these two uses of profit. They are likely to consider:
- How much money the firm needs to finance future plans
- How much dividend shareholders have received in the past
- Shareholders' expectations for this year's dividend.

If the majority of shareholders are unhappy with the recommendation, they can vote against this at the annual general meeting.

> **Overheads**, or **expenses**, or **overhead expenses** are payments for something that is of immediate use to the business, other than the actual products they sell.

Key information: assessing financial performance using a P&L account

REVISED

Sadly, company law does not require companies to publish a lot of detail in the profit and loss account. That shown above complies with the law. However, assessment of financial performance can be made by checking which direction profits are headed. Increasing profits suggest improving financial performance. However, before making a final decision on performance, ratios should be calculated, as explained in the next topic.

Shareholders will be particularly interested in levels of net profit. Those more concerned with the operating performance of the business will consider operating profit all important. Few will see gross profit as the most important profit figure, yet it does reveal information on the basic profitability of the business that will be of interest to competitors.

Now test yourself
TESTED

1 Using 140 characters or less, what does a balance sheet show?
2 Using 140 characters or less, what does a profit and loss account show?
3 Using 140 characters or less, what is meant by reserves?
4 State three stakeholders who will be interested in seeing a company's accounts and, for each, briefly explain why.

Answers online

> **Exam tip**
>
> Look out for profit and loss accounts where different profit figures move in different directions. These can provide great opportunities to show insight. If gross profit rises but operating profit falls, the firm has probably struggled to control its expenses for the year. A company whose gross and operating profits rise, but net profit falls, may have taken on significant extra borrowings, pushing up the net financing cost of the business.

Ratio analysis

Financial accounting statements provide useful data that can be helpful in assessing the performance and health of a business. However, the raw data itself can only tell the reader so much. More powerful analysis can be achieved by looking at financial variables in relation to others, calculating financial ratios.

Types of ratio
REVISED

The three main classifications of ratio are:
- Profitability: This shows the relationship between gross/operating/net profit and revenue, assets and capital.
- Liquidity: This shows the ability of a firm to meet its short-term debts with cash or near cash assets.
- Gearing: This shows the proportion of the long-term finance in a business that has come from loans.

Each tells us about a different aspect of the company's performance (profitability) and financial health (liquidity and gearing). Taken together, they can really unveil some of the secrets of the financial statements.

Liquidity ratios
REVISED

Both liquidity ratios — current and acid test — are calculated in order to understand the balance between the company's short-term debt and the assets it can use to meet that debt: cash or other current assets that can be speedily turned into cash.

Answers and quick quizzes at www.hoddereducation.co.uk/myrevisionnotes

Current ratio

$$\text{Current ratio} = \frac{\text{current assets}}{\text{current liabilities}}$$

The ideal value for the current ratio is 1.5, meaning that a business would have £1.50 of current assets for every £1 of short-term debt, which is deemed enough to be able to cover the debts comfortably without holding too many resources in unproductive forms, where they could be better invested elsewhere. If the ratio falls too low, this may indicate that the firm is suffering from a liquidity crisis, so is unable to find enough cash to settle debts as they become due.

Acid test ratio

A stiffer test of liquidity than the current ratio — the acid test ratio — discounts inventories as something that can be quickly converted to cash.

$$\text{Acid test ratio} = \frac{\text{current assets (excluding inventories/stock)}}{\text{current liabilities}}$$

The ideal value for this ratio is 1. This would mean a company has £1 of cash or receivables to cover every £1 of short-term debt.

Exam tip

If either liquidity ratio goes too high, the firm may have too much money tied up in stock, debtors or cash. This money could generate a far greater return if invested in non-current assets. Holding excessive current assets may feel safe but is likely to damage a company's return on capital employed (ROCE) ratio.

Gearing

REVISED

Measuring the long-term financial health of a business, the gearing ratio expresses long-term liabilities as a percentage of the total amount of long-term capital in the business.

$$\text{Gearing ratio} = \frac{\text{long-term liabilities}}{\text{capital employed}} \times 100$$

In other words, if a business is financed by £50m of loans and £50m of equity, the gearing ratio would be 50%. Indeed, 50% is regarded as the danger level over which it is normally inadvisable to pass. The problem with a high gearing is the cash drain it represents: with interest payments to make, as well as loan repayments, high levels of debt can suck the lifeblood from a business rapidly.

To reduce an unhealthily high gearing ratio, several options are open:
- Issue more shares
- Retain more profits
- Repay some loans.

Capital employed adds shareholders' capital (total equity) to loan capital (long-term liabilities) to work out the total long-term finance in the business.

Profitability ratios

REVISED

Assessing how profitable a business has been can be done using the actual figures for profit over several years. However, more powerfully, profitability can be assessed by calculating profit margins. These show profit as a percentage of revenue. The most profitable firms are able to ensure that a greater proportion of every £1 in revenue is left over as profit once costs have been deducted. Profit margins were covered in more detail in Topic 20 (see A-level textbook, p. 144). A summary is provided in Table 16.6.

Table 16.6 Summary of profit margins and profitability

	Gross profit margin	Operating profit margin	Net profit margin
Formula	Gross profit/ Sales revenue × 100	Operating profit/ Sales revenue × 100	Profit after tax/ Sales revenue × 100
What it shows	Gross profit per £ of sales	Operating profit per £ of sales	Net profit per £ of sales
How to improve it	Price up Unit variable costs down	Boost gross margin Cut overheads per £ of sales Increase sales	Boost operating profit margins Cut corporation tax bill (legally!)
Problem if it is too low	May not be enough gross profit to cover overhead expenses	May not be enough operating profit to reinvest into the business and so get growth	May be too low to provide shareholders with acceptable annual dividends

Return on Capital Employed (ROCE)

Another measure of profitability is the ROCE ratio. This expresses operating profit as a percentage of the capital that has been invested in the business. Therefore it shows a return on that capital that is comparable with other potential uses of capital, such as simply leaving money in the bank to earn interest.

$$\text{Return on Capital Employed} = \frac{\text{operating profit}}{\text{capital employed}} \times 100$$

Higher is better for this ratio, since a higher return means the money invested in the business is generating a higher return on that investment. Where ROCE falls below current interest rates, a business may question whether it would be better off closing, liquidating its assets and putting all the money in the risk-free bank for a higher return than the risky option of running a business.

Table 16.7 shows ROCE figures for several plcs; notice how significant the variations are.

Table 16.7 The return on capital employed (ROCE) achieved by a selection of public limited companies in 2014/2015

Company	Annual operating profit	Capital employed	ROCE
Costa UK* (coffee bars)	£132,500,000	£286,100,000	46.3%
Ted Baker (retailing)	£49,759,000	£140,574,000	35.4%
Marks & Spencer (retailing)	£600,000,000	£6,085,000,000	9.9%
Mandarin Oriental (hotels)	£120,800,000	£1,537,000,000	7.9%
*(in Costa's case it is a division of a company)			

> **Exam tip**
>
> Improving ROCE can be achieved by buying back shares from shareholders. It is this fact that explains the strange sounding notion of returning cash to shareholders; if share capital is reduced, capital employed falls, yet the transaction has no impact on operating profit.

In order to boost the ROCE ratio, two options are available:
1 Find a way to increase operating profit.
2 Reduce capital employed without damaging operating profit.

Interpreting ratios to make business decisions

Ratios can help to make key business decisions. Gearing and liquidity ratios help to identify whether a business can afford to invest money in new projects. Meanwhile, return on capital employed can help to assess the attractiveness of a new investment (alongside ARR), or identify underperforming parts of a business.

Table 16.8 shows how ratios can be useful.

Table 16.8 Interpreting ratios to make decisions

Decision	Ratios	Evaluation
Can we afford to spend £50 million on launching in China?	Acid test 0.95 Gearing 24.5%	Finance can come from extra borrowing (to a 50% gearing maximum) plus some use of working capital (to an acid test minimum of 0.6)
Do we need to put our prices up?	Gross margin This year: 8.7% Last year: 10.2%	The problem should be addressed, but price elasticity of demand must also be considered before proceeding
Should we focus on Divisions A and B and sell off Division C?	ROCE figures for: Division A 22.6% Division B 31.4% Division C 5.7%	Unless Division C produces something of value to Division A or B, there is a strong case for selling it off and focusing on the strongest areas of the business

Limitations of ratio analysis

Ratio analysis is a very helpful tool. Yet there are limits to its ability to tell us the whole story of a business. The major issue is the lack of detail provided within financial accounts. Often the true story of a firm's receivables or stock cannot be seen. If money owed by customers is mainly owed by reliable, regular customers, this should turn into cash, which will be received on time. However, if much of the receivables figure on the balance sheet consists of bad debts from failing customers, acid test and current ratio results will paint a misleadingly healthy picture.

If stock is about to go out of fashion and become virtually worthless, the current ratio will again present a misleading picture of health.

On the profit and loss account, net profit can be affected by one-off transactions such as selling a piece of property at a profit. Boosting net profit, this will improve the net margin for this year, but this will simply be a blip, perhaps misleading those who do not investigate further than a ratio result.

Now test yourself

5 Which ratio would be most useful to use when:
  (a) deciding whether prices are too low
  (b) deciding whether to borrow to buy new machinery
  (c) assessing whether to offer credit to new customer?
6 State two actions a business can take to reduce its gearing ratio.
7 What are the ideal values for the (a) current and (b) acid test ratios?
8 What is considered the danger level for the gearing ratio?
9 State two ways to boost a company's ROCE ratio.

Answers online

Human resources

Monitoring the effectiveness of human resources

Just as effective management of any business resource involves assessing how effectively it is being used, so HR management must find ways to assess the effectiveness of the way that people are managed in the business. As a result, a number of important HR indicators will be regularly monitored, especially:
- labour productivity
- labour turnover
- absenteeism.

Labour productivity

Perhaps the single most important measure of the effectiveness of staff is labour productivity.

$$\frac{\textbf{output per period}}{\textbf{number of employees per period}}$$

A business that is able to boost labour productivity without increasing pay will enjoy lower labour costs per unit. This should boost its competitiveness, allowing prices to be cut if needed, or a higher profit margin.

Labour turnover

Measuring the percentage of the workforce that has left during a year, this indicator can indicate staff discontent with how they are treated if it increases.

$$\frac{\textbf{Number of staff leaving the firm in a year}}{\textbf{Average number of staff during the year}} \times 100$$

Causes of increasing labour turnover could include those shown in Table 16.9.

Table 16.9 Some internal and external causes of increasing labour turnover

Internal causes	External causes
Poor recruitment and selection, resulting in the wrong people being appointed	More local vacancies arising, tempting staff to look for better opportunities
Poor motivation or leadership	Better transport links allowing staff to look for alternative jobs further away
Wage rates below the local norms	

High labour turnover has, on the whole, negative effects in most cases. However, some positives can be found in the right circumstances. The negatives of a high labour turnover include:
- extra recruitment costs to find replacements
- extra training costs for replacements
- time taken for replacements to settle in and become productive
- loss of productivity while replacements are found, trained and find their feet.

Exam tip

The context may determine the importance of employee performance data. During periods of rapid growth for a business, ideas and solutions, which are virtually unmeasurable, may be critical to ensuring that a business successfully moves to a new stage in its development. It is in mature businesses that indicators such as productivity can be crucial, since productivity gains may represent the best chance to increase profits — by boosting margins.

Potential positives of a high labour turnover include:
- new workers with new ideas and enthusiasm
- new workers with appropriate skills may be brought in to prevent the need to re-train existing staff where skill requirements have changed
- a new way of looking at problems in the business could bring solutions to long-standing issues.

Absenteeism

Measuring the amount of time missed by workers who do not come to work when they are supposed to can indicate discontent in the workplace. However, the weakness of this measure is that it fails to distinguish between avoidable and unavoidable absences.

$$\frac{\text{Total days (or hours) of absence in a period}}{\text{Possible total days (or hours) that could have been worked}} \times 100$$

There is no doubt that a high level of absenteeism causes extra costs and lost productivity that damages a firm's competitiveness.

Typical mistake

Be careful with both absenteeism and labour turnover. They are both indicators where high numbers are bad: beware interpreting rising levels of everything in business as good.

Using employee performance data to help make business decisions

REVISED

As with most data gathered by businesses, employee performance data can highlight areas where problems exist. The data is unlikely to pin down the cause, or provide the solution. However, analysis of data in this way can uncover major areas where improvements need to be made. This is especially true where comparative data for rivals is available. Where a business's HR data shows it is lagging behind rivals, competitiveness will suffer.

Human resource strategies to improve employee performance

REVISED

To improve employee performance, a range of strategies is available. Each may be appropriate in different circumstances.

Financial rewards

Using financial rewards such as performance-related bonuses can be hazardous. As Herzberg would point out, trying to use a hygiene factor such as pay to motivate staff will only create a temporary improvement in performance, which will disappear if the reward disappears. A further problem is in deciding how performance will be measured, before awarding a bonus. Measure performance in the wrong way and employees may adapt what they do simply in order to boost their bonus, perhaps in an unexpected and harmful way.

Employee share ownership

Though hypothetically logical, employee share ownership is more likely to work in small businesses than large ones, where staff may feel their own performance has no serious impact on the overall profits of the business.

Share ownership should work by aligning the goals of the business with those of staff. If staff work better, the company will make more profit, allowing higher dividends to be paid to shareholders, including the employees.

Consultation strategies

Finding an appropriate way to gather employees' views and, even harder, show that they are being genuinely considered, can boost employee engagement and performance. In small businesses, **consultation** can be a doddle — the boss chats things through with all five members of staff. If the business has 50,000 staff in 50 countries, this method is not viable. The use of technology can help — by setting up internal chat rooms or a forum where staff can have their say — but the challenge of consultation grows as a business grows.

> **Consultation** means seeking and listening to the views of employees as part of a decision-making process.

Empowerment strategies

Harnessing the theoretical ideas of Maslow and Herzberg, genuinely empowering staff can bring significant increases in employee performance. However, **empowerment** can be terrifying to managers, who will still be held accountable for the work of subordinates but cannot even tell them what to do, let alone how to do it. The key conditions required if empowerment is to be effective are:

- clear corporate aims and objectives
- a strong culture of trust
- a skilled and talented workforce.

> **Empowerment** means giving staff the authority not just to decide how to do a task, but to decide what tasks need doing in the first place.

Now test yourself

TESTED

10 Briefly explain what the data shows is happening at this business:

HR indicator	2 years ago	1 year ago	This year
Labour productivity (units per worker per week)	100	105	115
Labour turnover (%)	3%	8%	16%
Absenteeism (%)	6%	12%	20%

11 Identify two strategies the firm above could use to help improve employee performance.
12 State two possible reasons why the rise in labour turnover could be causing the increase in productivity.

Answers online

Exam practice

Use the following information to answer the question about assessing this business's performance.

Extracts from profit and loss account

	This year £m	Last year £m
Revenue	3,500	3,200
Cost of sales	2,500	2,000
Gross profit	1,000	1,200
Expenses	800	700
Operating profit	200	500
Net cost of finance	50	20
Tax	30	25
Net profit	120	455

Summary of current balance sheet

	£m	£m
Non-current assets		250
Inventories	50	
Receivables and cash	20	
Current liabilities	(40)	
Total assets less current liabilities		280
Long-term liabilities	(180)	
Net assets		100
Share capital	25	
Reserves	75	
Total equity		100

HR data

	This business	Industry average
Labour productivity (units per worker per week)	45	58
Labour turnover (annual %)	23	15
Absenteeism (annual %)	8	5

1 Analyse the information provided to help discuss whether the business should invest in new automated production machinery to replace staff on their production line. (20)
2 Assessing a business's competitiveness should not solely rely on basic financial and HR data. Do you agree? Justify your view. (20)

Answers and quick quiz 16 online

ONLINE

Summary

- A balance sheet (statement of financial position) shows what a business owns, owes and how much shareholders have invested.
- A profit and loss account (statement of comprehensive income) shows revenues and costs for a time period.
- Published financial statements provide useful insight for a range of stakeholders.
- Calculating financial ratios helps to uncover what a business's accounts show.
- The ratios you need to know focus on assessing three areas:
  - profitability
  - liquidity
  - gearing.
- Key measures of the effectiveness of HR management in a business are:
  - labour productivity
  - labour turnover
  - absenteeism.
- Strategies to improve HR effectiveness include:
  - financial rewards
  - employee share ownership
  - consultation strategies
  - empowerment strategies.

Causes and effects of change

The value of change

Though continuity may bring comfort, change brings opportunities. It is change that forces progress — which is generally positive.

Internal causes of change

A number of internally controllable issues can bring about the need to change. These include:

- Changes in organisational size: As a business grows, or shrinks, internal change is inevitable. Expansion can lead to the need to adjust budgets and add extra supervisory layers to the structure to prevent spans of control becoming too wide. Contraction is likely to lead to redundancies and the damaging impacts that can have on staff morale.
- Poor business performance: When profit, profitability or revenue growth are consistently below par, change is often made at the top of an organisation. The need to change a senior decision-maker is implied since they have the ultimate responsibility for underperformance of the business.
- New ownership: Following a takeover, aims, objectives, policies and procedures may well change in order to satisfy the vision that the new owners have for the firm. Even when a successful business has new owners, some change is likely since without the expectation that new owners can improve a business, takeover is unlikely to take place.
- Transformational leadership: For businesses that are struggling to survive, a new 'transformational leader' may be appointed to radically adjust almost everything the business does and how it does it, in the hope that they can find a new mission or purpose and thus revive performance.

> **Typical mistake**
>
> Do not slip into the misguided belief that it is only external factors that lead to businesses needing to make major changes. There are several internal factors that can lead to the introduction of major change programmes.

External causes of change

Frequently, it is changes in the external environment in which the business operates that will cause change to take place. These focus on the acronym PESTLE, while adding changes to the market as a sixth cause:

- Changes in the market: The emergence of new competitors, or radical change in relative market shares, can lead to major change being required within an organisation in order to counter threats. On the other hand, rapid growth in demand caused by fashion or trends may require swift changes in order to capitalise on this demand.
- Political change: Changes in the political party in government can have significant impacts, especially in businesses providing services at least partially financed by government spending. Less broadly, even a change of policy from a political party can bring about the need for a change in approach from a business, which perhaps will now need to adjust its approach to selling.

> **Exam tip**
>
> When multiple causes of change hit a business at the same time, this can explain why the business struggles to deal with these scenarios effectively. Revising for one exam can be hard enough, the problems become far greater when you have several papers in several subjects to revise for at the same time.

- Economic change: Changes in economic growth, as the economy follows its cycle of expansion and slowdown, affect most businesses depending on their income elasticity. The major impact is likely to be on demand, and therefore an element of business change will be required to adjust capacity to suit current demand.
- Social change: How society expects to live — lifestyle changes — can create huge forces for change for businesses, which may need to adjust what they sell, how they deliver products and services or what alternative functions consumers may expect from existing products. Anticipating social change can be a tremendous way to steal market share from rivals, if change can be spotted and acted upon rapidly.
- Technological change: New technologies can create whole new markets for products that may not have existed a few years earlier. In addition, technology can make new processes possible, allowing new ways to manufacture or deliver products and services.
- Environmental change: For business, perhaps the most important aspect of environmental change to consider is consumers' attitudes to the environment. No doubt many consumers care enough about the environment to factor this into their buying decisions. The trick for businesses is to react to the shifting environmental concerns of their consumers.

Possible effects of change

REVISED

- Effect of change on competitiveness: Much change is focused on the need to improve a firm's ability to compete in the market with its rivals. Following Porter's advice, cost leadership or differentiation are the only two viable long-term routes to improved competitiveness (see Table 17.1).

Table 17.1 Possible changes designed to boost competitiveness through cost leadership and differentiation

Possible changes designed to boost competitiveness through cost leadership	Possible changes to boost competitiveness through differentiation
Finding new suppliers	Redesigning the product
Redesigning the product to reduce the cost of making it	Re-branding the product or service
Boosting capacity utilisation through branch closures	Adding extra features to the product or service

- Effect of change on productivity: In a manufacturing context, change that is focused on processes is likely to have as a fundamental goal the desire to increase productivity, thus reducing unit costs. This may come from **automation** or simply updating the technology already being used. In the service sector productivity improvements are harder to find, with generally more labour-intensive processes meaning that it is improvements in motivation that can make a difference, but perhaps only marginal improvements.

Automation means replacing people with machines, switching from a labour intensive to a capital intensive approach to a task.

- Effect of change on financial performance: Change generally means short-term pain for long-term gain (see Table 17.2).

Table 17.2 Long-term financial improvement and short-term pain

Long-term financial improvement	Short-term pain
Reducing labour costs	Redundancy payments
Lower unit costs	Investment in new production robots
Improved revenue growth	Increased advertising budget
Better profit margins through increased price	Cost of redesigning product

● Effect of change on stakeholders: Change brought on by an external threat or negative internal aspects is likely to have painful impacts on several stakeholder groups. To deal with poor financial performance, cost-cutting may well hurt staff, suppliers and customers.

Key factors in change

Successful change

REVISED ☐

Many change initiatives fail. Key reasons for this include:
● What motivates leaders does not motivate most of their staff.
● Leaders can believe that they themselves are the change.
● Money is the most expensive way to motivate people.
● The change process and the outcome of the change must be fair.

Therefore, to make sure that a change initiative, such as a quality initiative, a new customer service approach or a management reorganisation succeeds managers need to ensure that:
● All staff understand the need for change.
● All staff understand in advance, what the new changed world will be like.
● All staff understand the plan for moving from A to B.

Key issues in the likely success of change are dealt with in more detail below.

Organisational culture

REVISED ☐

Organisational culture affects the success of change in two main ways:
1 Some organisations have cultures that welcome change as a chance to improve, to enhance the way the business strives to achieve its mission. Successfully managing change in these organisations is far easier than in those where the culture is wary of any change to the current way of doing things.
2 Major change can require a change in culture within the organisation. Success comes when change managers find ways to subtly adjust the culture, without trying to radically move it in an opposite direction. Attempts to change culture that try to shift perspective on 'how we do things' through 180 degrees are unlikely to succeed, generating far more resistance to proposed changes.

Size of the organisation

REVISED ☐

Instinctively, many believe that successful change is easier in a small organisation than a large one. Little evidence exists to support this view. Issues faced by managers of small- to medium-sized firms include:
● Smaller firms may have fewer financial resources to help to move the change forward and ensure a smooth transition.

- Often dominated by one person or family, the alternative perspectives required to understand the need for change and method of change may be lacking.
- With a smaller workforce, the range of skills available may be limited, reducing the flexibility of the workforce to adjust to new ways of working.

In larger firms, problems are still likely to exist:
- Senior managers may struggle to get a real feel for the views of their thousands or tens of thousands of staff.
- Different parts of the business may need different approaches from the change programme; these differences can be hard to accommodate in a coherent plan.
- Explaining change to staff can be hard. Even if the CEO can passionately explain the change to her underlings, they are likely to explain the change in a slightly less effective way to their subordinates, and so on, until junior managers struggle to generate any enthusiasm explaining the changes to staff.
- Changing the way the organisation functions creates chances for co-ordination problems as different departments must adjust to different working relationships.

> **Typical mistake**
>
> Avoid lazy assertions that change is easier in a large or small organisation. Use the issues raised here to recognise that managing change is tough in both large and small firms but for different reasons.

Time and speed of change

REVISED

External change factors can lead to a changed environment over an extended period of time, perhaps a decade or two. The result is that a business can manage the internal changes needed more easily, making small adjustments over a period of time that are more easily introduced. When change happens more rapidly, perhaps through the release of a new technology, radical adjustments are required. These disruptive changes force major internal shifts which may well be difficult to pull off effectively for managers.

> **Incremental change** occurs when change is slow and happens in small steps.
>
> **Disruptive change** occurs suddenly, unpredictably, and has major effect on entire markets.

Managing resistance to change

REVISED

Kotter and Schlesinger suggested three successful approaches to managing the resistance to change generally experienced by firms looking to make significant internal changes.

1 Education and communication: Effectively explaining to staff why change is needed, then how the proposed changes will address the problems causing the need to change, can work well. If much resistance to change is caused by staff not understanding exactly why the current status quo is not good enough, enlightening them as to what makes change necessary can break this barrier.

2 Participation and involvement: If unofficial leaders are consulted on how to make changes, allowing them to feed colleagues' views into a change process, the changes are more likely to be successful. The reason is that if people feel they 'own' the changes, they will try hard to make them work, instead of dragging their feet if change is imposed.

3 Negotiation and agreement: Sometimes resistors may need to be 'bribed' to accept changes, perhaps with a pay rise or adjustment to working conditions. Trade unions may often be involved in this process, with the union negotiating on behalf of their members to reach an agreeable solution to the problems preventing successful change.

> **Exam tip**
>
> When trying to explain why a change has not succeeded, if there is little evidence of Kotter and Schlesinger's suggested approaches, perhaps their least favoured method has been used. Kotter and Schlesinger were clear that using force and coercion is the least likely method to successfully overcome resistance to change.

Now test yourself

4 State the three basic challenges that successful change management must meet.
5 Briefly explain why change may be easier to manage in a young technology business than a long-established DIY retailer.
6 State the three main successful ways to overcome resistance to change.

Answers online

Scenario planning

Planning ahead allows better decision-making. This is because:
- time can be taken to analyse possible actions
- resources needed can be secured.

In order to plan ahead, it is necessary to imagine the future. **Scenario planning** looks to harness the benefits of planning ahead. It does so by regularly imagining issues that may affect the business in the future. The most common purpose of scenario planning is in preparing for threats, though it can be used to plan future growth paths.

> **Scenario planning** means visualising possible future situations for a business and then devising plans for how to exploit likely opportunities and minimise the effects of likely threats.

Identifying key risks through risk assessment

The first stage to scenario planning is **risk assessment**. This involves:
- identifying possible major risks or threats faced by the business
- quantifying the possible cost to the business if the event occurs
- attaching a probability to the chance of the risk occurring.

This allows a firm to make a considered judgement as to which risks to prioritise preparing to handle, by combining the magnitude of their effect with the probability of the risk occurring.

Common risks that many businesses identify include:
- Natural disasters: Floods, storms, earthquakes and other natural disasters can cause havoc, especially for manufacturers whose supply chains can be disrupted. Suppliers may be unable to harvest, mine, produce or deliver materials and components. The company's own manufacturing facilities may be disrupted if the disaster strikes locally, while onward distribution can be hampered by damage to infrastructure.
- IT systems failure: The trouble with computerising operations systems, such as ordering and replenishment, automated banking and online sales, is that an extra area of significant vulnerability is added to businesses. From an internal system malfunction, to viruses and malware, to major hacking events, companies whose IT systems fail to function effectively may find the consequences are a failure to deliver their product or service. This is likely to lead to reputational damage.
- Loss of key staff: While more staff than you may expect can be replaced with relative ease, some businesses have 'superstars' who are so special at their role that they may be irreplaceable. Apple designer Jonathan Ive or Ted Baker's Ray Kelvin may be irreplaceable. The business would need to find a way to try to work around their loss, often by bringing in several people who can each do part of what their superstar once did.

> A **risk assessment** is a process used to identify, quantify and decide on the likelihood of negative future events occurring.

> **Typical mistake**
>
> Do not assume that a natural disaster only represents a problem to businesses local to the site of the disaster. Perhaps the most significant business problem of natural disasters is the disruption they can cause to a well-oiled supply chain, potentially messing up the entire chain of production. This could be true even if the disaster occurred on the other side of the world if that is where the supplies come from.

Planning for risk mitigation

The whole point of scenario planning is to give decision-makers time to consider how they might deal with the effects of a major risk occurring. Mitigation involves lessening the impact of the risk, generally through laying out plans in advance showing what will be done if a crisis strikes. The idea of **contingency planning** builds on the benefits of planning in advance which was outlined at the start of this topic.

> **Contingency planning** means preparing plans in advance that can be implemented if a company is hit by a major crisis.

Table 17.3 Examples of risk mitigation planning

Potential crisis	Risk mitigation
Natural disaster	Have relationships in place with alternative suppliers
	Organise potential outsourcing of production
	Figure out alternative transport routes for major items within the supply chain
IT systems failure	Have a back-up system ready to switch on
Loss of key staff	Succession planning

Identifying and training potential replacements for key personnel — **succession planning** — allows a business to gain the benefits of internal recruitment for key positions. Knowing the logic behind existing business strategies can really help a new leader seamlessly take over the helm of a business, in a way that an external replacement would find impossible.

> **Succession planning** means preparing replacements for key personnel in advance of their departure.
>
> **Business continuity** means getting a crisis-hit business back to functioning normality as quickly as possible after a major disruption.

Business continuity relies on a number of components:

- A secure financial position that will enable a firm to spend the cash required to deal with an emergency without threatening its long-term financial stability.
- Clearly defined responsibilities laid out in advance, confirming who will deal with what aspects of possible problems. This allows training to be provided in crisis management to these personnel.
- Effective communication systems prepared, perhaps including special emergency numbers to call for stakeholders who want to contact the business and also methods for the business to contact the media to begin handling the marketing and PR implications of a crisis.

Now test yourself

TESTED

7 What three-step process is involved in risk assessment?
8 List three common risks for which businesses can prepare in advance.
9 Briefly explain why scenario planning is a better alternative than dealing with a crisis once it has happened.

Answers online

> **Exam tip**
>
> Management in scenario planning and crisis management illustrate how there is no one right management style. Preparing for a disaster relies on consultation in order to get a rounded perspective on likely risks and possible mitigating actions. Once a crisis strikes, however, speed of decision-making is key, for which autocratic decision-making is the best way. This illustrates nicely how different styles suit different situations.

Exam practice

1 'The ability to effectively manage change is the key to long-term financial success in all markets in the twenty-first century.' Discuss. (20)
2 Assess the impact of Britain leaving the EU on a UK-based manufacturer which exports 80% of its output to EU markets. (20)

Answers and quick quiz 17 online

ONLINE

Summary

- Internal causes of change include:
  - changes in organisational size
  - poor business performance
  - new ownership
  - transformational leadership.
- External causes of change include:
  - changes in the market
  - political change
  - economic change
  - social change
  - technological change
  - legal change
  - environmental change.
- Change is likely to have significant effects on:
  - competitiveness
  - productivity
  - financial performance.
- Successful change management relies on:
  - all staff understanding the need for change
  - all staff understanding, in advance, what the new changed world will be like
  - all staff understanding the plan for moving from A to B.
- Managing change is influenced by:
  - corporate culture
  - time and speed of change
  - size of the organisation.
- Managing resistance to change is best done through:
  - education and communication
  - participation and involvement or
  - negotiation and agreement.
- Scenario planning starts with risk assessment.
- Scenario planning helps businesses deal with major crises by preparing in advance.
- Preparing in advance means risk mitigation can take place.

Answers and quick quizzes at **www.hoddereducation.co.uk/myrevisionnotes**

18 Globalisation

Growing economies

Economic development is happening: a greater proportion of the world's population is now living above the poverty line. The cause is not redistribution of the world's wealth; it is the development of economies which had previously been relatively inefficient and unproductive. The key drivers behind economic development for the countries that have developed significantly in recent years have been:

● willingness to accept inward investment from multinationals
● more enterprising behaviour from local businesses
● more stable government
● easier access to export markets due to improvements in communication and transport: globalisation.

Growth of UK economy compared to developing economies

REVISED

To contextualise the term developing economies, it is worth comparing growth rates around the world with the economy of the UK. For the past 200 years, economic growth in the UK has averaged 2.25% per year. That means the size of the economy doubles every 30 years or so. Other economies that would be classified as developing economies have recently been experiencing more rapid growth (see Table 18.1).

Table 18.1 Economic growth of selected developing countries

Country	Average annual growth in real GDP per head 1990–2013 (%)
Bangladesh	3.8
China	9.4
India	5.0
Bolivia	1.8
Nigeria	3.4

> **Typical mistake**
>
> Do not underestimate the growth rates of countries such as Bangladesh. As growth rates are cumulative, Bangladesh's growth rate means their economy will double in size every 18 years. This level of economic development makes a significant impact on life in developing economies — just 3.8% per year.

Growing economic power of countries within Asia and Africa

REVISED

The next two topics will cover China, India and Africa in more detail. What needs to be raised here is the broader impact of development in the wider South East Asia. China has acted as something of a hub. Manufacturers in China are looking for suppliers from whom transport costs will not be great. As a result, other Asian economies, notably Vietnam, Indonesia and Cambodia have seen rapid growth in the last two decades. Not only do these countries represent a viable source of supply for China, they are also building their own manufacturing base.

They offer lower cost production than China, where increases in real wages and other costs are putting off some companies looking for cheap production locations.

Implications of economic growth for businesses

REVISED

New export opportunities

As developing countries see incomes rising, UK businesses may discover new markets to which they can export. The UK is particularly good at providing services including:
- fashion design
- design engineering and architecture
- culture (books and entertainment)
- financial and other business services.

As economies reach the latter stages of development, the demand for services grows, meaning that UK exporters should be targeting China right now.

Offshoring production

Many UK manufacturers have closed their UK manufacturing facilities and re-opened them in developing countries. Dyson's move to Malaysia some 20 years ago is an example. The goal is to exploit the lower production costs, boosting profit margins, even if transport costs rise as a result. In recent years, more service businesses have found ways to offshore their work, with jobs as diverse as call-centre enquiry and complaint handling and basic analysis of medical x-rays being shifted to lower cost economies.

> **Offshoring** means moving a business function to another country, generally in order to lower costs.

Increased domestic competition

As countries develop, entrepreneurs, increasingly able to access capital and credit, will start up businesses that may be so successful that they can start exporting to countries such as the UK. This leads to increased competition for UK businesses, both globally and in their own home market.

Implications of economic growth for individuals

REVISED

As an economy grows, the types of jobs done change. Initial stages see those employed in agriculture moving into manufacturing jobs. This shift is both cause and effect of development, as manufacturing processes add more value than primary sector jobs, stimulating growth. However, the change in employment patterns will have a variety of impacts:
- rural to urban migration
- increased need for managers, expanding the middle class
- increasing skill levels within the economy.

In addition, developing economies represent opportunities for entrepreneurs to start up and grow businesses that depend on increasing disposable incomes.

GDP per capita

Rising levels of income per person should be a clear indicator of economic development. If, on average, the people of a country are earning more, they will spend more, creating a virtuous circle. Therefore, watching **GDP per capita** over time provides an excellent indicator as to the level of purely economic development taking place within a country.

Literacy

Although money is a component, there is more to economic development than just rising incomes. Illiteracy rates — the number of people who cannot read or write — should see a dramatic improvement as an economy passes through the stages of economic development.

A literate workforce will be more productive, capable of performing tasks that add more value to production, thus hastening further economic development.

Health

Levels of health should improve as an economy develops. Key ways to measure health focus on the start and end of life. Simply measuring life expectancy gives a good clue as to the health of a nation; economic development leads to healthier living along with better treatment of later life diseases.

Human Development Index (HDI)

The **HDI** combines measures of economic progress with health and education to try to provide a well-rounded picture of a country's economic development. The figures in Table 18.2 illustrate HDI for selected countries.

Table 18.2 HDI ranking and scores, selected countries 2014

Source: Courtesy of the United Nations and reproduced under the Creative Commons License. http://creativecommons.org/licenses/by/3.0/igo/legalcode

	Rank (out of 180 countries)	HDI score (out of 1.0)
Norway	1	0.944
UK	14	0.892
Cuba	44	0.815
Mexico	71	0.756
China	91	0.719
India	135	0.586
Kenya	147	0.535
Nigeria	152	0.504

These figures help to illustrate that, as with any weighted average, there will often be debate over the relative importance of different factors. Cuba has relatively low GDP per capita, but the government prioritises both health and education, perhaps nudging the country higher than expected. Mexico's performance reflects what is not there; crime rates are not included.

> **GDP per capita**, or strictly Gross Domestic Product per head of population at Purchasing Power Parity, needs a little unpicking. Gross Domestic Product (GDP) is a measure of the total output of a country's economy. Dividing this by the population adjusts for countries with much larger populations. Purchasing Power Parity is a further adjustment that factors in differences in the cost of living.

> The **Human Development Index (HDI)** is an attempt to provide a single measure of economic development encompassing income, education and health.

China versus India

China and India matter because of their populations. Both are home to around 1.3 billion people: two countries, each with early 20 times the population of the UK. Neither country has reached the level of development of the UK, however both are catching up. China is further down the path of development than India, but both will be enormous features of the global economy for the foreseeable future.

China?

REVISED

Not only does China have a huge population, it has also undergone an incredible period of economic growth over the past 25 years. A growth rate that has averaged around 10% per year in that period has transformed the country. That 10% growth means the economy doubled in size every eight years or so. The result has been an explosion in markets for a range of consumer goods.

As GDP per head grows in China, and total GDP continues to grow at around 7% per year, China's economy seems likely to wrestle the title of global economic superpower from the USA.

Or India?

REVISED

India has one major advantage over China in the race to be the twenty-second century's dominant economic power: its population. India's population is growing faster than China's. In addition, its population is younger, the result of Chinese attempts to limit their population over the past 20 years.

Which has been growing faster?

REVISED

China. Largely as a result of investment in construction and infrastructure, allied with huge export growth, China is well ahead. The investment has come from two main sources:

- Government spending: This focused first on infrastructure (roads and dams, for power and water). Subsequently the focus has turned to housing, railways, schools and hospitals. Spending on these areas helps to reinforce the growth path on which the Chinese economy continues to travel.
- Foreign Direct Investment: Western companies have been building factories in China for the past 20 years to take advantage of low wage costs.

India has lagged behind on this kind of **fixed capital formation** although its performance has improved in the last ten years or so.

China's export growth was originally built on incredibly low-cost labour. However, as wage rates have risen, China has retained its place as the

> **Fixed capital formation** is the term used to describe investment in long-term assets from roads to buildings.

world's largest exporter of manufactured goods. Notably, these exports contain a huge proportion of high technology products: higher than India, the UK or even the USA.

India's exports are less obvious. Its major export successes have been 'invisibles' such as software engineering and running call centres. Its export advantages over China are:

- English (the global language) is widely spoken.
- The outstanding top end of the education system turns out world class managers and software engineers.

Can India grow rapidly and consistently?

REVISED

The three key weaknesses facing the Indian economy are:

- Poor infrastructure: India's democratic system of government (China is not a democracy) means that if the voters don't agree with a policy, the government cannot ultimately force it on the population. China's government can dictate that over 40% of spending will be on investment in improving infrastructure, notably motorways and utilities such as water and electricity supply. India's road system is far worse than China's and undoubtedly a drag factor on attempts to grow the economy.
- Narrow education system: Despite the very top end of India's education system being excellent, education for the masses is poor, with 29% of the population being unable to read and write. These individuals will not be able to effectively take on higher skilled jobs needed as the economy looks to grow. In China, 96.5% of the population is literate.
- Balance of payments deficit: Compared to China's current account surplus of $290 billion in 2015, India's deficit of $25 billion shows that Indian consumers are buying more imports than foreigners want to buy Indian exports. Without a fall in the value of the rupee (which will prompt even more inflation), this problem will be hard to fix.

A further issue is the tendency of the Indian economy to 'overheat' when industrial production accelerates. This overheating shows as inflation, which the Bank of India curbs by increasing interest rates, thus halting growth. India's inflation rate has been consistently higher than China's.

Can China outstrip America?

REVISED

Wages present the key challenge to China for sustaining its remarkable growth. As the economy develops, wage rates rise. This is already evident in China. The problem is that much of China's growth has come because it offers low wage manufacturing. As multinationals interested only in low wage locations pull out, the question is whether enough higher added value manufacturing can be attracted to sustain the overall growth.

China's GDP has overtaken the US, if measured at PPP. Of course, this adjustment for the cost of living is significant: prices in the US are significantly higher for many items than in China.

As China's economy, especially its manufacturing sector, continues to steam ahead, emissions present a major concern. Environmental legislation and regulation in China leave much to be desired. Although the Chinese government is now taking active steps to ensure better environmental standards, particularly regarding air pollution, scenes of smog in Chinese cities are all too common.

> **Typical mistake**
>
> Although China's GDP will outstrip America's, it is more interesting to ask whether GDP per capita will get close in the foreseeable future. With a population over four times the size of the US, China's economy would need to be over four times the size of America's for that to happen. Make sure you state clearly whether you are discussing total GDP or GDP per capita.

What are the opportunities for British business?

Export opportunities, along with scope to directly invest in China and India, exist. However, British firms have not yet shown significant levels of success in either country, despite the odd one-off hit, such as Jaguar Land Rover in China (though it is Indian-owned). Major stumbling blocks include:

- Short-termism in UK plcs: Cracking such major markets will take time. Shareholders have often shown themselves unwilling to wait.
- Underestimating market potential: Over the past 20 years, during which China has seen such astounding growth, many British commentators have continually predicted that its economy would implode; it's still going strong.
- Ponderous decision-making: Some UK firms have dithered over China and India. Waiting for too long to commit has allowed foreign competitors, notably Germany, to get into China, and to a lesser extent India, and establish themselves securely.

However, two key opportunities do present themselves:

1 India may be a more comfortable market for UK businesses, given the countries' shared past (India was a British colony for some 150 years). Having more cultural similarities than with China, British firms may stand more chance in India, which continues to offer opportunities that have already been missed in China.

2 As China's economy continues to develop, its service sector is likely to show higher growth rates. Of course, many of the UK's global success stories can be found in the service sector. There may still be time for British financial services companies, designers and musicians to establish themselves in a rapidly growing sector of the Chinese economy.

Now test yourself

4 To the nearest 100 million, what is the population of both China and India?
5 State three key drivers of Chinese growth over the past 25 years.
6 State two factors that have held the Indian economy back relative to China.
7 Why do UK businesses have reason to be optimistic about (a) China and (b) India?

Answers online

Business potential in Africa

What is Africa like?

Although some generalities can be made about 'all' African countries, vast differences exist: there is wealth and development (South Africa, Nigeria) as well as great poverty and underdevelopment (Malawi). Meanwhile Africa is frequently split along economic, religious and social lines, between North Africa (Egypt, Tunisia, etc.) and sub-Saharan Africa.

The focus of this topic is mainly sub-Saharan Africa. North African countries are further along the path to development, and represent a

Typical mistake

Africa is a continent. Never refer to it as a country.

smaller population than the part of the continent that lies south of the Sahara desert. Some generalities include:

● It is less economically developed than most other parts of the world.
● Huge reserves of natural resources are yet to be exploited.
● There are difficulties in maintaining reliable stable government (not true for all countries).
● Corruption represents a significant disincentive to foreign investment.

However, other, less 'known' common threads are developing:

● Many countries are experiencing strong economic growth around the 5% per year mark.
● There is major FDI especially from China and Japan.
● There is a broad improvement in governance, with fewer civil wars and a slow growth in democracy.

Opportunities for business in Africa

REVISED

In Africa's richest nations, especially oil-rich Nigeria, there is tremendous wealth in the very top few per cent of the population. This wealth can be attracted by British retailers, hotels and public schools and, perhaps in the future, a broader range of high-end UK businesses.

As countries like Nigeria lead the continent in economic development, middle classes will emerge. Indeed, soft drinks sales in Nigeria and Cameroon have rocketed in recent years as shown in Figure 18.1.

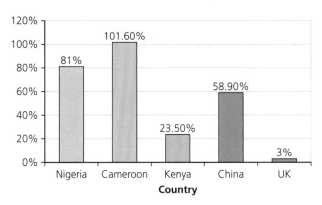

Figure 18.1 Percentage increase in soft drinks sales volume 2009–2014

Source: Euromonitor 2015

Consumer goods markets are beginning to mature, with international brands starting to make their mark. Britain's Unilever has made strong inroads into the continent. Other multinationals to have invested directly in Africa in a major way are Wal–Mart and Microsoft.

Problems doing business in Africa

REVISED

Corruption

Corruption is a problem in most African countries (similarly in many less economically developed countries globally). Its prevalence offers businesses two major headaches:

1 Costs can rise as local or national officials expect payment to allow a firm to receive the necessary licences and permissions to do business.
2 Companies that value CSR cannot condone conducting business in a corrupt manner.

Poor infrastructure

Issues relating to infrastructure include substandard:
- electricity supply
- road networks
- rail networks
- waste disposal facilities.

Investor concern about stability

Health epidemics, government collapse and inconsistent application of the rule of law create instability in many African nations. Even the mighty Nigeria has not managed to effectively deal with terrorist insurgents in the northeast of the country. These concerns over stability represent a major obstacle to investment — which by its nature takes time to pay back — during which investors are more likely to meet major disruption.

> **Exam tip**
>
> If exploring problems of investing in Africa, consider the length of time most major investments take to pay off: years rather than months. The continent is changing so rapidly, this brings uncertainty, which investors hate. Meanwhile, it is often not a single problem, but instead several problematic factors working together.

> ### Now test yourself   TESTED ☐
>
> 8 Which two countries have already made significant investment in many sub-Saharan African countries?
> 9 List three major problems of doing business in Africa.
>
> Answers online

International trade and business growth

The logic behind foreign trade: international specialisation   REVISED ☐

Trade is necessary because economic history has taught the world that if each country specialises in the things they do best, then trades with others to get products and services they do not produce domestically, the global economy is more productive as a whole.

Distinguishing between imports and exports   REVISED ☐

Imports

Britain imports goods and services worth over £40 billion per year. These imports may be:
- foreign brands that add to the choice available to UK consumers
- goods or services that Britain no longer mass produces
- materials and components used by British businesses, especially manufacturers, which may be produced far more cheaply, perhaps at better quality, abroad
- services, such as tourism, involve importing services from foreign hotels.

> **Imports** are products and services produced abroad and consumed domestically.

> **Exports** are products and services that are produced domestically and consumed overseas.

Exports

Exporting offers businesses the chance to increase sales, to achieve growth which enables them to enjoy economies of scale. Another major reason for exporting is to avoid reliance on the domestic market. If a firm's home economy enters recession, there may be a drastic fall in sales. If the firm can export to a country unaffected by recession, the damage caused by the fall in domestic sales is less significant.

> **Exam tip**
>
> Remember that for imports, goods and services arrive and cash flows out of the UK. For exports, it is goods and services that flow out and cash that flows in to the UK.

The link between business specialisation and competitive advantage

REVISED

Business specialisation

Choosing to produce only one product, or products for a single market, is a common strategy used by businesses. Porter's focused differentiation or focused cost leadership are examples of strategies based on specialisation.

How specialisation can boost efficiency

For a business choosing to produce just one product, fewer machines will be needed than by a multi-product firm. Therefore the cost associated with purchasing or funding those machines will be lower. There is a similar effect with training costs pushing down total costs; there is no need to provide training to help multi-skill staff working in a single product firm. F.W. Taylor believed that specialisation enhanced efficiency on the basis that 'practice makes perfect'. An employee who repeats one simple task over and over gets quicker and quicker at that task, boosting the efficiency of the process in which they are involved.

How efficiency gains created by specialisation can create competitive advantage

Increased efficiency has one simple but substantial benefit: lower unit costs. If specialisation can be used to lower unit costs, a business finds itself with an ideal choice of two attractive options:

1 Lower selling price by the same amount as unit costs have been reduced. This preserves the profit margin on each unit, but lowering prices boosts competitiveness of the business within its market, thus boosting sales.
2 Alternatively, a company may simply decide not to adjust prices or its price competitiveness and settle for a higher profit margin on every unit it sells as a result of lower unit costs.

> **Exam tip**
>
> Perhaps the key determinant of which route to choose is price elasticity. For a firm selling a price elastic product, the former option should lead to a significant increase in sales, boosting total revenues. For a company whose product is price inelastic, cutting price makes no sense, since the increase in unit sales will be relatively small.

Foreign Direct Investment (FDI) and business growth

REVISED

Outward **Foreign Direct Investment (FDI)** occurs when a British business buys assets abroad. Typically this may involve building production facilities or buying retail outlets, although takeovers of foreign businesses are also considered as outward FDI. FDI can also flow inwards. When foreign companies buy British assets, buying property or building factories in the UK, money flows in to Britain. It is important to note that subsequent earnings from these investments will flow out of the UK, so rent on a foreign-owned UK property leaves the UK.

> **Foreign Direct Investment (FDI)** occurs when a business purchases non-current assets in another country.

Outward FDI offers businesses opportunities to grow abroad. The key benefits of actual FDI, rather than simply exporting products made in the UK, include:

● Avoiding problems involved in exporting
● Avoiding transport costs
● Avoiding trade barriers
● Access to natural resources
● Lower operating costs.

> **Typical mistake**
>
> Too many simplistic responses to questions about the benefits of FDI never make it past lower operating costs. Note that several other benefits exist, some of which may be of particular relevance in the context provided.

10 Why does international specialisation create the need for countries to trade with one another?
11 When you pay for a hotel room in Ayia Napa for a week, does that count as an export or an import for the UK?
12 List three potential benefits of FDI instead of exporting domestically produced products.

Answers online

Factors contributing to increased globalisation

It is the growth in international trade that best illustrates the concept of globalisation. Figure 18.2 shows 25 years of strong growth, then raises the interesting question of whether the pace of globalisation has slowed, especially with the US moving towards a more **isolationist** stance.

> **Globalisation** is the trend towards closer ties between economies and businesses within the global economy.
>
> **Isolationism** refers to a nation whose trade policies are designed to put the interests of domestic businesses first by imposing trade barriers to hamper imports.

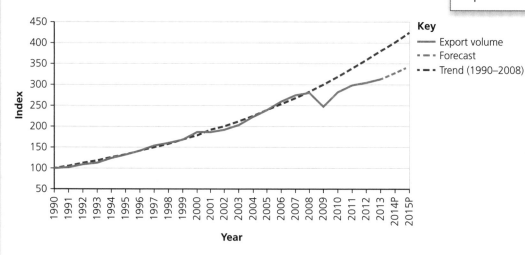

Figure 18.2 The volume of world merchandise exports, 1990–2015 (index 1990 = 100)

Source: WTO

Trade liberalisation   REVISED ☐

Trade liberalisation involves removing trade barriers, such as:
● Tariffs: This is a tax imposed on imports that raises the price of imported products, aiding sales of domestic rivals.
● Quotas: These are physical limits on the quantity of a type of good that can be imported in a year. Once the limit is reached, consumers must buy from domestic producers.
● Regulations: Rules, paperwork and systems can be put in place to make it harder for imports to enter a country.

Liberalisation will generally follow a new trade agreement between two countries, on the basis that both remove trade barriers between one another.

Table 18.3 Opportunities and threats caused by trade liberalisation

Opportunities from trade liberalisation	Threats caused by trade liberalisation
Companies that rely on imported materials and components will enjoy lower costs, enabling them to reduce prices to compete with cheaper imported rivals	Allowing imports into a domestic market does increase competition for domestic firms. The most efficient should survive; those who could only survive due to the barriers will lose that protection and possibly face closure
Due to the bilateral nature of trade agreements, liberalisation can lead to increased export opportunities with the removal of barriers in the other direction	

Political change

REVISED

The key political change prompting the wave of globalisation shown above is political change in China. Following the death of Chairman Mao, the 1980s and 1990s saw a move away from hard-line communism, with private ownership of business allowed. Then, in 2001, China joined the WTO (World Trade Organization), giving it access to rich western markets and offering the country the chance to enjoy an amazing export-led boom.

Britain's decision to leave the EU, along with the election of Donald Trump as US president during 2016, offer hints that political changes may now slow down the march of globalisation.

Reduced cost of transport and communication

REVISED

The extra costs involved in moving goods around the world can prevent trade by lowering profit margins. However, the last 50 years have seen significant reductions in the cost of transport for three main reasons:
1 Oil prices have remained stable or fallen, contrary to fears that the supply of oil may run low, driving costs up.
2 Technological developments have led to the development of more efficient engines, reducing fuel consumption and therefore cost.
3 Technology has also enabled the building of bigger trains, boats and planes which allow container economies of scale.

Communication's major revolution has been the arrival of the internet as a technology. Hard as it may be to imagine a world before the internet (or email), organising trade through phone lines and possibly fax machines lacked efficiency. Now, linked with the hardware involved, especially high capacity fibre-optic cable, immediate worldwide communication of complex data is normal.

Increased significance of transnational corporations

REVISED

Global giants, selling in hundreds of markets, seek growth by entering new markets in order to boost sales year by year and keep shareholders happy. Whenever a transnational corporation enters a new market, local businesses face an incredibly powerful new competitor, one that will benefit from enormous economies of scale. These, of course, are companies that will be transferring resources and products from one country to another, boosting international trade. In addition, when major global transnationals are able to sell their product in so many markets, consumer choice from nation to nation declines: different national markets become less different.

Increased investment

REVISED

Communication and trade liberalisation have both driven increased trans-border capital flows. As financial markets are more willing to invest capital in businesses based elsewhere in the world, so the world seems to become a smaller place. The downside to this globalisation of financial markets is the interconnectedness which has evolved. With banks in one country investing elsewhere in the world, and lending to foreign customers, a financial crisis in one part of the world can spread rapidly throughout the whole global financial system, as seen in 2008.

Migration

REVISED

Many people who migrate to other countries do so for economic reasons. The vast majority of these migrants tend to share two key characteristics:
1 They are proactive and determined, willing to uproot and move to an entirely new country to work and live.
2 They tend to be relatively well-educated.

These traits help to explain why increased migration can stimulate economic growth.

> **Typical mistake**
>
> There is a huge amount of well-researched evidence to show that inward migration has a strong positive effect on the success of UK businesses.

Growth of the global labour force

REVISED

Companies have managed to reduce their labour costs by seeing the market for labour as global, rather than local or national. Many UK businesses have offshored production in order to benefit from cheaper labour elsewhere in the world. Meanwhile, other UK businesses facing shortages of skilled staff have recognised the benefits of recruiting from abroad in order to fill jobs that would otherwise have to be offshored, or left undone — losing sales.

Structural change

REVISED

All economies that experience economic development see structural change, with reduced reliance on agriculture as economic activity shifts first to manufacturing, and then into services. Major economies that have experienced rapid development in the past 40 years have increasingly specialised in order to improve their international competitiveness. They have been able to find export markets that have enabled the acceleration of development and the related trade to sustain the rise of globalisation.

Now test yourself

TESTED

13 State three barriers to trade that a government can use to hamper imports.
14 Briefly explain two potential benefits to domestic businesses of agreements to liberalise trade.
15 List three technological developments that have encouraged globalisation.

Answers online

Protectionism

> **Protectionism** means giving preference to domestic producers by making it harder for foreign companies to export to your country.

The goal of **protectionism** is to increasing a nation's prosperity by increasing the amount exported and/or decreasing the amount imported to the country. It is the opposite of free trade. Protectionism usually features the use of trade barriers to make it harder for foreign firms to import their goods. The three major forms of trade barrier are:

- tariffs
- quotas
- legislation and regulation.

Tariffs

REVISED

Imposing a tax on a product being imported automatically reduces its competitiveness, as the **tariff** will drive up the price. This reduces the ability of the product to compete with domestically produced rivals.

> A **tariff** is a tax imposed on an imported product to allow it to enter a country.

The two main scenarios in which governments tend to use tariffs are:

1 To protect a declining industry
2 To protect 'infant' industries.

Table 18.4 Benefits and drawbacks of tariffs

Benefits of tariffs	Drawbacks of tariffs
As tariffs help firms to survive, they protect jobs of firms whose rivals are being taxed	Imposing tariffs pushes up prices, reducing consumers' ability to buy the product, reducing standards of living
Tariffs also indirectly protect the other businesses that rely on these firms for trade: suppliers and local firms that would suffer if unemployment rose	Tariffs help inefficient firms to survive, potentially harming competitiveness. Without tariffs there is far greater incentive for these firms to improve what they do
Tariffs raise tax revenues, allowing governments to increase spending on public services	

Import quotas

REVISED

The effects of **quotas** are almost identical to tariffs. The mechanism differs, since instead of directly manipulating the price of imports, this control happens indirectly, through the market mechanism.

> A **quota** is a physical limit on the volume of a product that can be imported in a year. Once the quota is used, only domestically produced goods will be available.

Quotas are designed to protect and encourage domestic producers. If imports are limited, this is likely to push prices up. This should encourage domestic producers to increase the amount they are willing to supply. In addition, quotas are likely to improve the current account of a country's balance of payments.

Table 18.5 Benefits and drawbacks of quotas

Benefits of quotas	Drawbacks of quotas
Domestic firms face less competition, improving their competitiveness. This improves profit for shareholders and job security for workers	No extra tax revenue is gained by the government
Preventing unemployment theoretically reduces government spending on benefits	They push up prices domestically for consumers

Government legislation

REVISED

Legislation relating to consumer protection and environmental protection can act as a barrier to imports. If a government imposes new, stronger standards for safety or emissions in certain industries, importers may find their products suddenly become illegal. This in turn necessitates design change, which takes a significant period of time, before importing can resume.

In trading blocs, such as the EU, where one goal is the harmonisation of laws within the bloc, these problems are less likely since the same standards apply across the whole trading bloc.

Domestic subsidies   REVISED

Instead of acting to make importing harder, domestic subsidies are a protectionist measure that looks to actively support domestic firms. The government pays a figure, usually per unit of output, to sustain firms that would otherwise be unable to compete.

The **subsidy** can be thought of as reducing the unit costs by the amount of the subsidy, thus boosting margins, or allowing companies to cut their selling price. Boosting margins may keep some businesses operating in markets from which they would otherwise withdraw, protecting jobs and domestic supply of that product.

The other consequence is to make it easier to export these products, as with a lower selling price they may be more price competitive in foreign markets.

> A **subsidy** is a payment made by government to a business producing a certain product or located in a particular area that the government wishes to support.

Table 18.6 **Benefits and drawbacks of paying subsidies**

Benefits of paying subsidies	Drawbacks of paying subsidies
Subsidies in effect stimulate demand, perhaps allowing struggling businesses to boost order books, allowing investment in more efficient production	Artificially inflating profit margins of inefficient businesses can prevent them pushing for efficiency gains that would allow them to compete without the subsidies
Subsidies have a positive effect on the balance of payments by reducing imports and boosting exports from firms receiving the subsidies	Subsidies must be funded, meaning the government must increase taxation — in a sense punishing firms in industries where no subsidies are provided

Exam tip

The USA is clearly heading towards a protectionist outlook under the presidency of Donald Trump. This gives you a great opportunity to bring in examples from your reading of business news stories to help illustrate answers to questions on protectionism with current examples.

Now test yourself   TESTED

16 In what two types of industry are governments most likely to use tariffs?
17 State one protectionist measure designed to cut imports and one that also stimulates exports.
18 List three stakeholder groups who would support paying subsidies to a struggling manufacturer.

Answers online

Trading blocs

The latter half of the twentieth century saw a move away from protectionism in favour of free trade. One result has been the creation of a number of major **trading blocs** allowing free trade between member states.

In addition to free trade, some trading blocs have, or are working towards:

- harmonisation of laws (all members have the same legal standards governing business operations)
- free movement of labour.

> A **trading bloc** is a group of countries that sign up to free trade between them, protected by a tariff wall against imports from outside.

The attractions of trading blocs

REVISED

Despite Britain's decision to leave the EU trading bloc, attractions of belonging to a trading bloc remain. These include:

- Harmonisation of laws allows one product to be made that meets legal requirements in all member countries. This allows companies to benefit from economies of scale.
- Countries working together within a trading bloc have more power than individual nations to stand up to non-member countries using techniques such as **dumping**.
- Competing in a larger 'home' market incentivises the boosting of efficiency for firms in member states.

> **Dumping** is a term used to describe the practice of selling off excess production in a foreign market at an exceptionally low price, which destroys sales for local producers. China is frequently accused of dumping excess products, such as steel, elsewhere in the world.

Expansion of trading blocs

REVISED

Table 18.7 shows a selection of the biggest trading blocs around the world.

Table 18.7 Expansion of trading blocs

	Starting date	Main members	Total GDP 2014 (bn)	Total population 2014 (m)
European Union (EU)	1958	Germany, France, UK (28 in total)	$16,000	515
Association of South-East Asian Nations (ASEAN)	1967	Indonesia, Thailand, Vietnam (10 in total)	$2,600	625
MERCOSUR (Spanish for South American Common Market)	1991	Brazil, Argentina, Uruguay (6 in total)	$3,600	300
North American Free Trade Association (NAFTA)	1994	USA, Canada and Mexico (3 in total)	$21,000	480
East African Community (EAC)	2000	Kenya, Tanzania (5 in total)	£110	150

The EU and the single market

Although Britain is currently in the process of leaving the EU, the post-Brexit EU will still have 27 members and a total population of around 445 million consumers. These consumers, in global terms, are relatively affluent. The EU's single market remains an incredibly attractive market for EU companies to access. This explains why probably the critical aspect of Brexit negotiations is the terms of access to the EU's single market for British firms.

What the EU has achieved, which other trading blocs have yet to do, is to introduce a single currency (though not among all members). It is perhaps here that EU supporters may have gone too far.

The ASEAN trading bloc

The ten full members of ASEAN (see Table 18.8) operate in an Asia dominated by the economic success of China, Japan and South Korea. ASEAN's members try to work constructively alongside these giant neighbours. After all, much of ASEAN's success has been in feeding the might of their bigger neighbours' manufacturing machines.

Table 18.8 ASEAN's full member states

ASEAN's full member states				
Brunei	Cambodia	Myanmar (Burma)	Laos	Malaysia
Thailand	Vietnam	Philippines	Indonesia	Singapore

NAFTA trading bloc

With only three members — Canada, Mexico and the USA — NAFTA is a tense trading bloc. At the heart of the tension is low-cost Mexico's ability to attract companies looking for a low-cost manufacturing base from which they can import freely to the world's largest domestic market: the USA. Resentment of this aspect of NAFTA's existence was probably the underpinning reason behind the election of Donald Trump to the US presidency in 2016. The next few years will be interesting for NAFTA.

Impact on businesses of trading blocs

> **Typical mistake**
>
> A mistake made by some students and most campaigners in the Brexit referendum is to try to generalise about the impact of trading bloc membership on all businesses in a country. Factors such as whether they import supplies, export finished products, whether they are a manufacturer or service provider, or whether suitably skilled staff are available domestically mean that generalisation about the positivity of trading bloc membership should never be made.

> **Exam tip**
>
> With the Trump administration in the USA looking to build a wall on the US–Mexican border, the very existence of NAFTA may be in question between 2017 and 2021, when the next US election is due. Watch the news to monitor what is happening in this major current business issue.

It is impossible to generalise about whether membership of a trading bloc is overall beneficial or negative to businesses in any country. Different industries will benefit more from free trade than others. In general, it tends to be manufacturing firms that benefit more than others from membership of a trading bloc. However, even within an economic sector, the balance of benefits to drawbacks can vary widely. The key impacts on business of being located in a country within a trading bloc are summarised in Table 18.9.

Table 18.9 Advantages and drawbacks of trading blocs to businesses

Advantages of trading blocs	Drawbacks of trading blocs
● Free movement of goods between members gives the potential to create a large 'single market'	● Competition increases due to freer trade, so those with monopoly power may find it competed away
● External tariff walls insulate the business from competition from another part of the world	● To create a single market, new rules and regulations may be agreed, including minimum wage rates
● As trade grows between neighbours, it becomes economic (and necessary) for governments to provide infrastructure support	● The availability of easily accessed neighbouring markets may reduce enterprise in relation to distant but dynamic ones such as China
● The advantages become much greater if there is free movement of labour as well as free movement of goods	● Within a geographically proximate bloc, there may be common factors that together become common problems, e.g. low commodity prices

Now test yourself

TESTED

19 State three major trading blocs and in which part of the world they can be found.
20 Briefly explain how being based in a free trade area helps to make economies of scale available.
21 State two possible features of a trading bloc apart from free movement of goods and services.

Answers online

Exam practice

Keith Glazebrook, owner of Lamination Station Ltd, a successful chain of high street printing and copying stores throughout the UK, decided that the time was right for expansion. With contacts all over the world, Keith, an entrepreneur who valued networking, had figured out that, in order to grow his business, he wanted to enter a rapidly growing market. He had narrowed down his choices to just two potential markets: India and Kenya. His research had discovered the following information:

	India	Kenya
Population (million 2014)	1,262	46
GDP per capita at PPP	$5,900	$3,100
Economic growth % change 2014	7.2%	5.3%
% of GDP from agriculture	29.3%	17.9%
% of population working in agriculture	75%	49%
Adult literacy (as % of population)	71.2%	78%

Keith knew that much of his custom would come from people who would have no copying or printing facilities at home. Some trade would come from entrepreneurs looking to produce promotional materials. Much of the rest would come from normal householders looking to copy legal or other important documents. In order to grow his business, Keith wanted to find the market with the most growth potential. With healthy profits from his UK operations, he is willing to wait for his investment to pay off, but his goal is to double the size of his business in the next 15 years.

1 (a) Explain two potential problems that Keith may face doing business in either country. (6)
  (b) The current Indian government have launched a number of protectionist measures. Explain two possible protectionist measures and the effect they may have on Keith if he opens branches in India. (6)
  (c) Should Keith choose to expand to India or Kenya? Justify your decision. (12)

2 'An increasing trend to protectionism, led by Donald Trump's US Government, will inevitably lead to negative consequences for a UK business that exports 50% of its output to the US.' To what extent do you agree? (20)

Answers and quick quiz 18 online

ONLINE

Summary

- Economic growth can be measured in several ways:
  - GDP per capita at PPP
  - literacy
  - health
  - HDI.
- Major economic growth has been evident in several countries within Asia and Africa in the last 20–30 years.
- China is now arguably the world's largest, or at least second largest, economy.
- China and India have roughly similarly sized populations, and thus markets.
- China has grown more rapidly than India for the last 25 years.
- China is more developed as an economy than India.
- Factors holding India back include:
  - poor infrastructure
  - narrow education system
  - balance of payments deficit.
- Africa may be the last major opportunity for massive growth available to multinationals.
- Problems doing business in Africa include:
  - corruption
  - poor infrastructure
  - lack of stability.
- International trade allows international specialisation.

- International trade consists of:
  - imports
  - exports
  - foreign direct investment (FDI).
- Eight major factors have contributed to increased globalisation in the last 30–40 years:
  - trade liberalisation
  - political change
  - reduced cost of transport and communication
  - increased significance of transnational corporations
  - increased investment flows
  - migration
  - growth of global labour force
  - structural change.
- Protectionism is the opposite of free trade.
- Protectionist measures include:
  - tariffs
  - quotas
  - government legislation and regulations
  - domestic subsidies.
- Protectionism seeks to take action to discourage imports and encourage exports.
- Major global trading blocs include NAFTA, EU, ASEAN.
- Membership of a trading bloc allows significant benefits to businesses located within them, especially a much larger market to sell to without any barriers to trade.

Answers and quick quizzes at **www.hoddereducation.co.uk/myrevisionnotes**

19 Global markets and business expansion

Conditions that prompt trade

Trade between businesses in different countries, or a business in one country and consumers in another, tends to be prompted by one or more of a number of common factors. These factors can be grouped into two categories:

1 Push factors: These are reasons driving a firm away from its domestic market.
2 Pull factors: These are reasons to attract a business to a new foreign market.

Although the desire to trade internationally is often driven by a corporate objective of growth, other goals may be survival, cost minimisation or reduction of risk.

Push factors

Reasons why a firm may wish to leave its domestic market, or at least remove a sole reliance on it, include:

Saturated markets

Where a firm is keen to grow, new customers must be sought. If everyone in a domestic market that wants the product has already bought it, especially in the case of consumer durables such as TVs, growth can only come in one of two ways:

1 Widen the range of products being sold
2 Sell to new markets.

For a business that does not feel it has the talent or assets to broaden its product range, new markets must be found.

> **Exam tip**
>
> Don't forget to use Ansoff's Matrix when assessing the risk and causes of risk involved in entering a new international market. The lack of understanding of the market is what causes this strategy to be higher risk than simple market penetration.

Competition

Particularly if a giant new competitor enters a market, existing businesses may recognise that in the long term, their survival lies in fleeing the competition. A huge new player entering a market could call upon tremendous financial and distributive strengths to quickly eliminate smaller rivals. Those smaller rivals may decide to leave the market and seek their fortune in new international markets as a route to survival.

Extending product life cycle

As a product nears the decline phase of its life cycle, entering new international markets may represent a viable extension strategy. Sustaining a high level of sales ensures the product continues to generate a positive cash flow which can be invested in new product development. In some cases, entering new markets may be a way of prolonging the growth stage of the life cycle.

Pull factors

REVISED

The pull factors are features of international trade which operate as a force attracting a business into foreign markets.

Economies of scale

The opportunity to boost unit sales through successfully entering new international markets brings with it the opportunity to benefit from economies of scale. These will be accentuated if production is concentrated in a few locations globally. Not only will purchasing economies of scale be likely, but also managerial and technical economies of scale may arise. With economies of scale comes a reduction in unit costs, boosting profit margins.

Possibility of offshoring and outsourcing

The lure of lower costs is great, especially when the differentials between the costs of land, labour and support services are so great between the UK and many developing economies. Therefore, this opportunity to significantly reduce costs can act as a very strong pull factor for UK-based businesses to shift production abroad.

Risk spreading

Selling in only one country is a little like putting all your eggs in one basket. Entering more international markets is an effective way of spreading risk. If sales fail in one country, there are other markets where sales may remain stable. Although the process of entering a new market may carry an element of risk, as Ansoff pointed out, if that entry is successful, the overall risk faced by the business is reduced.

> **Exam tip**
>
> Generally speaking, push factors are threats which drive a business to trade internationally, while pull factors are more likely to be opportunities a business recognises as being involved in trading internationally.

> **Offshoring** means moving one or more business functions to a foreign country, usually to take advantage of lower labour costs.
>
> **Outsourcing** means contracting another business to perform a business function on your behalf. Frequently that function will be production, often performed by a business located in a lower cost country.

Now test yourself

TESTED

1 State three pull factors encouraging international trade.
2 List three push factors that encourage international trade.
3 List three possible corporate objectives that may be behind a business's decision to begin to trade internationally.

Answers online

> **Typical mistake**
>
> Do not use the terms outsourcing and offshoring interchangeably. While they may both be actions designed to reduce costs, they are distinctly different and examiners expect to see the best students use terminology with accuracy.

Assessment of a country as a market

Once a business has decided to pursue a strategy involving overseas expansion, it must choose carefully which markets to enter. This decision-making process will focus on a range of factors that determine the attractiveness of a market.

Market attractiveness

REVISED

Assessing a market's attractiveness should be done in the most objective manner possible. The result is that companies considering overseas expansion are likely to set a range of criteria that will apply across potential markets. The country that scores best when assessed against all the criteria will be chosen as the market most likely to offer success.

Common criteria are shown in Table 19.1.

Table 19.1 Common factors determining market attractiveness

Common factors determining market attractiveness		
Levels of disposable income	Growth of disposable income	Ease of doing business
Quality of infrastructure	Political stability	Exchange rates

Levels and growth of disposable income

REVISED

The level of **disposable income** is a key reflection of standards of living in a country. Thus, low disposable income countries will be unattractive markets for companies selling expensive luxuries such as VR headsets. However, it is not only the level of disposable income that matters, it is the direction and size of changes in disposable income that suggest what the future holds.

Growing levels of disposable income represent an opportunity for business. As people earn more, they spend more. In addition, they spend differently. As disposable incomes rise, new niche markets emerge, satisfying consumer wants rather than needs. Getting into these niches early can be a major step to success in a new country.

Countries with growing levels of disposable income represent opportunities to firms looking to expand abroad. The crucial judgement for a business looking to enter these markets is timing. Enter too early and there may not be a large enough market to break even. Enter too late and rivals may have already established brand loyalties.

> **Disposable income** is the money a household has available to spend from income after income tax has been deducted.

Ease of doing business

REVISED

The World Bank (among others), regularly produces statistics on the ease of doing business in different countries. The way 'ease of doing business' is measured is typically via an assessment of the time taken for many common business activities such as:

- days to start a business
- days to wait for a construction permit
- days to get electricity
- total tax rate as a % of profit
- days to import an item
- days to enforce a contract.

Quality of infrastructure

REVISED

Infrastructure describes the services needed to make modern life function, including:

- roads
- railways
- running water
- reliable electricity
- WiFi and broadband connection.

Transport networks and basic services matter for businesses looking to enter a market. The speed with which goods can be transported has a major operational impact, while for service providers as well as manufacturers, basic utilities are crucial.

Political stability

The term 'political stability' covers issues such as:

- policy instability
- tax regulations
- labour regulations
- government bureaucracy
- corruption.

The level of political stability is vital in the planning process for any business. The more stable a potential market, the more confident a business will feel about forecasts of its future performance in that market. Some firms will favour stability over other factors, while more entrepreneurial businesses may be willing to accept the risks involved in instability if other factors make a market attractive.

Exchange rates

Exchange rates fluctuate, meaning that any firm that expects them to remain stable is being naïve. Although some currencies may gain or lose strength in the long term, perhaps dependent upon long-term economic performance, the volatility of exchange rates makes them seem a factor that is hard to assess usefully. Indeed, exchange rates are unlikely to affect a decision as to whether to enter a new market. They will, however, be an important consideration in deciding when to enter a new market.

Now test yourself

TESTED

4 For what type of products might levels of disposable income be a more important factor than growth in disposable income?
5 State three aspects considered when measuring the ease of doing business in a new market.
6 List three components of infrastructure required by modern businesses.

Answers online

Assessment of a country as a production location

As a company decides to expand, or shift production to another country, several factors will be considered. For UK businesses moving abroad, costs of production will play a key part in the decision. However, several other factors that affect costs directly or indirectly will also play a part.

Costs of production

REVISED

Given the fact that cost is often the key driver behind decisions to move production to a new country, the costs of production in that country will be assessed carefully. Table 19.2 shows costs of manufacturing in selected countries relative to the USA. Perhaps most notable is the rise in the costs of manufacturing in China between 2004 and 2014.

Table 19.2 Boston Consulting Group data on manufacturing costs in selected countries relative to the cost of manufacturing in the USA

Source: www.bcgperspectives.com

Country	Indexed manufacturing costs 2004 (USA = 100)	Indexed manufacturing costs 2014 (USA = 100)
China	86.5	95.6
Germany	117.4	121.1
Japan	107.2	111
UK	107.4	108.7
Indonesia	82.3	83.1
India	86.8	87.2
Mexico	92.1	91.5

The assumed reason for lower costs in many countries is lower wage costs. However, this factor can be overstated. The key is to consider how **labour intensive** the production process is. For many products, even in a lower cost country, production will be **capital intensive**. This is shown well by the breakdown in Jaguar Land Rover's costs in Figure 19.1.

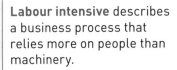

Labour intensive describes a business process that relies more on people than machinery.

Capital intensive describes a business process that relies more on machinery than people.

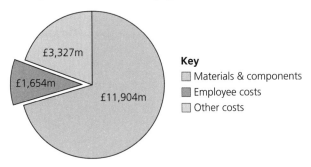

Key
- ☐ Materials & components
- ▨ Employee costs
- ☐ Other costs

£3,327m
£1,654m
£11,904m

Figure 19.1 Jaguar Land Rover cost breakdown 2014

Source: JLR accounts; all figures in £ms; total costs: £16,885m

Often the cost differential will be down to the ability to source materials and components more cheaply abroad, along with lower costs of land and business services.

Skills and availability of workforce

REVISED

Producing abroad needs a skilled, or at least semi-skilled, workforce. The skills required to operate machinery may not be available in many less economically developed locations. In addition, to function in a modern manufacturing plant, literacy will be an important skill. Topic 25 showed literacy to be an important indicator of the level of development of an economy. Without a strong education system to provide literate staff with the necessary skills, some countries will struggle to be seen as attractive locations for production.

Infrastructure

REVISED

As for firms assessing the attractiveness of a new country as a market (Topic 33), so infrastructure will be an important consideration for those looking for a production base. Transport and utilities must be up to scratch for a modern manufacturing facility to be able to reliably service the markets it is designed to serve. This explains why some major multinationals will take responsibility for improving local infrastructure in a location they choose, as well as building their own production facilities.

Location in a trading bloc
REVISED

Often a vital pull factor for a location will be its presence within a trading bloc. When Britain was still a member of the EU, it became an extremely attractive manufacturing base for non-European firms. The reason was that for a company such as Toyota, seeking to serve the European market, building their cars in the UK meant that they avoided tariffs that would have been charged on cars imported from Japan, or indeed anywhere outside the EU.

> **Exam tip**
>
> With the UK outside the EU, there is no doubt that its attractiveness as a production location for global businesses will be reduced. Without tariff-free access to the single market, foreign direct investment flows may fall considerably. It is well worth monitoring the terms of Brexit that will be thrashed out between 2017 and 2019 to see whether the UK can find a way to maintain tariff-free access to the single European market.

Government incentives
REVISED

National governments may well be keen to attract foreign companies to set up production facilities in their country. Reasons for this include:
- job creation
- extra tax revenues
- a boost for local suppliers
- increasing skill levels among local labour force
- potential for a positive impact on the balance of payments.

In order to attract businesses to their country, governments will use a variety of possible incentives, such as:
- grants to help purchase land and machinery
- tax breaks
- investment in local infrastructure
- investment in local training.

Ease of doing business
REVISED

As explained in Topic 33, a business planning to operate in a new country will need to assess how much regulation, government interference and bureaucratic inefficiency it may suffer from. Typical issues to consider include:
- days to start a business
- days to wait for a construction permit
- days to get electricity
- total tax rate as a % of profit
- days to import an item
- days to enforce a contract.

Political stability
REVISED

As well as assessing a country as a potential market, it will also need to be assessed as a production location. Businesses expect to be able to plan for the future, something which is made almost impossible if governments change frequently and make drastic policy changes as a result. This factor is likely to be more important when assessing a country as a manufacturing base, rather than simply a market to sell to. This is because the level of investment needed to start producing is likely to be higher, thus these investments will take longer to pay back and generate a positive return on investment.

Natural resources

It is likely that the availability of natural resources will play a key role in attractiveness for businesses further back along the supply chain. Generally, companies that initially process raw materials at the start of a supply chain will need large quantities of relatively bulky resources. These will be expensive to transport over large distances. This makes it logical for these firms to select locations near a plentiful supply of natural resources.

Likely return on investment

Ultimately the test of a production location will boil down to the likely return on investment. Cheaper locations will seem more attractive, since the initial investment will be lower. However, where a cheap location provides limitations to the likely future revenues the location can earn, this may be a false economy. A country where the investment will be 50% higher that can generate revenues that are 100% higher will ultimately offer a better return on investment for firms that are willing to take a long-term view.

Now test yourself

7 Are low wages in a country more important for capital or labour intensive businesses?
8 Based on Table 19.2, was production in India or China cheaper in 2014?
9 State three reasons why a country's government may offer incentives to businesses setting up production facilities.

Answers online

Reasons for global mergers or joint ventures

As we saw in Topics 8 and 9, growth can occur organically or inorganically through **mergers** and **takeovers**. With speed of reaction to changing markets and technologies globally, inorganic growth, via merger or takeover, can represent a huge temptation to companies from different countries. For those unwilling to make adjustments to the ownership structure of their business, a **joint venture** represents an alternative approach to working with a business in another country.

A **joint venture** is a formal agreement between two separate businesses to work together for a fixed time on a specific project.

A **merger** occurs when two firms agree to come together to create a new, single business.

A **takeover** occurs when one business buys a controlling interest in another business.

Spreading risk

For a successful business selling in just one or two national markets, a downturn in one or both markets can spell disaster. It may therefore make sense to ensure that the business is selling across a range of national markets, in order to ensure that some of their markets are likely to remain buoyant, even if some fail. Moving into foreign markets may be easiest achieved by merger or takeover.

> **Exam tip**
>
> If spreading risk is the motive, it is most likely that getting into quite different markets would do a better job of spreading risk. In these cases, it makes a lot more sense to harness the expertise of another business, through inorganic growth or a joint venture, instead of a company trying to break into a very different market on its own.

Entering new markets/trade blocs

REVISED

Having explored the benefits of operating in a trading bloc in Topic 31, the reasons for operating production facilities in a new country, especially as a way of avoiding trade barriers such as tariffs, are clear. Similarly, entering a new foreign market in order to boost sales is a common strategic approach to achieving a growth objective.

However, as Ansoff stressed, the danger of entering a new market is a lack of understanding of that market, and a failure to comprehend how deep the lack of understanding may be. Mergers or takeovers can be a smart way to overcome this problem; buying a business filled with local experts can be the route to acquiring that missing local understanding. Alternatively, joint ventures with domestic firms, without the permanence of a takeover or merger, can also overcome this initial lack of understanding.

> **Exam tip**
>
> The Chinese government does not allow foreigners to take over large Chinese businesses. This is why so many large western firms have entered China using joint ventures with Chinese partners.

Acquiring national/international brand names/patents

REVISED

The opportunity to buy intellectual property — especially brands and patents — can drive global mergers or takeovers. Buying up a strong portfolio of brands offers a lower risk way to penetrate new international markets. Though expensive, global players are likely to have access to the finance needed to buy nationally dominant brands. Thus, by using their substantial financial muscle, large firms can enter new international markets by buying up market leaders and harnessing the power of their brand and distribution networks in each market.

Buying businesses that hold patents is a quick route to effective new product development. Once an idea or new process has been patented, the resources of a global firm may be able to bring that idea to market more successfully than smaller, national businesses. With design and marketing departments, along with distribution networks, this can be clever strategy for international growth.

Securing resources and supplies

REVISED

For companies using natural resources, especially minerals that can only be found in far-flung corners of the world, ensuring secure, reliable and reasonably priced supplies can represent a problem. The solution can be setting up a joint venture, with the company extracting the resources. However, this can lead to problems if the joint venture partner is not maintaining standards of quality or ethical treatment of staff. Bad publicity would rub off on both partners. To gain more control, a full takeover may be a better option. This gives full control over how the former supplier operates, in a way that a joint venture does not. This form of backward vertical integration is increasingly common in both Africa and South America.

Maintaining/increasing global competitiveness

REVISED

Boosting competitiveness by driving down unit costs may help to explain many global mergers or takeovers. It is the economies of scale that such deals promise that entice firms to come together, as a means to drive costs down ensuring that the business can undercut any rivals it may need to. Porter's low-cost strategy could be a perfectly viable route for one business in each market. As Porter pointed out, there is only room for one cost leader in any market. However, following Porter's generic strategies suggests that competitiveness can be maintained by ensuring differentiation. Buying similar businesses across the world, with similar points of differentiation, can also explain a number of global mergers and takeovers.

> **Typical mistake**
>
> In the heat of an examination, too many students forget Porter's truism: that there can only be one cost leader in any market. Using the phrase 'this could help them become another cost leader' screams of a lack of understanding.

Challenges of global growth via merger or takeover

REVISED

Just as discussed in Topic 9, the major problem of any merger or takeover is overcoming the potential for a clash of cultures as two businesses come together. These problems are likely to be intensified when the deal crosses national boundaries. Of course, other problems of mergers and takeovers may also arise, including:

- synchronising IT systems
- agreeing new policies and procedures
- adjusting organisational structure
- dealing with staff uncertainties over job security.

Now test yourself

TESTED

10 Briefly explain the difference between a merger and a joint venture.
11 Explain why a takeover may be preferable to a joint venture when a business wants to work closely with a supplier in a low wage country with minimal labour laws.
12 How does a joint venture help to overcome Ansoff's concerns over market development?

Answers online

Global competitiveness

If a business can achieve the ability to compete effectively on a global scale, the key benefits are likely to be:

- dominating their domestic markets with minimal penetration from imports
- ease of entry and strong competitiveness in foreign markets due to global brand recognition.

> **Global competitiveness** measures the ability of a business to succeed against both domestic rivals and foreign competitors in international markets.

As Porter has pointed out, competitiveness can be achieved through cost leadership, since the firm with the lowest costs should always be able to undercut their rivals' prices. Porter's alternative strategy is to compete through a high level of product differentiation. This is especially feasible in wealthier markets where price is likely to be less important, with consumers valuing other features such as design, branding and functionality.

The impact of movements in exchange rates on competitiveness

Movements in the relative values of currencies can have a major impact on the competitiveness of global firms. The three major contexts to consider are:

1 Companies which rely on export markets
2 Companies whose domestic market is subject to competition from imports
3 Companies which need to import significant quantities of raw materials or components.

Impacts of a high exchange rate

Considering the case of a UK-based business, an appreciation in the value of the pound is bad news in two of the three key scenarios.

For example, if £1 is worth $1.50, and the exchange rate changes to £1:$2, the pound has strengthened against the dollar.

● Companies which rely on export markets will find it harder to sell their goods in foreign markets due to increased prices, or must accept lower profit margins. For a company selling a product for which they need to receive £10 of revenue, at the original exchange rate they would need to charge $15 in the USA. Once the pound has appreciated in value, they will need to charge $20 to achieve the same £10 of revenue, or accept a lower revenue of £7.50 if they maintain the $15 selling price in the USA.

● Companies whose domestic market is subject to competition from imports will find their foreign rivals' imported products seem cheaper to UK consumers if the pound increases in value. An American product that sells for $150 would have cost a UK consumer £100 at the £1:$1.50 exchange rate. When the pound appreciates to £1:$2, the $150 item will now only cost a UK consumer $75, giving imported goods a significant advantage over domestic rivals.

● Companies which need to import significant quantities of raw materials or components may be the only ones to celebrate an appreciation in the value of the pound. The stronger pound buys more foreign currency, meaning that their imported materials will cost them less in pounds, lowering their production costs.

Impacts of a low exchange rate

The effects of depreciation in the value of the pound will be the precise opposite of those shown above when the pound rises in value, as shown in Table 19.3.

Table 19.3 Effects of depreciation in the value of the pound

Context	Effect of a falling pound
Companies which rely on export markets	Products will seem cheaper in foreign markets, boosting export sales
Companies whose domestic market is subject to competition from imports	Imported products will become more expensive in sterling terms, increasing the competitiveness of domestic producers in their home markets
Companies which need to import significant quantities of raw materials or components	Imported materials will now cost more, pushing up production costs unless the same materials can be sourced at home

Competitive advantage through cost competitiveness

The ability to produce goods and deliver services cheaper than anyone else in the market provides a secure competitive position for a business. The ability to lower its prices below any rival yet still make a profit when others are making a loss means the business can always rely on value-seeking customers. However, being the cheapest supplier in a market is a difficult and relentless challenge. Three key strategies to achieving cost leadership are outlined below.

Raising productivity

Productivity gains will come from increasingly efficient use of resources. Key resources from which more efficiency may be squeezed are:
● human resources
● tangible non-current assets.

Finding a way to increase labour productivity is a fundamental principle behind Topics 16–21. Clearly, motivated staff are likely to achieve higher levels of productivity. However, it is important to consider that overall productivity within a business may have just as much to do with how well planned and organised processes are. Therefore management and organisation play a key role in the quest for higher productivity, thus lower unit costs.

The assets that a business uses to generate revenue include property, machinery and equipment. If a way can be found to gain more output or revenue from the same assets, the unit cost will fall. Opening an automated car wash for longer hours can generate higher revenues without adding too much to the costs. Finding a way to ensure that a piece of machinery breaks down less often — thus producing more output — will again reduce average cost per unit.

Outsourcing

One way to reduce costs is to find another business that can perform a business function more efficiently than you can 'in-house'. This is called **outsourcing**. Not only can this reduce running costs, it can also free up capital and space to invest further in those processes which you can do cheaper than anyone else.

Offshoring

If a business can do something more efficiently than any other, but unit costs are high simply because of the prevailing local rates of wages and land, the solution may be **offshoring**: transferring the business's successful methods and expertise abroad.

> **Outsourcing** means contracting another business to perform a business function on your behalf. Frequently that function will be production, often performed by a business located in a lower cost country.
>
> **Offshoring** means moving one or more business functions to a foreign country, usually to take advantage of lower labour costs.

> **Typical mistake**
>
> Remember that with offshoring, the original business still owns the facilities that have been moved abroad. Outsourcing, which need not mean a change of country, means paying another company to perform a process for you.

Competitive advantage through product differentiation

REVISED

Businesses based in the UK (or other developed economies) will find it hard to be cost competitive. Instead, they are far more likely to achieve global competitiveness through effective and long-lasting product differentiation. As outlined in Topic 4, differentiation can come from several possible sources shown in Table 19.4.

Table 19.4 Possible sources of product differentiation

Actual product differentiation	Perceived product differentiation
Design	Branding
Different functions	Advertising
Engineering	Sponsorship
Performance	Celebrity endorsement

Skills shortages and their impact on international competitiveness

REVISED

If companies have failed to plan for future workforce needs, or provide appropriate training for staff, they may find themselves lacking in staff with appropriate skills to cope with changes in the market. To overcome the problem of being unable to fill newly created positions with appropriately skilled staff, a company may need to poach staff from other businesses. This will almost certainly require paying higher wages to coax staff from their existing employers. So the failure to invest, which may have been seen as a way of boosting competitiveness by cutting costs, may result in damaging competitiveness by leaving roles unfilled, or necessitating the payment of higher wages in order to fill those gaps.

Where this failure to plan and invest is mirrored by that of the government, a company may find itself unable to access any suitably skilled staff to fill vacancies. Where a national skills shortage exists, businesses may need to consider outsourcing abroad, or even relocating a particular function to a country where the required skills are more readily available.

Now test yourself

TESTED

13 What type of businesses will benefit from a strong pound?
14 List three potential strategies that a firm might follow to try to achieve cost leadership.
15 State four methods to achieve long-term product differentiation.

Answers online

Answers and quick quizzes at **www.hoddereducation.co.uk/myrevisionnotes**

Exam practice

1 'A company adopting a strategy of global cost leadership will always be more vulnerable to changes in exchange rates than a company using differentiation as a strategy.' To what extent do you agree? (20)

2 Key issues that businesses usually consider when choosing an international market to enter are:
   - levels and growth of disposable income
   - ease of doing business
   - quality of infrastructure
   - political stability
   - exchange rates.

Assess which ONE is likely to be most important for a UK mobile phone network provider looking to build new overseas markets. (20)

Answers and quick quiz 19 online

ONLINE

Summary

- Trading internationally is likely to be prompted by push and/or pull factors.
- Push factors that prompt trade include:
  - saturated markets
  - competition
  - extending the product life cycle.
- Pull factors that prompt trade include:
  - economies of scale
  - possibility of offshoring or outsourcing
  - risk spreading.
- Key considerations when assessing new international markets include:
  - levels and growth of disposable income
  - ease of doing business
  - quality of infrastructure
  - political stability
  - exchange rates.
- Key considerations when assessing international production locations include:
  - costs of production
  - skills and availability of workforce
  - infrastructure
  - location in a trading bloc
  - government incentives
  - ease of doing business

- natural resources
- likely return on investment.
- Global expansion may be pursued through joint ventures or mergers and takeovers.
- Motives for global mergers or joint ventures include:
  - spreading risk
  - entering new markets or trading blocs
  - acquiring brand names or patents
  - securing resources or supplies
  - boosting global competitiveness.
- Global competitive advantage can come through cost competitiveness or product differentiation.
- To boost competitiveness through cost competitiveness, three clear strategies can be followed:
  - raising productivity
  - outsourcing
  - offshoring.
- Changes in exchange rates have an impact on global competitiveness.
- Global competitiveness can be affected by skills shortages.

20 Global marketing

Global marketing

Global marketing strategy and glocalisation REVISED

During the twentieth century, some brands were able to spread their sales worldwide through a consistent and unchanging product and promotional approach. Coca-Cola's success is unlikely to be repeated, as the nature of global markets has changed. The need to adapt products to suit local market tastes has led to an approach to global marketing known as **glocalisation**.

A summary of the strengths of both approaches is shown in Table 20.1.

Table 20.1 Global versus glocal branding

Strengths of global brands	Strengths of localising your brands (glocalisation)
● Huge sales provide production opportunities to enjoy significant economies of scale	● Tailoring to local tastes and habits should boost market share, e.g. green tea Magnums in Japan
● Over 1.1 billion people travelled abroad in 2014; global brands can be bought for reassurance and familiarity, i.e. globalisation helps sales	● Local buyers can assume you are a local producer, which may help sales (e.g. many British people believe Ford to be a British car maker, not American)
● Many promotional tools are global (e.g. sponsoring Formula 1 or buying the rights to Arsenal's shirt front) and can only be economic if the brands sell globally (e.g. Emirates airline)	● An innovative product designed for local tastes may end up being a global success, e.g. the Nissan Qashqai, designed in Sunderland, but now an important global brand
● Global scale provides strong negotiating power with retailers (helping those 'power brands' get better display and distribution)	● Localising brands probably means localised production, which cuts costs and may help establish a greener image for the business

Glocalisation is a term used to describe an approach to global marketing that maintains a consistent brand and image across the world, but makes adaptations, especially to products, to suit local markets.

Exam tip

It is only at the higher priced end of markets where global consistency still pays. Luxury brands seem loved throughout the world without adaptations. It is in mass markets where local changes tend to be needed.

Different approaches REVISED

Domestic/ethnocentric

This approach to global marketing stays focused on the home country. The attitudes of the company's senior managers will be heavily influenced by their national culture. This leads to an approach that expects consumers in foreign markets to welcome the company's products as they are.

Ethnocentric attitudes can also be found among consumers, sometimes unwilling to consider imported products worthy of their attention. This gives domestic producers a competitive advantage in their home markets.

However, when it comes to breaking into foreign markets, this could breed an ethnocentric approach from managers, who will assume foreign consumers will buy products just because they come from their country.

International/polycentric

A polycentric approach is founded in the belief that all markets are different. Thus, decisions are made at a local level, specifically designed to suit the needs of local customers. The empowerment of local managers to develop new products and brands with local tastes in mind can undo some of the advantages of operating on a global scale. However, the firm will still look to benefit from advantages of size, such as purchasing economies of scale.

Mixed/geocentric

Perhaps the best approach, this combines ethnocentric and polycentric perspectives. The approach is underpinned with the belief that people all over the world share some characteristics, thus the creation of global brands with a level of consistency worldwide is possible. However, the approach also accepts that local differences exist, necessitating localisation. The geocentric approach would empower local managers, but on the understanding that where possible, global is best. So local managers can take decisions that suit their area where the company's global approach cannot be applied effectively.

Applying the marketing mix to global markets

REVISED

The judgement of marketing managers will be crucial in deciding the extent to which the four Ps should be adjusted to suit local needs. Although consistency with the company's global approach will generally be desired, especially under an ethnocentric and a geocentric approach, different Ps may need to be adjusted. Examples of local adjustments needed could include:

● Product: Size, taste/flavour, packaging
● Promotion: Methods and content
● Place: Typical outlets may vary; a delivery service may be expected
● Price: Some local markets may need to see pricing strategies adjusted due to local competition.

Applying Ansoff's Matrix to global markets

REVISED

Ansoff helps businesses assess the level of risk associated with their choice of strategic direction. Measuring markets and products on its two axes, as firms consider entering new foreign markets, they can assess how similar or different new markets are to their existing markets. On the other axis, they can judge risk by the extent to which local market conditions require them to change their product portfolio or enter the market with existing products.

Now test yourself

TESTED

1 Which approach to global marketing is founded on the belief that all international markets have such significant differences that a global approach to marketing will fail?
2 What name is given to the recognition that successful global marketing needs some recognition of local differences?

Answers online

Global niche markets

Differences between different countries' markets mean that from a global perspective, each country could be seen as a niche within the global market. As covered in Topic 15 of the AS book, selling products to a niche market tends to allow firms to take advantage of the following benefits:

- benefits of successful niche market strategy
- able to meet consumer needs more precisely
- able to charge a higher price than mass market products
- less direct competition.

Cultural diversity

REVISED

> **Typical mistake**
>
> Do not confuse national cultures with corporate cultures, as covered in Topic 16. Although both refer to common acceptable norms of behaviour, one refers to behaviours acceptable in a country while the other refers, far more specifically, to those behavioural norms found in a business.

Cultural diversity is caused by many factors, but predominantly driven by:

- Economic factors: Particularly differing levels of average disposable income in different countries.
- Weather: Particularly temperature influences how and where people work, relax, eat or generally live their lives.
- History and tradition: These features of a country may have a wide-ranging impact on so many issues relevant to business, including diet, attitudes to religion, gender, racial diversity and lifestyle.

> **Cultural diversity** describes the differing interests and values of people from different national backgrounds.

The impact of cultural diversity is to make the delivery of a single global strategy very hard to pull off. With consumers in different niches sharing different needs and wants, the pressure to adapt to local diversity is great.

Features of global niche markets

REVISED

Wealthy people tend to travel a lot, picking up tastes and habits that are remarkably similar at the higher income end of markets globally. This explains why niches at the higher income end of most luxury goods markets, from perfume to cars or champagne to designer clothes, tend to develop as global niche markets. For products that are not luxuries, or for luxury goods aimed at lower income consumers, there is less commonality globally. Thus these markets tend to differ by country. Therefore, it is safe to assume that most global niche markets cater to the wealthy in supplying luxuries. On the other hand, most mass markets tend to have local variations that make a standardised, global, ethnocentric approach less likely to work.

Adapting the marketing mix to fit global niche markets

REVISED

Critical aspects of a successful global marketing mix vary according to the type of market. For businesses aiming at those top end luxury niches, key features include:

- aspirational price levels
- products with a strong brand heritage

- distribution through world famous luxury stores such as Harrods and at airports
- promotion in glossy style and travel magazines and through glamourous PR events.

However, for companies attempting to compete in other global niche markets, with less commonality, a deep understanding of local tastes is critical in designing the marketing mix. Cultural diversity can affect each aspect of the mix:

- Different features expected of the product
- Different price expectations depending on the value placed on the product or service locally as well as levels of income
- Differences in traditional channels of distribution from country to country
- Different expectations of how promotional messages are received from country to country and market to market.

Without the availability of staff with a deep understanding and experience of local market differences, the marketing mix produced for a global brand may fall victim to failing to appropriately read the conditions that would allow a successful brand launch.

> **Exam tip**
>
> Carrying out market research in a foreign market may fail to uncover every relevant aspect of consumer behaviour. Market research exercises tend to be limited in scope: they only discover what they set out to ask. Too often, a failure to understand local markets means that research fails to ask the right questions.

Now test yourself

TESTED

3 State three key sources of cultural diversity within markets.
4 Which niche markets are most likely to share common features globally?
5 What is likely to be the key for successfully marketing a product in a new country in markets typified by cultural diversity?

Answers online

Cultural and social factors in global marketing

As discussed in the previous two topics, there can be remarkable differences between different national markets. This makes global marketing fraught with possible problems. The previous topic suggested that a deep understanding of local conditions is likely to be the key to a successful marketing mix. This topic summarises six common causes of marketing mistakes for firms looking to market their products in different national markets.

Cultural differences

REVISED

Behavioural norms can be very different from country to country. The way people meet and greet one another in formal and informal settings can be vastly different from country to country. Similarly, typical behaviours within business meetings can vary. Even yes and no can mean different things in different countries, with yes often meaning perhaps in some environments. Meanwhile, societies may have vastly different perceptions of certain marketing methods; consider the use of singing and dancing cows, which are amusing and brand-building in the UK, but likely to cause offence in cultures where cows are sacred animals. Indeed, religious beliefs can form a strong part of the set of values that influence cultural differences.

> **Culture** describes normal, acceptable behaviours in a certain context.

Exam tip

It is hard to overestimate how many businesses fail to fully grasp cultural differences when entering new international markets. Linking this to the problems of carrying out effective market research explains why so many firms get it wrong when trying to break into an unfamiliar market.

Different tastes

REVISED

Most obviously, tastes can vary in food and drink markets. Different national cuisines, influenced by the types of food most commonly grown locally, as well as historical factors, may dictate the likely success of different flavours of food or drink. Global coffee shop brands have found the need to feature far more tea on their menus in traditional tea-drinking markets such as China and India.

Other markets, however, can be strongly influenced by local differences in taste. Clothing, especially fashions, will see tastes varying depending on local media as well as local climate. Meanwhile markets for products such as cars (different features or interior designs), electronics (different ways of using them) or books (different genres preferred) may be hugely influenced by local tastes.

Language

REVISED

Assuming your level of English is close to fluent, you can consider yourself lucky in a global business sense. Table 20.2 shows the popularity of English as a language of international communication in a business environment.

Table 20.2 The five most popular languages being learned around the world 2015

Source: www.themindunleashed.org

Language	Learners (million people)
English	1,500
French	82
Chinese	30
Spanish	14.5
German	14.5

It is clear which language many people want to be able to speak to 'get on' in the world. However, English is not the most commonly spoken language globally. Table 20.3 shows it only features mid-way up the most commonly spoken languages in the world.

Table 20.3 The five most widely spoken languages in the world 2015

Source: www.themindunleashed.org

Language	Speakers (million people)
Chinese	1,197
Spanish	399
English	335
Hindi	260
Arabic	242

Answers and quick quizzes at **www.hoddereducation.co.uk/myrevisionnotes**

Combining these facts with the widely recognised business practice that speaking to a consumer in their own language helps hugely in successfully selling to them, should help you see why studying a foreign language can increase your employability. Fluent linguists working for a business offer two key benefits in trying to sell to foreign markets:

1 Customers will be impressed if spoken to in their own tongue.
2 Marketing errors caused by linguistic misunderstanding in product naming, branding or promotion are likely to be avoided.

Typical mistakes

General references to language barriers do not impress examiners. Try to be specific as to the types of language problems that can occur in global marketing.

Unintended meanings

REVISED

The problems with literal translation is that all languages have their own idiom: phrases that should not be taken literally, such as English phrases like 'flogging a dead horse' or 'back in a second'.

At times a literal translation can cause a significantly different meaning to be understood by consumers in a local market, a meaning that may be far from the intended meaning behind the promotion.

Inappropriate or inaccurate translations

REVISED

The major causes of problems relating from translations include:
● Wrong words: Choosing the wrong word to use in a local language can confuse or obscure meaning.
● Sounds like something else: A brand name that sounds like something else in the local language can lead to problems.
● Slang: Local slang can make some words used as brands or in advertising slogans carry unexpected and inappropriate meanings.

Inappropriate branding or promotion

REVISED

Wording and imagery used in branding may clash with local values and cultures causing negative publicity for a brand in a local market. Carefully designing a TV advert that 'works' in Western Europe does not mean that the advert's message and content will be effective, or even acceptable, in all global markets. A major area for problems here is religious beliefs and cultural diversity.

Now test yourself

TESTED

6 List the six major causes of international marketing mistakes caused by cultural and social factors.
7 List three markets in which different local tastes can lead to the need to make adjustments to products.
8 Is it more important to speak somebody else's language when you are buying from them or selling to them?

Answers online

Edwards and Edwards is a high street food retailer, specialising in high-end, luxury, specialist food products including caviar, champagne and specialist cold meats. Edwards and Edwards has been successfully operating across a number of European markets for the last ten years. In order to satisfy its shareholders' desire for continued growth, the company has now decided to enter both the Japanese and Chinese markets. With no previous experience of these markets, the firm has commissioned local market research companies to gauge local consumers' reactions to the likely success of the expansion. Results have been broadly positive and are summarised below.

Question	% of positive responses in China	% of positive responses in Japan
Would you like to be able to buy high-end European food products?	46	32
Have you ever heard of Edwards and Edwards?	18	12
Would you be willing to pay a price premium for these products?	55	12
Would you expect to see premium locally sourced products in-store?	12	67

1 (a) To what extent does the research data support the use of an ethnocentric/domestic marketing strategy? (20)

(b) Evaluate the main marketing challenges that Edwards and Edwards may face in entering these two new markets. (20)

2 'Increased globalisation will inevitably lead to reduced differences between national markets for consumer goods over the next 20 years.' Do you agree? Justify your answer. (20)

Answers and quick quiz 20 online

ONLINE

Summary

- Glocalisation means thinking globally and acting locally.
- There are three broadly different approaches to global marketing:
  - ethnocentric/domestic
  - polycentric/international
  - geocentric/mixed.
- The marketing mix is likely to need adapting to suit local markets.

- The Boston Matrix can be used to help to assess the attractiveness of new international markets.
- Cultural diversity means local markets can have major differences, based especially on economic factors, weather and history and tradition.
- Major causes of problems in operating in international markets include cultural differences, different tastes and language issues.

21 Global industries and companies (multinational corporations)

The impact of multinational corporations

The impact of MNCs on the local economy REVISED

Employment

Table 21.1 Positive and negative impacts of multinational companies

> A **multinational** company is one that has branches or manufacturing plants in several countries.

	Positive impact of MNCs	Negative impact of MNCs
Local labour	• Western training methods may make the local workforce more productive/ employable	• Western employers may attract over-qualified people — possibly stripping local businesses and public services of skilled staff
Wages	• MNCs usually pay higher wage rates than local firms, improving standards of living	• Some locals may feel bitter that they are paid less than westerners for doing exactly the same job
Working conditions	• MNCs have international reputations to maintain, so they will tend to provide above-average conditions • Yum Foods has a 'Human and Labour Rights Policy' and claims to employ it in all 125 countries	• Conditions may be above average, yet still quite shocking to westerners • Some MNCs may have impressive policies in place, yet the workplace reality may be worse than the paper theory
Job creation	• Yum Foods employs 1.5 million people worldwide; in Africa it provides more than 20,000 jobs	• The success of MNCs may sometimes be at the expense of local independent firms; the key measure is net job creation

Local businesses

When a multinational sets up operations in a new area, the impact on most local businesses is likely to be positive. A new factory that creates hundreds of jobs will look to local businesses for some supplies, will create more spending power locally — to be spent in local shops and restaurants — and will add income to the area that local entrepreneurs can exploit. However, if the operation started by a multinational provides direct competition to an existing business, it may have too much power for local rivals.

Local communities and the environment

The impact of multinationals on local communities and the environment is too complex to be considered in absolute terms. Examples of multinationals investing in local communities, raising standards of healthcare, education and infrastructure can be found. Alongside these are examples of multinationals whose approach can cause damage to local communities, disrupting social structures and indirectly bringing problems of crime that can be associated with suddenly newly found wealth.

Likewise, although there are examples of multinationals that have had a damaging effect on the physical environment, local businesses may be just as, if not more, guilty of causing environmental damage. This may be especially true where local environmental regulations are minimal or non-existent: at least a multinational may need to stick to globally laid down internal environmental standards.

The impact of MNCs on the national economy

REVISED

FDI flows

When multinationals choose to invest directly into other countries, they are injecting cash into the national economy. That cash creates jobs and injects extra money into the local economy. However, there are concerns that the FDI flows may not entirely work in that direction. Once a multinational is generating profit, the likelihood is that the profit will be sent out of the country, back to the multinational's home country.

> **Foreign Direct Investment (FDI)** occurs when a business purchases non-current assets in another country.

Balance of payments

Countries that import more than they export run a current account deficit. This is likely to lead to a fall in the value of the currency, which creates a risk of inflation. However, if the country attracts FDI, the inflow of cash from multinationals cancels out the current account deficit.

The potential problem to this occurs when a multinational decides to withdraw its FDI. This represents a further outflow from the country, thus further damaging the balance of payments current account. One company's decision to withdraw FDI would have a minimal impact on a major economy, but the effect of a large multinational withdrawing from a smaller less economically developed country can be significant.

Technology and skills transfer

When multinationals open facilities in a new host nation, they are likely to introduce ideas and methods that may be new to the country. This allows the local economy to copy or 'borrow' the techniques and methods being used, improving the efficiency of local businesses. Access to new technology can be the key to unlocking economic development. Skills can be developed among the local workforce, which sustains the ongoing development.

Consumers

As multinationals enter new countries, consumers within those countries gain more choice. This is broadly seen as a good thing. However, problems may emerge if the competition from the multinational drives domestic firms out of business. Though this is the reality of capitalism, concerns over the fairness of the competition are often attached to the entry of multinationals to foreign markets.

> **Exam tip**
>
> The impact of multinationals on consumers in host countries is a classic example of one where you should be able to introduce ethical concerns as a counter-argument against classic benefits such as increased choice. Introducing the ethical issues involved in the operations of multinationals can be a handy way to produce counter-arguments or offer evaluative thoughts within an exam answer.

Business culture

Multinational businesses are run in a professional and generally consistent way. This consistency of operation may not be commonly found in host countries. In just the same way that technology and skills transfer helps domestic businesses, so will the experience of seeing how a multinational operates. As domestic suppliers deal with the multinational they are likely to adapt a more consistent and professional business culture.

Tax revenues and transfer pricing

Different countries charge different rates of tax on business profits. As multinationals operate across several countries, it is logical for a multinational to try to maximise their profits in countries where tax rates are lowest, declaring minimal or no profits in high tax countries.

The mechanism that multinationals use to engineer this is **transfer pricing**. A multinational will move products between its different locations, charging an 'internal price' for components or partially finished goods as they are transferred between the multinational's locations.

This allows high prices (therefore low profits) to be charged by branches in high tax countries, with most profits engineered into the operations based in low tax countries.

Laws on transfer pricing vary from country to country, but clever tax accountants can generally ensure that multinationals using this technique are not breaking any laws.

The implication for host countries is that multinationals are able to minimise the tax they pay locally using transfer pricing. This potentially places undue pressure on host countries' governments to keep tax rates low.

> **Typical mistake**
>
> Most multinationals that use transfer pricing, or base themselves in tax havens, are not actually breaking the law. The term used for not paying tax which is legally due is tax evasion. The multinationals are using tax avoidance strategies: not illegal, but ethically dubious.

> **Transfer pricing** is a technique used by multinationals to adjust the internal prices paid by one branch of their operations to another as a way of minimising the total tax bill paid by the company.

> **Now test yourself**
> TESTED ☐
>
> 1 Briefly explain why the reputation for environmental damage that tarnishes multinationals may not be deserved.
> 2 What global inconsistency makes transfer pricing possible?
> 3 State three negative impacts that a multinational may have on local labour markets.
>
> Answers online

Ethics in global business

What are business ethics?

REVISED ☐

First covered in Topic 18, business ethics concerns the morality of business decision-making and actions. The natural conflict between operating in a morally acceptable way and boosting profit can be intensified when a multinational begins operating in a less economically developed country.

Stakeholder conflicts

REVISED ☐

Large businesses operating on a global scale are most likely to be pursuing an objective of maximising profit, under pressure from their shareholders. Given the power of large shareholders, they are likely to be the dominant stakeholder group, who get their way. Table 21.2 shows examples of stakeholder conflicts and summaries of the ethical problems posed.

Table 21.2 Conflicting stakeholders – ethical solutions

Conflicting stakeholders	Example	Ethical problem
Retailers and their suppliers	In 2015, Arcadia plc (Topshop) cut 2% from all payments to suppliers from 1 September. Young designers squealed at the threat to their finances	Price negotiations should be tough, but once a price is agreed, it is unethical to bully a small supplier into receiving less
Directors and staff	In May 2015, Tesco told staff it would in future contribute 5% of pay towards their pensions; before it was 11%. New boss Dave Lewis gets 25% of his salary paid 'in lieu of pension'!	Staff understand that bosses receive higher remuneration, but unfairness such as this is quite simply unethical
Management and shareholders	Bafflingly, owners of bank shares have allowed senior bank staff to pay themselves bonuses that strip the banks of their profitability (Lloyds Bank shares: 976p in 1999; 575p in 2007; 75p in 2015)	Ethics should apply in all cases; using negotiating power is fine, but many bonuses were for things that cost the bank in the long term, e.g. mis-selling Payment Protection Insurance (PPI)

Pay and working conditions

REVISED

Before deciding on the morality of pay rates around the world, it is imperative to view local pay rates in a local context. Paying a factory worker the same in Vietnam as a factory worker in the UK fails to take account of differences in the costs of living.

Ethical issues relating to pay and working conditions include:
- Should wealthy consumers feel comfortable wearing clothes made by factory workers paid pence, rather than pounds, per hour?
- Should firms in less economically developed countries be allowed to produce goods for developed economies in working conditions that would be unacceptable in the markets being sold to, but which are legal in the host country?
- Should a multinational company that outsources some of its production be responsible for the pay and working conditions in their suppliers' factories?

Table 21.3 indicates how a line can be drawn between ethically acceptable and unacceptable working conditions in developing economies.

Table 21.3 Working conditions and ethics

Working conditions that could be seen to be ethically acceptable	Working conditions that are unconditionally unacceptable
● Cramped and hot, where profit margins are too low to allow more space and air conditioning	● Dangerous conditions with machinery and fire risk — and perhaps chemical air pollution
● Long working hours, perhaps up to 12 hours a day	● Forcing people to work long hours. perhaps by threats of dismissal
● Agricultural workers planting rice — bending over for perhaps 12 hours a day	● Long back-breaking hours in agriculture with little pay — while farmers and dealers get rich

Answers and quick quizzes at **www.hoddereducation.co.uk/myrevisionnotes**

Environmental considerations

Emissions

For products that produce emissions that are harmful to the environment — perhaps most obviously cars — the emissions produced are regulated in all developed countries. In addition, consumers may also be attracted by products with lower emissions.

Ethical issues arise when considering who measures emissions. Although independent testing takes place, if the manufacturer itself has to pay an independent tester, the company doing the testing may be tempted to adjust results in the hope of securing a long-term customer. A further issue can be seen if a company discovers an emissions problem with a product. Failure to communicate this information externally, perhaps in the hope of fixing it quickly without tarnishing the company's brand, is unethical.

Waste disposal

Many products produced by businesses pose problems of disposal when their life is complete. Getting rid of old consumer electronics products which often contain poisonous elements presents problems with an ethical dimension. In developed economies, disposal of hazardous substances is highly regulated and thus expensive. However, some businesses see less economically developed countries with their weaker or non-existent regulations as a cheap solution. Dumping hazardous products or by-products on less developed countries is unethical.

Supply chain considerations

The major ethical issues highlighted on the specification are the exploitation of workers and child labour. Both of these practices are clearly wrong. However, two interesting issues can be raised:

1 What is the alternative for the worker or the child? If this is the only job available to the worker, no matter how exploitative, how else could they feed their family? Should the job be withdrawn? If the child is working for their parents, perhaps on a family farm or in a family factory, would the removal of that extra pair of hands cause the business insurmountable problems?
2 Should a business be responsible for the employment practices of their suppliers, or their suppliers' suppliers? Large businesses producing or selling complex products may well be buying from suppliers who buy materials from other suppliers. If one of the suppliers' suppliers is using child labour, does the original business deserve censure?

Marketing considerations

Misleading product labelling

Although tight product labelling legislation is in place to ensure that labels don't lie, ethical issues still surround labelling. Many of these relate to food products, but by no means all. Issues include:

● implications of messages about the vague benefits of a product
● inferences about a product's ingredients or methods of production, perhaps implying it is 'all natural' but without being clear about the level of highly processed ingredients used in it
● unhelpful imagery on packaging or in adverts, which is designed to infer, suggest or imply something untrue, without explicitly claiming an untruth.

Inappropriate promotional activities

A range of promotional activity that businesses undertake can be criticised for being unethical. Examples include:

● Promotions that encourage consumers to buy more than they need can lead to food waste.
● Food retailers have also received criticism for running Buy One Get One Free promotions on sugary drinks and foods, encouraging over-consumption of foods best consumed in small quantities.
● Advertising has also been blamed for social issues, such as body image issues, especially among teens, by using touched up images of models to set unattainable beauty goals.
● Companies offering credit to try to encourage people to buy products they really cannot afford can also be accused of unethical promotion.

The fundamental issue here is where to draw the line between a business objective of maximising sales and consumers' inability to resist the bombardment of promotional messages they receive every day.

Controlling multinational corporations

Influence or control?

REVISED

The subtle difference between influence and control can be illustrated by considering a company's stakeholders. While stakeholder groups such as pressure groups and customers may influence a business, control lies with major shareholders and the directors they appoint, as well as with government (through laws and regulations).

Figure 21.1 shows different stakeholder groups according to their level of control or merely influence.

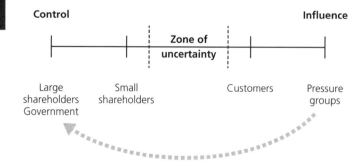

Figure 21.1 The subtle boundary between influence and control

Notice the dotted arrow showing that pressure groups can influence governments as well as businesses.

> **Exam tip**
>
> Some argue that customers can exert control over businesses, while many would suggest that they merely have influence over what businesses do. Examples can be found to illustrate both, but, as the zone of uncertainty marked on Figure 21.1 shows, customer power can offer excellent opportunities to explore the issue of control versus influence.

The need to control MNCs

REVISED

Unlike most governments, the leaders of multinationals are not answerable to the citizens of the countries in which they operate. Instead multinationals do the bidding of their directors, appointed by major shareholders. It is this issue that lies behind the belief that the activities of multinational companies need to be controlled to an extent by external agencies such as governments. Specific situations raised are outlined below.

Safety concerns

Multinationals producing in less developed countries with lax regulations on factory safety may be able to squeeze extra life out of unsafe machinery that has had to be retired from plants elsewhere. If local regulations cannot ensure safe equipment for workers, some other form of control may be needed.

Short-term mineral extraction

By their nature, minerals can only be extracted once. Where a multinational enters a host country to extract minerals, it is therefore crucial that the country receives appropriate reward for its irreplaceable natural resources. What an appropriate level of reward is can be debated. However, in circumstances like these, with vast sums of money changing hands, it can be too easy for local politicians to benefit personally by allowing the multinational in, rather than ensuring that rewards are shared equitably within the host country.

Weakening local cultures

Using their marketing budgets and techniques, honed over many years, multinationals can be highly adept at selling foreign products to locals. Concerns are often raised when the success of a multinational's marketing leads to consumers changing their habits and lifestyles as a result. This can lead to a loss of traditional local cultures, to be replaced by some kind of global corporate consumerist culture.

Lack of commitment to the host country

A multinational lacks the strong bonds tying it to a country that characterises domestic focused companies. As a result, multinationals may be willing to leave a country, perhaps creating significant unemployment or social problems, in the event of problems that a domestic producer may have the commitment to work through, such as a recession.

MNCs and political influence

REVISED

Lobbying key political decision-makers is something that multinationals tend to do exceptionally well. With money and power, multinationals can exert a worrying level of influence over politicians.

This influence can be used to achieve many things that aid the operations of multinationals, including:
- granting licenses to run phone, rail or electricity networks
- granting licences to extract raw materials
- encouraging changes in laws and regulations affecting the multinationals' operations
- offering tax breaks
- overlooking instances where a multinational has failed to adhere to regulations.

> **Lobbying** describes the process of directly trying to influence key political decision-makers to act in the best interests of a business.

Typical mistake

These actions, which multinationals can influence politicians to take, may all seem to refer to less economically developed countries. Look more carefully and you can see that all could apply to developed countries too. There are plenty of examples of multinationals gaining political influence in countries such as the UK in order to get their way; this is not simply a developing world phenomenon.

Legal control

REVISED

Multinationals have to abide by the laws of each country in which they operate. However, the two legal areas where multinationals cause confusion are in takeover law and tax law.

Although takeover deals involving domestic companies will be dealt with by competition authorities in that country, who can stop a multinational from one country taking over a multinational based in another country? Even though trading blocs such as the EU can exert control, cross-border takeover involving multinationals can in some ways seem ungoverned by any law.

As covered in Topic 40, multinationals can use transfer pricing between the different countries in which they operate in order to avoid paying tax in countries where corporation tax rates are high. Without an effective global body to police the operations of multinationals in areas such as this, there is no clear legal control over this.

In developing economies the issue of legal control may be more fundamental. In some countries, laws governing the operations of companies, such as they exist, may not be effectively enforced. In some ways, this allows businesses, especially large, powerful multinationals, to operate beyond the law in some parts of the world.

Pressure groups

REVISED

There is no doubt that powerful pressure groups can exert some influence over multinationals. They can also influence governments in order to try to curb business actions they do not support. Their power, though, is limited to influencing rather than controlling the actions of multinationals. However, in many cases, multinationals have stopped or adjusted activities that powerful pressure groups objected to.

Social media

REVISED

Table 21.4 Impact of social media on company behaviour

Why social media may impact on company behaviour	Why social media may have little impact on company behaviour
Social media's power is to be able to almost instantaneously shine a light on events to audiences of millions. Bosses of multinational businesses are aware of the potential number of customers who may discover mistakes or malpractice that cast their business in a poor light. If this publicity leads to customers going to rivals to buy, it is little surprise that multinational bosses will pay close attention to how their businesses operate in order to avoid a potentially catastrophic social media storm.	The speed with which issues appear on social media is tremendous, but they also disappear from social media quickly too. If a company can 'weather the storm' for a week or so, Twitter users are likely to have moved on to the next issue.

Now test yourself

7 State two stakeholder groups that (a) have some control over multinationals and (b) merely influence but do not control multinationals.
8 Briefly explain two examples of situations that illustrate the need to control multinationals.
9 What two areas of business operations does the law find it hard to deal with where multinationals are involved?

Answers online

Exam practice

1 'As multinationals operate across borders and have such huge financial resources, national governments now lack the ability to control their operations.' To what extent do you agree with this statement? (20 marks)
2 'The experience of China shows that inviting multinationals to set up in any developing economy brings more positives than negatives.' To what extent do you agree with this statement? (20 marks)

Answers and quick quiz 21 online

ONLINE ☐

Summary

- The major impacts of multinationals on local economies are:
  - effects on local labour markets
  - effects on local businesses
  - effects on the local community and environment.
- These effects can be both positive and negative.
- Effects of multinationals on national economies of host countries include:
  - FDI flows
  - balance of payments
  - technology and skills transfer
  - effects on consumers
  - development of business culture
  - tax revenues.
- Again, these impacts can be both positive and negative.

- The operations of multinationals raise a number of ethical issues, particularly relating to:
  - stakeholder conflicts
  - pay and working conditions
  - environmental impacts
  - supply chains
  - marketing methods.
- The need to control multinationals' operations is highlighted by issues including:
  - safety concerns
  - mineral extraction
  - loss of traditional local cultures.
- Multinationals have proved capable of softening the control exerted over them by:
  - laws
  - politicians
  - pressure groups.